IMAGES
of America

SEVIERVILLE

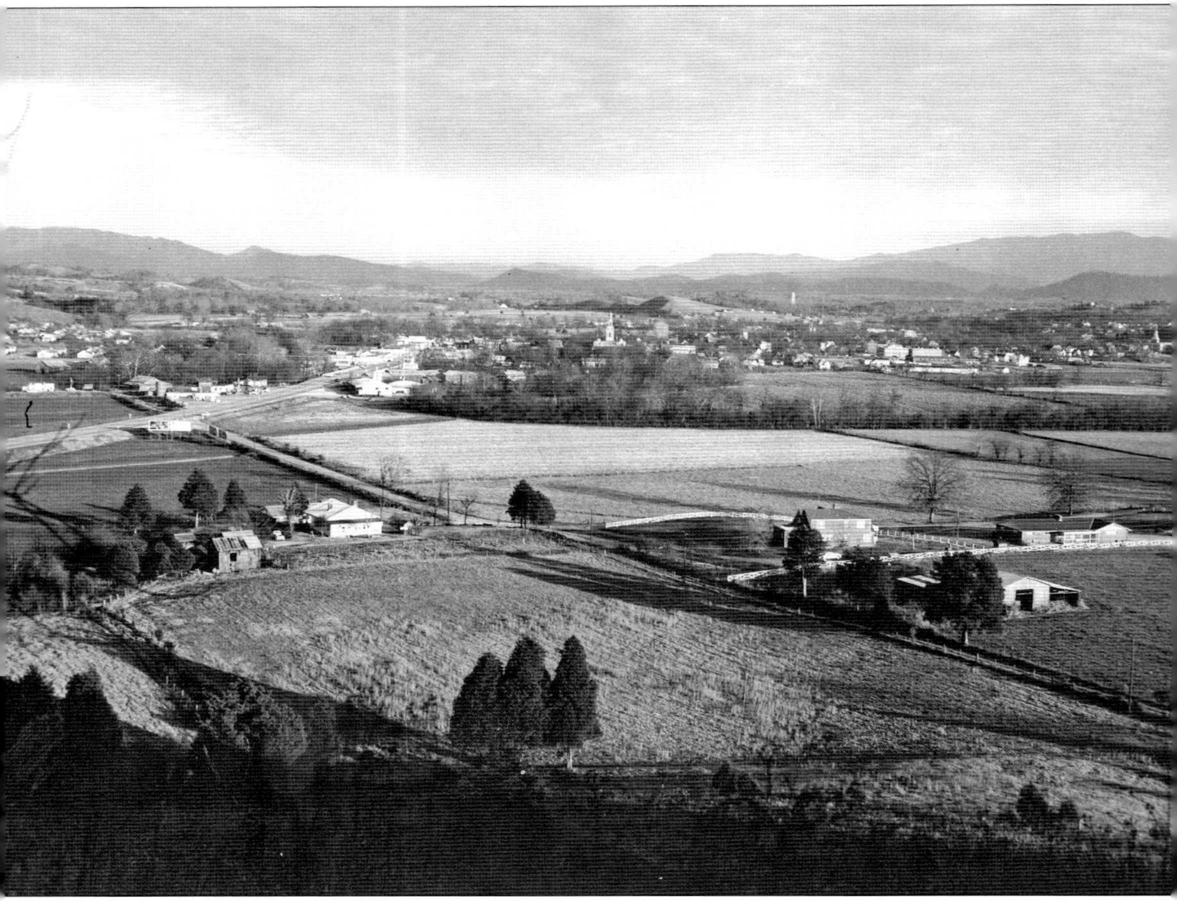

Anyone who has ever lived in Sevierville and returned home by traveling south on Chapman Highway has enjoyed this picturesque view of the historic courthouse tower with the Great Smoky Mountains as a backdrop. This photograph, taken before the West Prong of the Little Pigeon River was rechanneled in 1967, captures a view that has greeted returning residents and captivated visitors for generations. (Courtesy of Jimmie and Marie Temple.)

On the Cover: A photograph taken of Court Avenue facing north captures the unhurried atmosphere of the 1940s in Sevierville. The buildings on the right face the Sevier County Courthouse. In those days, Sevierville merchants knew most of their customers by name and an atmosphere of trust prevailed. Very few residents locked their doors at night. (Courtesy of King Family Library History Center, Herbert Lawson Collection.)

IMAGES
of America

SEVIERVILLE

F. Carroll McMahan

ARCADIA
PUBLISHING

ISBN 978-0-7385-9377-7

Published by Arcadia Publishing
Charleston, South Carolina

Printed in the United States of America

Library of Congress Control Number: 2011945701

For all general information, please contact Arcadia Publishing:
Telephone 843-853-2070
Fax 843-853-0044
E-mail sales@arcadiapublishing.com
For customer service and orders:
Toll-Free 1-888-313-2665

Visit us on the Internet at www.arcadiapublishing.com

For my wife, Michelle, the love of my life,
thank you for your love and support

Contents

Foreword

Webster defines heritage as something that passes from one generation to the next, e.g. a way of life or culture. Based on that definition I have to ask myself a question. Just how rich is our heritage? We are very fortunate in Sevierville to have such rich and fulfilling history. For many years our ancestors worked hard at building families, business and relationships that have endured through the years. We can see many of those things on a daily basis but many we have only heard about from our parents or friends down through the years. I feel it is very important to get this spoken history documented for all of those who will follow us in this cherished place. We can learn from our history and some of it is worth repeating and remembering.

—Bryan Atchley
Mayor of Sevierville

Acknowledgments

Publication of this book would not have been possible without the support and assistance of my family, friends, and colleagues. Every individual I have approached with questions or requests has offered an encouraging response. Special thanks go to Elizabeth Bray, editor with Arcadia Publishing, for her enthusiasm and unwavering support for this project. I owe an extraordinary debt of gratitude to my brother-in-law Richard E. Atchley Jr. and the King Family Library History Center staff, especially Tim Fisher and Theresa Williams.

I would also like to thank Jimmie and Marie Temple, John B. Waters Jr., Mary Louise Hailey, Steve Madison, Betty Madison Ogle, Marie Cameron, Betty May, Amanda Marr, Chad Branton, Allen Robbins, Becky and Lanning Wynn, Hulet Chaney, David Kerr, Ersa Rhea Smith, Chelsie Teague, Veta King, Mary Bob Rowe, Jeff Matthews, Johnnie Faye McClure, Ruby Hatcher, Martha Bowden, Robert Allen, Brandon Barnes, Gail Clevenger, Clara Hodge, Bryan Atchley, Jim McGill, Brenda McCroskey, Johnny Sims, Steve Holbert, Alfred Newman, Travis McCroskey, Terry Bryan, Eddie Helton, Stan Voit, and Andy Madson.

The vast collection of vintage photographs and information contributed by the estate of Herbert Lawson was immeasurably helpful for compiling this book. I have made every effort to assure historical accuracy. My primary sources were the King Family Library History Center, *The Mountain Press*, the Sevierville Chamber of Commerce archives, and oral interviews with numerous individuals. Finally, thanks to my wife, Michelle, for her understanding and steadfast support and sparing time for me to bring this project to fruition.

INTRODUCTION

It is not the honor that you take with you, but the heritage you leave behind.

—Branch Rickey

According to archaeological research, "the land at the forks of the rivers" has been inhabited for at least 10,000 years. Prehistoric inhabitants often established villages on floodplains near rivers. Locally, the most notable example of this practice is the McMahan Indian Mound, located along the Fork-of-the-River Parkway in downtown Sevierville. In 1881, Dr. Edward Palmer of the Smithsonian Institution excavated the mound, recovering burial-site objects and ancient relics used by those who lived in that early village. During a subsequent dig in the 1930s, archaeologists from the University of Tennessee recovered additional artifacts for study. When the Tennessee Valley Authority rerouted the West Prong of the Little Pigeon River in the 1960s, the mound was compromised. Fortunately, in 1987, Effie Benson Temple (widow of John E. Temple) conveyed the McMahan Indian Mound site to the city of Sevierville to be held in public trust, protected from further disturbance, based on its historical significance.

The first permanent white settlement in the Fork-of-the-River area was established about 1780. Isaac Thomas, a Virginian in trade with the Cherokee Indians, was the first to arrive. Later, large land grants were awarded to three veterans of the American Revolution, near the confluence of the East Prong and West Prong of the Little Pigeon River. Spencer Clack received 400 acres on the north side of the East Prong. James McMahan settled on 400 acres between the East Prong and West Prong, and Isaac Thomas received 1,000 acres located west of the river's west fork.

In 1785, Sevier County was established and named in honor of Col. John Sevier, who shortly thereafter served as governor of the state of Franklin, which existed from 1784 to 1788. The state of Franklin failed in 1788, and settlers governed themselves until 1794, when the area became part of the area known at the time as the Southwest Territory. James McMahan donated 25 acres along the south bank of the East Prong to establish a county seat. The settlement consisted of two streets: Main Street and Cross Street. A courthouse, jail, and stocks were constructed using proceeds from a land auction of half-acre lots. New property owners were required to construct a well-framed, square-logged, brick or stone building at least 16 by 16 feet (256 square feet). The village formerly known as Forks-of-the-River was officially renamed Sevierville, also in honor of John Sevier.

By 1795, the Southwest Territory reached a population of 60,000, the minimum needed to apply for statehood, and in 1796 the state of Tennessee was created. Five men were elected to represent Sevier County in the first Tennessee Legislature, which convened in Knoxville in 1796. Sevierville's rapid growth was halted by a devastating fire in 1856. The blaze, which started in the county jail, spread quickly and leveled the entire town. There was one fatality.

For over 100 years after Sevierville was named, residents grappled with the issue of permanent incorporation, voting for and against it several times. As a result, the city was not permanently incorporated until 1901. A dispute defying the arbiters of 200 years' time is alcohol sales in Sevier County and Sevierville.

From the start, Sevierville was vulnerable to major, crippling floods because of its proximity to the rivers. The first recorded flood occurred in 1875, and since then, 11 major floods have been recorded. The last occurred in 1965, two years after a series of floods over a two-week period left Sevierville a federal disaster area. The 1963 flood led to the Tennessee Valley Authority implementing protective measures, and by 1967 the West Prong had been rechanneled out of harm's way. There have been no serious floods since then, and the town has grown extensively. The spectacular beauty and recreational opportunities have supplied the area with a robust economy cultivated by tourism.

Although not a definitive history, this book attempts to capture some of the people, places, and stories that have shaped Sevierville—a name borne no place else on Earth.

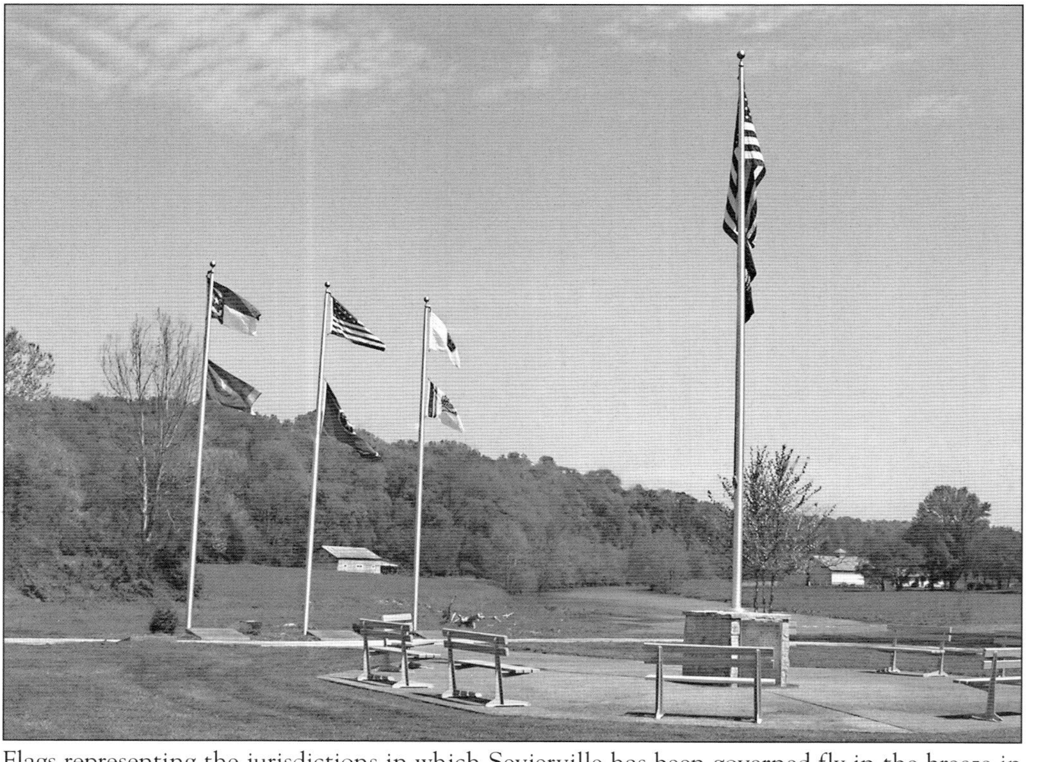

Flags representing the jurisdictions in which Sevierville has been governed fly in the breeze in Forks-of-the-River Cemetery Park. Many of the town's early settlers, including Spencer Clack, Isaac Thomas and James McMahan, are buried in the old cemetery that dates back to the late 1700s. In addition to the American flag, the Tennessee state flag, Sevierville flag, and Sevier County flag, the park has replicas of the North Carolina flag, because the area was once part of that state; a state of Franklin flag, for the period from 1984 to 1788 when the town was part of that state; and the Territory South of the Ohio, a historic organized territory whose boundaries conformed to the modern state of Tennessee and which lasted from 1790 until 1796. (Courtesy of Sevierville Chamber of Commerce.)

One

A Firm Foundation

Optimism is the foundation of courage.

—Nicholas Butler

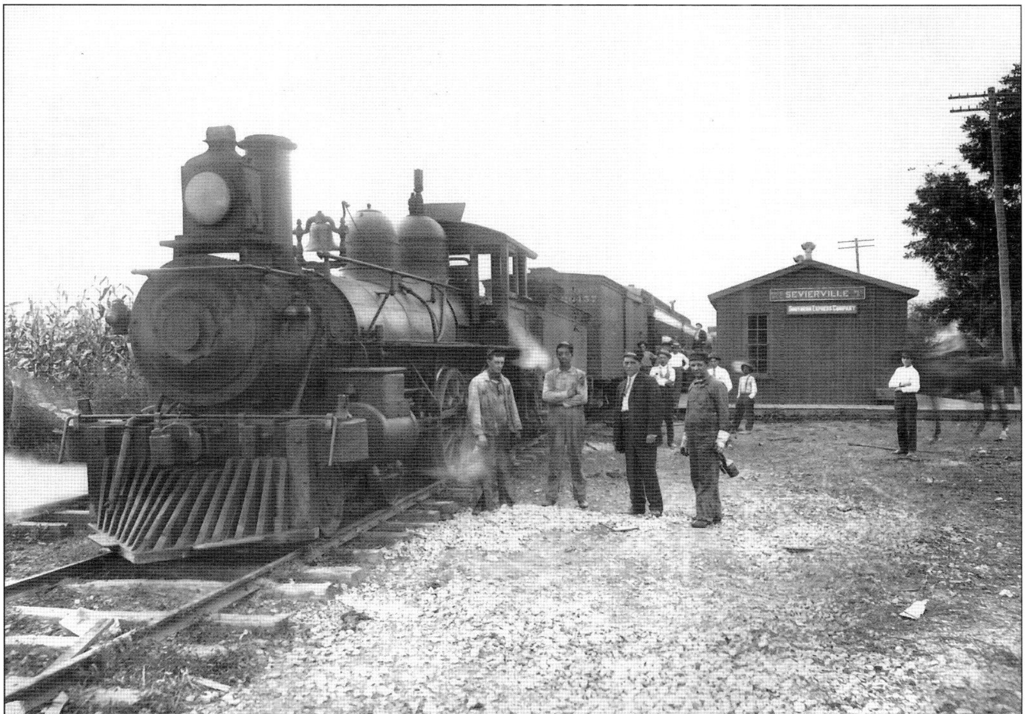

The first train to arrive in Sevierville was the Knoxville, Sevierville, and Eastern. After several aborted attempts to acquire railroad service between Knoxville and Sevierville, the first train was greeted by a joyous fanfare of over 600 people on a cold January day in 1910. The tracks stopped west of the river until 1916, when a trestle was constructed and tracks continued along and beyond Bruce Street. (Courtesy of King Family Library History Center, Herbert Lawson Collection.)

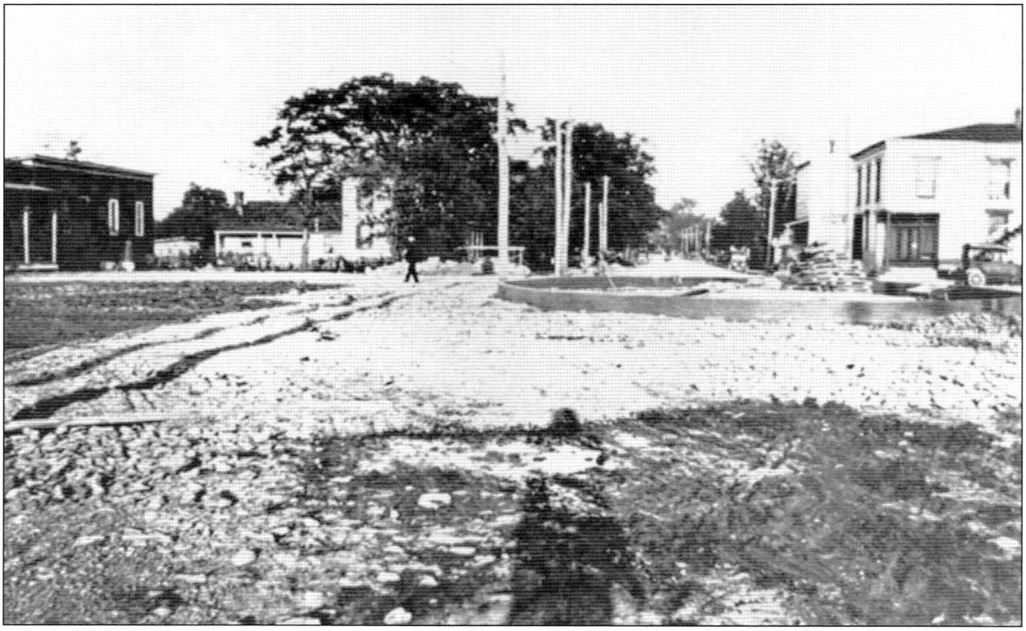

Commonly called the Run-Around, the public square, which was actually oval, was constructed in 1924. The grassy area in the center was used for the community Christmas tree for several years. The public square was located at the intersection of Main Street and Court Avenue (formerly named Cross Street). (Courtesy of King Family Library History Center, Herbert Lawson Collection.)

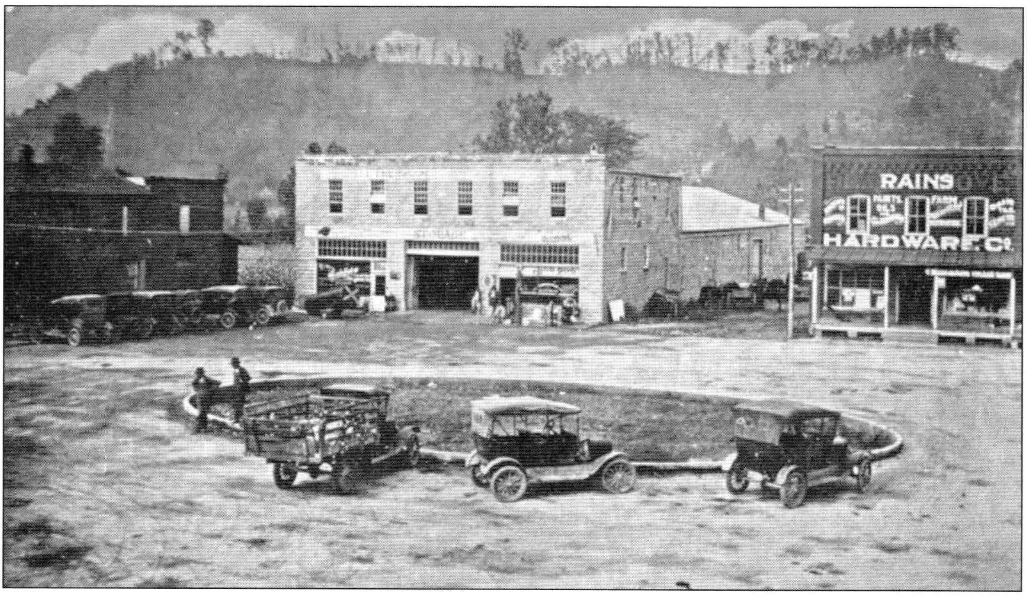

Some of the town's prominent businesses faced the public square, shown in this 1925 photograph. Rains Hardware Store and Thurman's Garage occupied the north side. The Yett building, which later became Lewelling's Market, was west of Thurman's Garage. The photograph was taken from the porch of the New Central Hotel. (Courtesy of King Family Library, Herbert Lawson Collection.)

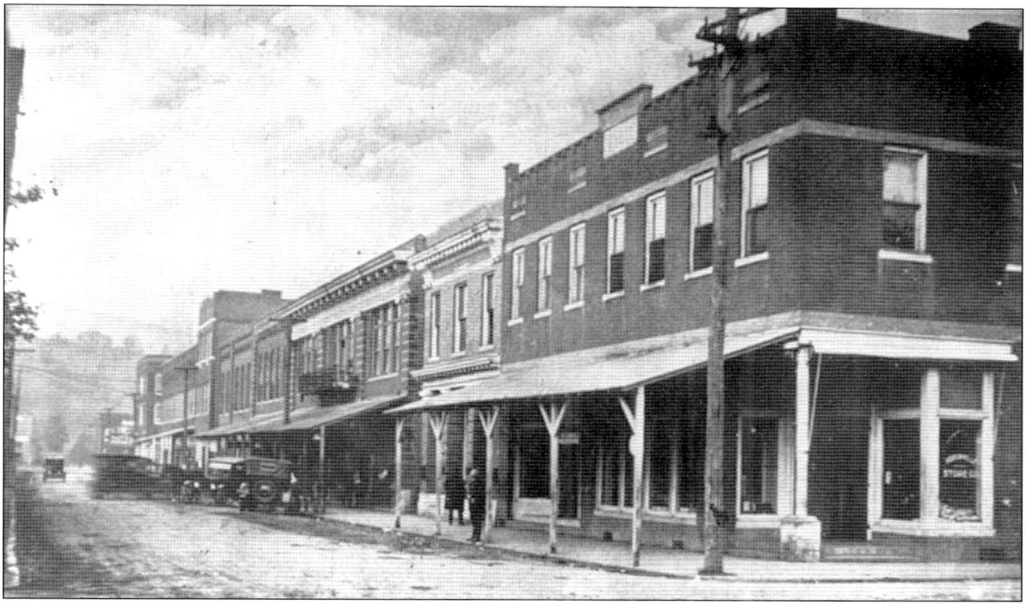

This photograph, facing north Cross Street, was taken about 1912. Several years after the new courthouse was built on the street, the name was changed to Court Avenue. (Courtesy of King Family Library History Center, Herbert Lawson Collection.)

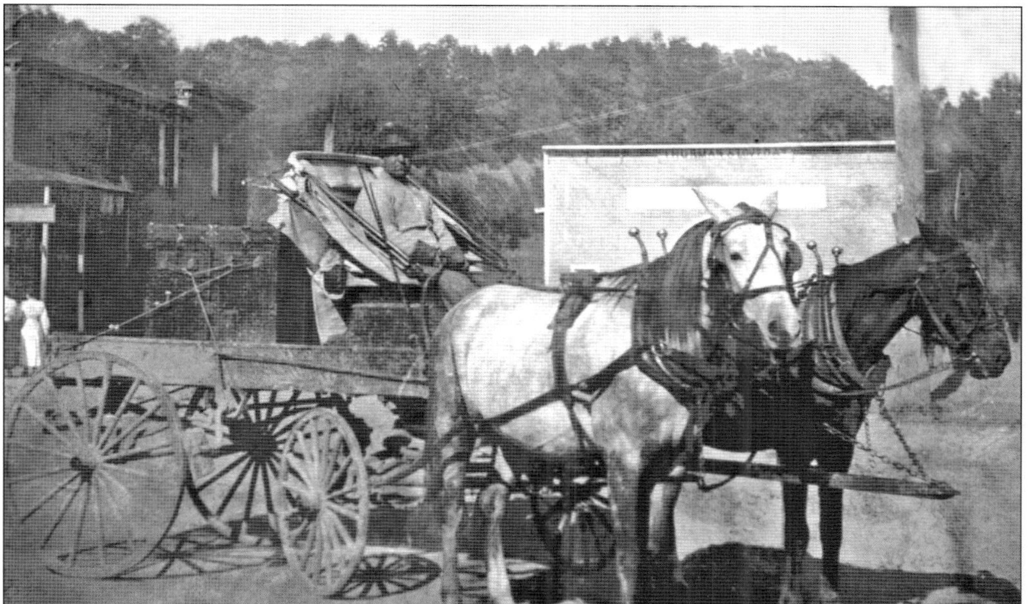

A horse-drawn mail and passenger coach ran between Knoxville and Sevierville in the early part of the 1900s. The 28-mile trip took three hours, one way. A coach pulled by a pair of horses left Sevierville at 4:00 p.m. A second pair of fresh horses awaited in Boyds Creek and another at Shook's Gap. The return trip from downtown Knoxville departed at 4:00 a.m. from the post office. For the next trip to Knoxville at 4:00 p.m., the teams of horses were switched. (Courtesy of King Family Library History Center, Waters Family Collection.)

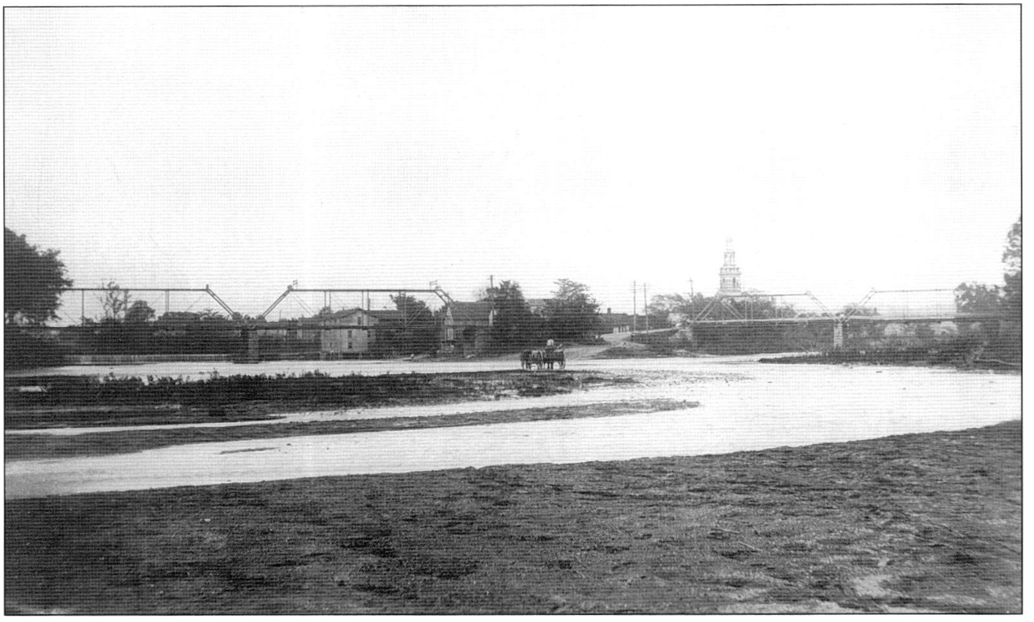

In 1893, these steel bridges were constructed over the East and West Prongs of the Little Pigeon River. The bridge over the West Prong was at the end of West Main Street. The other bridge constructed over the East Prong was on the north side of West Main Street, just west of the milldam. (Courtesy of King Family Library History Center, Herbert Lawson Collection.)

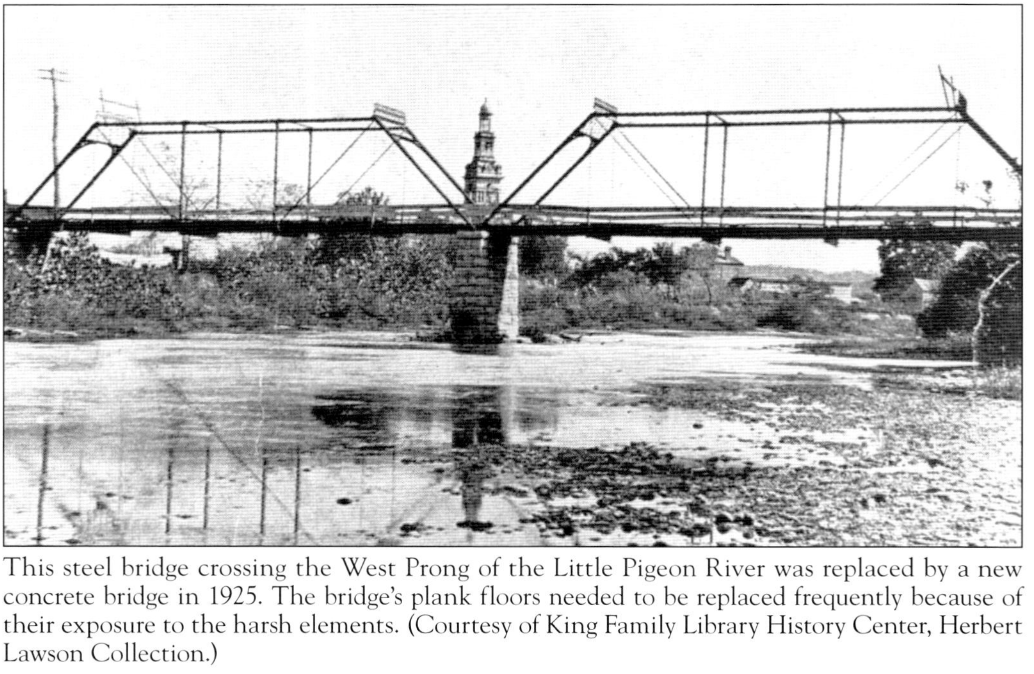

This steel bridge crossing the West Prong of the Little Pigeon River was replaced by a new concrete bridge in 1925. The bridge's plank floors needed to be replaced frequently because of their exposure to the harsh elements. (Courtesy of King Family Library History Center, Herbert Lawson Collection.)

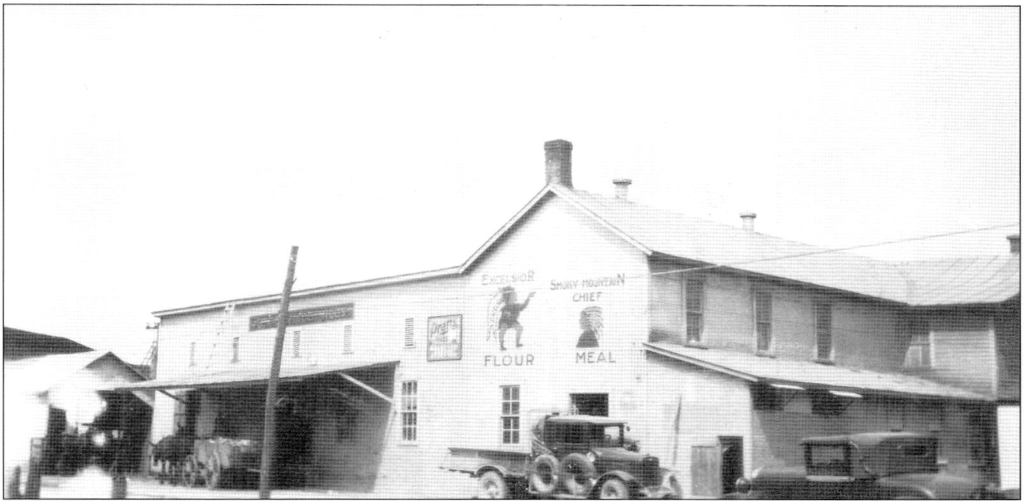

Sevierville Mills was built in the mid-1800s on West Main Street, along the banks of the East Prong of the Little Pigeon River. Proprietors included Archemides Chambers, Jerome Bowers, J.S. Ballard, J. Reed Wade, and Clifford Frost. The mill added an ice plant in 1915. The Tennessee Valley Authority removed the dam in the mid-1960s. Shortly thereafter, the buildings were demolished. (Courtesy of King Family Library History Center, Herbert Lawson Collection.)

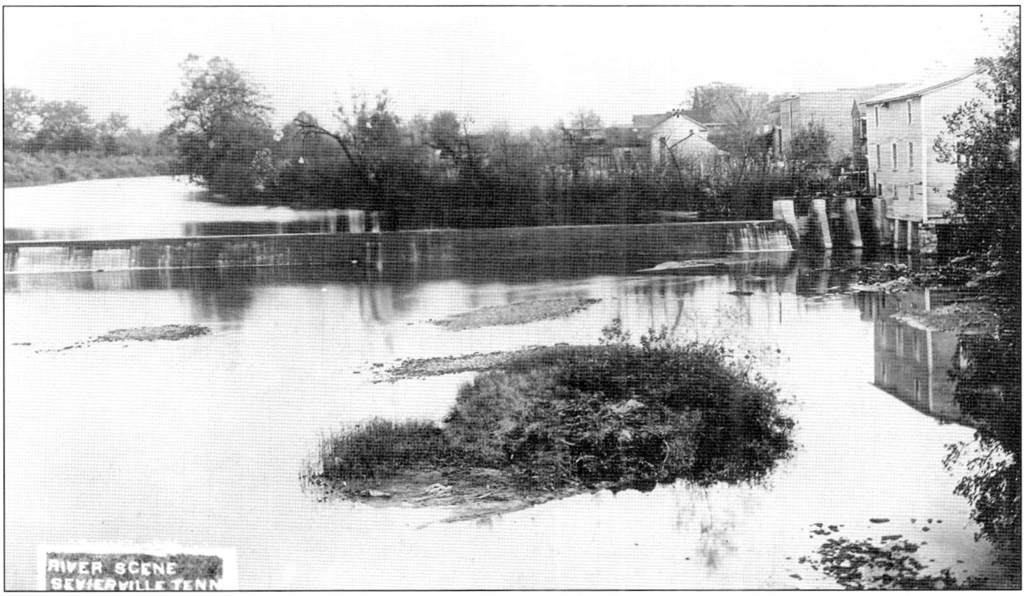

A concrete dam, shown here, replaced the original log dam behind Sevierville Mills in 1900. The scenic dam and millpond could be seen from the bridge crossing the East Prong of the Little Pigeon River. When the pond froze during extremely cold weather, local youngsters used the frozen river for ice-skating. (Courtesy of King Family Library History Center, Herbert Lawson Collection.)

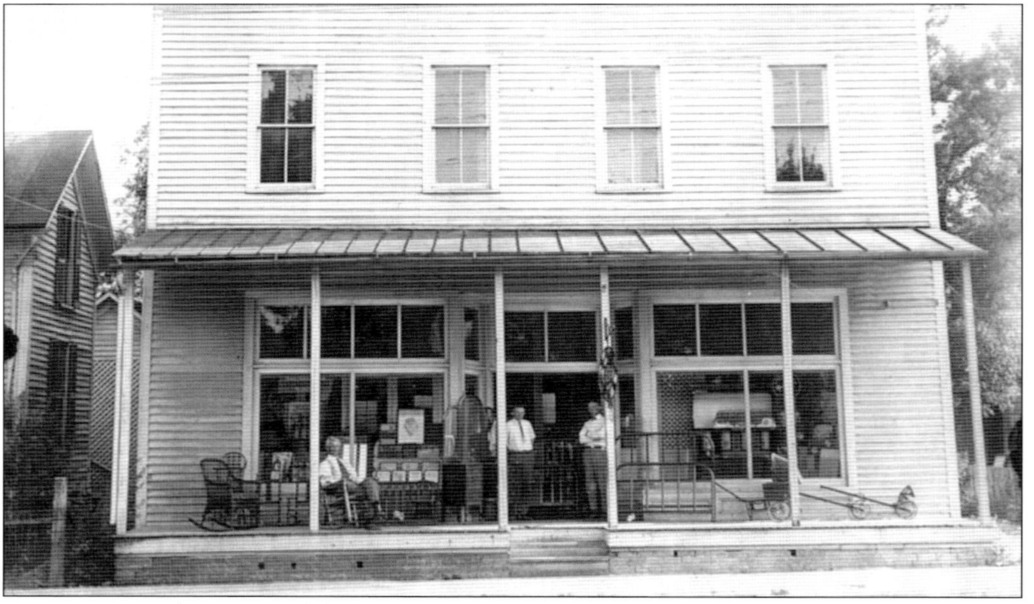

In 1902, K. Rawlings opened this new furniture store two doors west of the old Masonic temple on Main Street. Rawlings drove from Knoxville to Sevierville with a wagon filled with furniture he purchased for $100, every cent he had saved. The successful business grew, and members of the Rawlings family expanded to include the funeral trade, as well. (Courtesy of King Family Library History Center, Herbert Lawson Collection.)

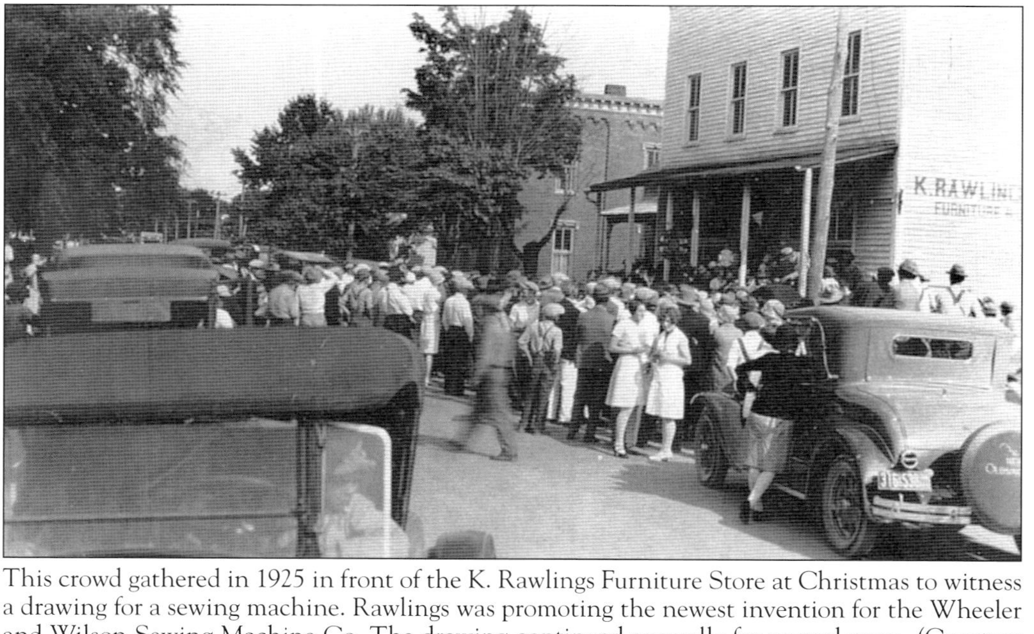

This crowd gathered in 1925 in front of the K. Rawlings Furniture Store at Christmas to witness a drawing for a sewing machine. Rawlings was promoting the newest invention for the Wheeler and Wilson Sewing Machine Co. The drawing continued annually for several years. (Courtesy of King Family Library History Center, Herbert Lawson Collection.)

Several hundred supporters of Sam R. Sells of Johnson City gathered on the grounds of the Sevier County Courthouse to hear a speech delivered by the congressional candidate in 1910. Sells won the election and served as the first district representative in Congress for the next 10 years. (Courtesy of King Family Library, History Center, Herbert Lawson Collection.)

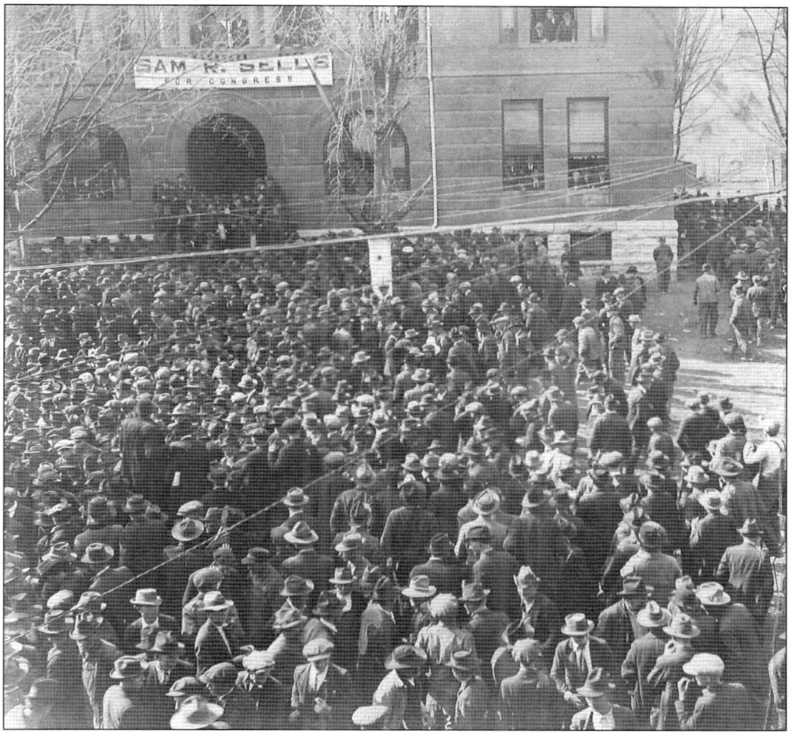

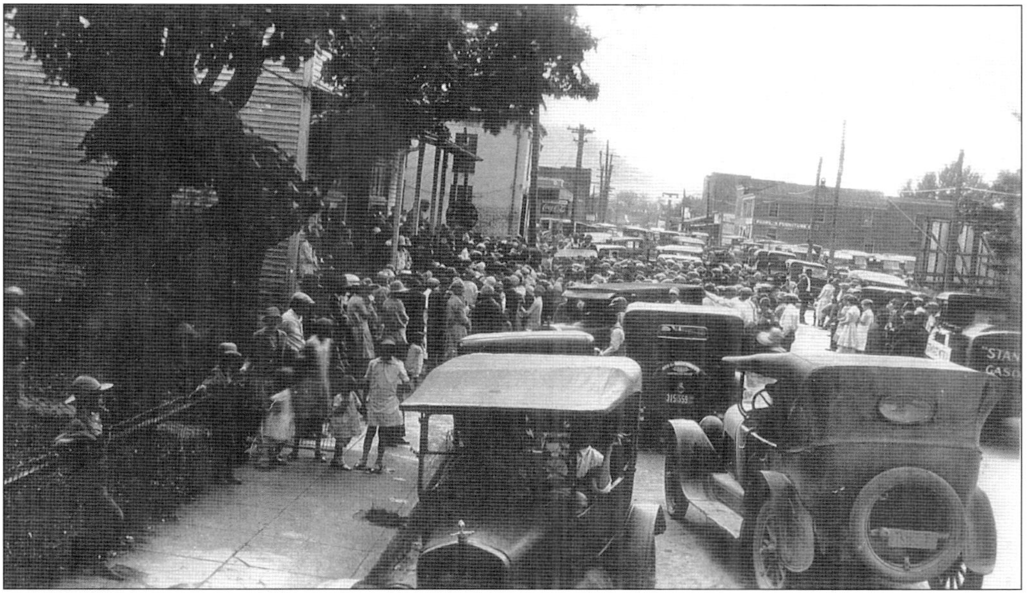

Main Street in 1925 buzzed with activity on Saturdays as residents from every county and rural demographic came to town to shop and conduct business. (Courtesy of King Family Library History Center, Herbert Lawson Collection.)

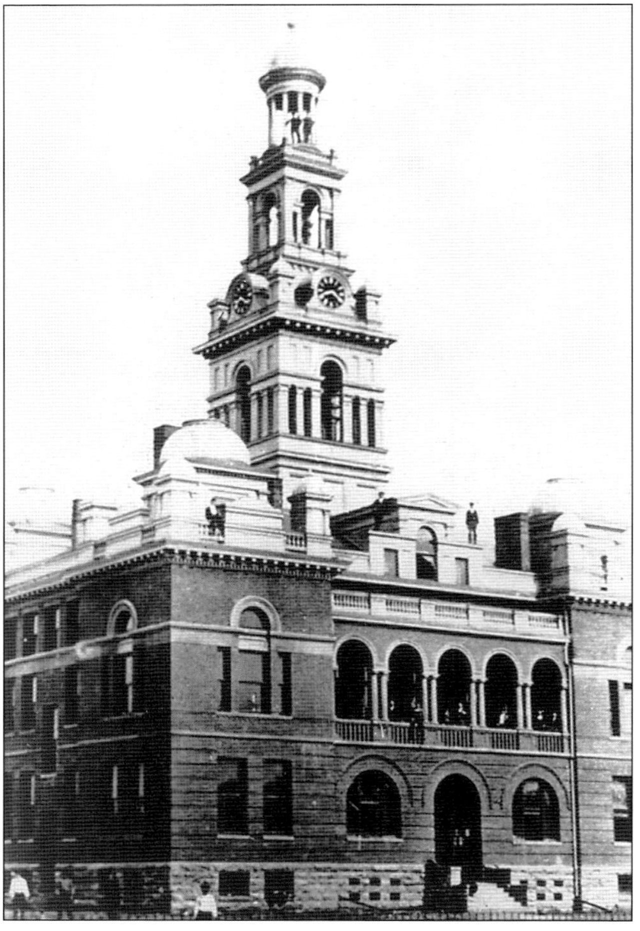

The historic 1896 Sevier County Courthouse features an imposing tower and clock. It is the fifth courthouse constructed since 1794. Enhanced by several additions and renovations, the courthouse has stood at the heart of Sevierville for more than a century. (Courtesy of King Family Library History Center, Herbert Lawson Collection.)

In 1893, a new county jail was constructed to replace the original jail that was located by the public square. This new jail, photographed here from the courthouse lawn, was built on the north side of Bruce Street. It was used until 1953, when it was demolished and replaced with a new structure. (Courtesy of King Family Library History Center, Herbert Lawson Collection.)

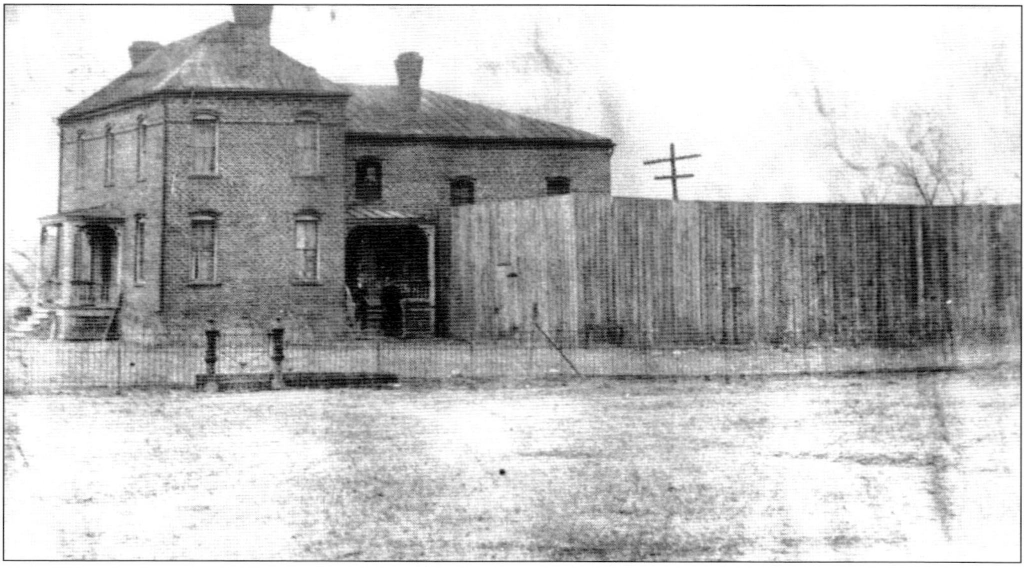

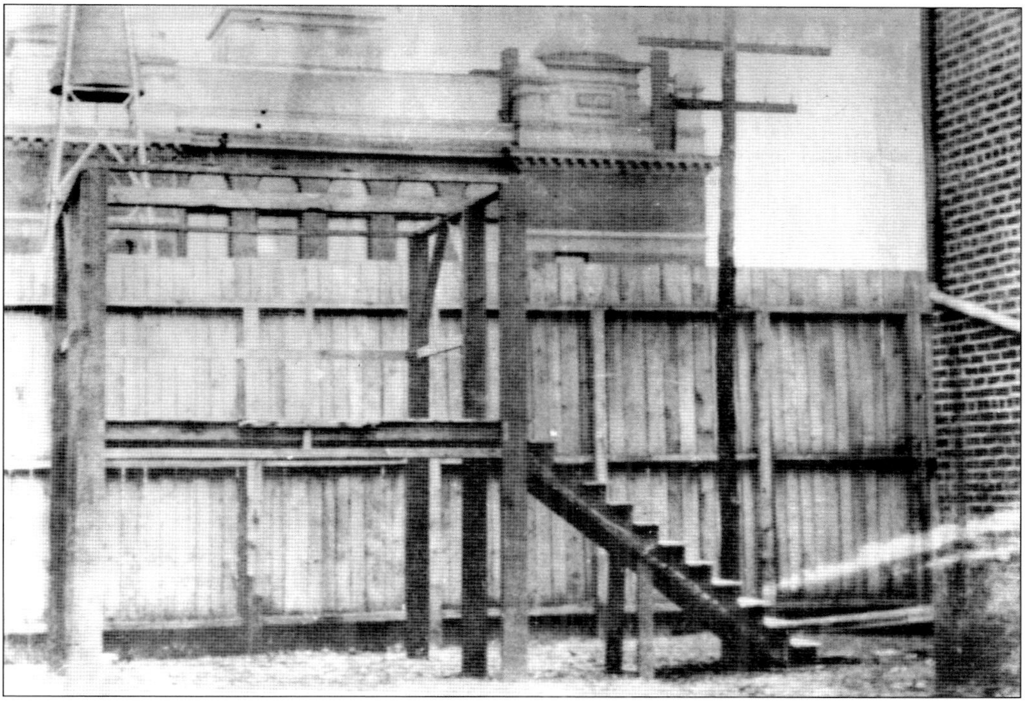

These gallows were located behind a tall wood fence adjacent to the 1893 Sevier County Jail. The last execution by hanging in the state of Tennessee took place here in 1901. (Courtesy of King Family Library History Center, Herbert Lawson Collection.)

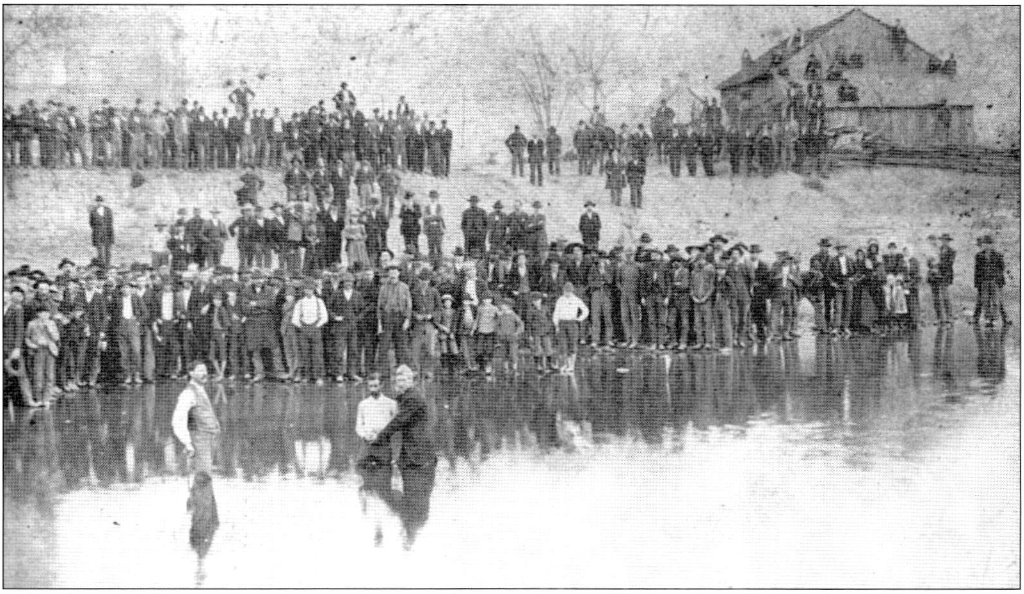

The baptism of Pleas Wynn drew a crowd, because shortly after, he and Catlett Tipton were hanged for the 1896 murders of William and Laura Whaley. Tipton and Wynn were members of a notorious vigilante organization called the White Caps. The group reigned terror throughout Sevier County for a decade. (Courtesy of King Family Library History Center, Herbert Lawson Collection.)

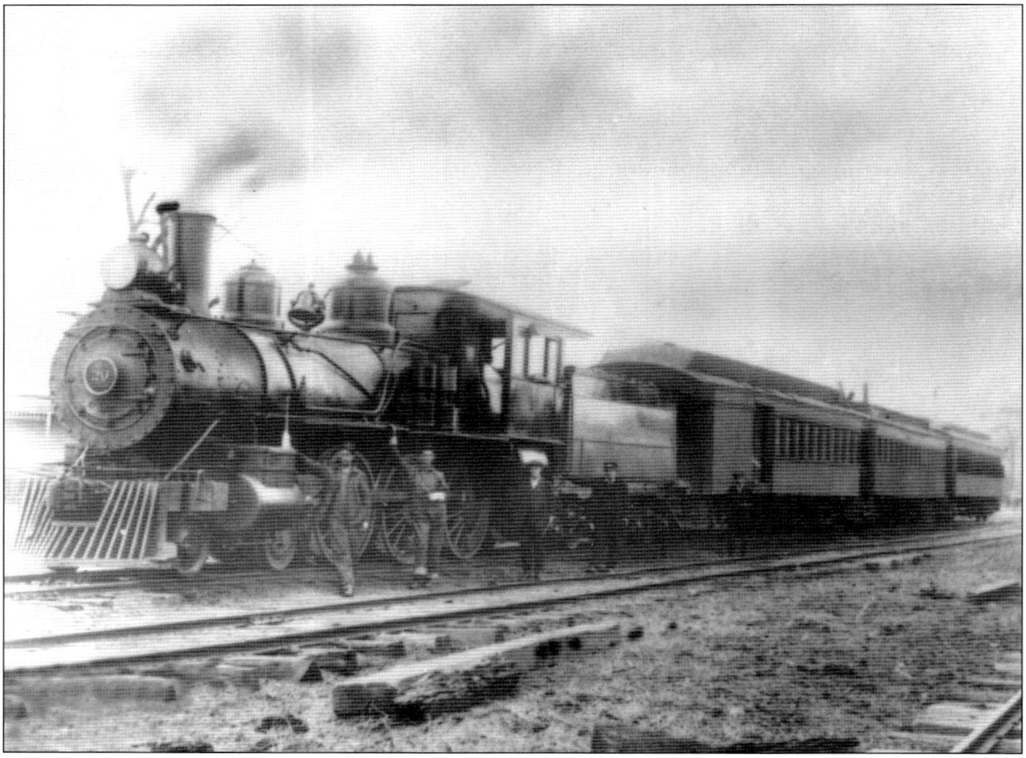

Shown here is the town's first train, the Knoxville, Sevierville, and Eastern. Residents of Sevierville soon bestowed a nickname "Slow Poke and Easy," due to the fact that the train was notoriously slow. The railroad meandered across the Boyds Creek valley. (Courtesy of King Family Library History Center, Herbert Lawson Collection.)

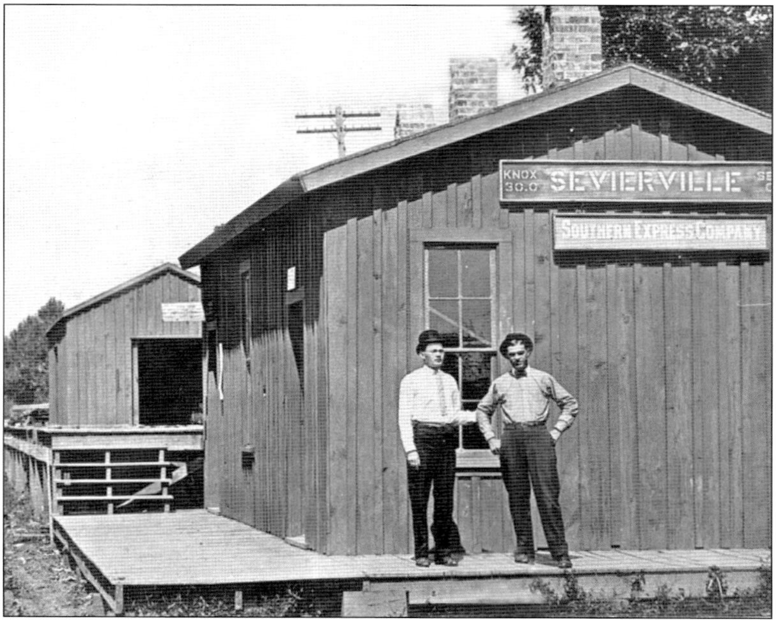

Tom Stafford and Jack McAfee await the arrival of the Sevierville, Knoxville, and Eastern at the Sevierville Depot. The depot was located near the west bank of the West Prong of the Little Pigeon. The location was chosen because tracks did not extend across the river until 1916. (Courtesy of King Family Library History Center, Herbert Lawson Collection.)

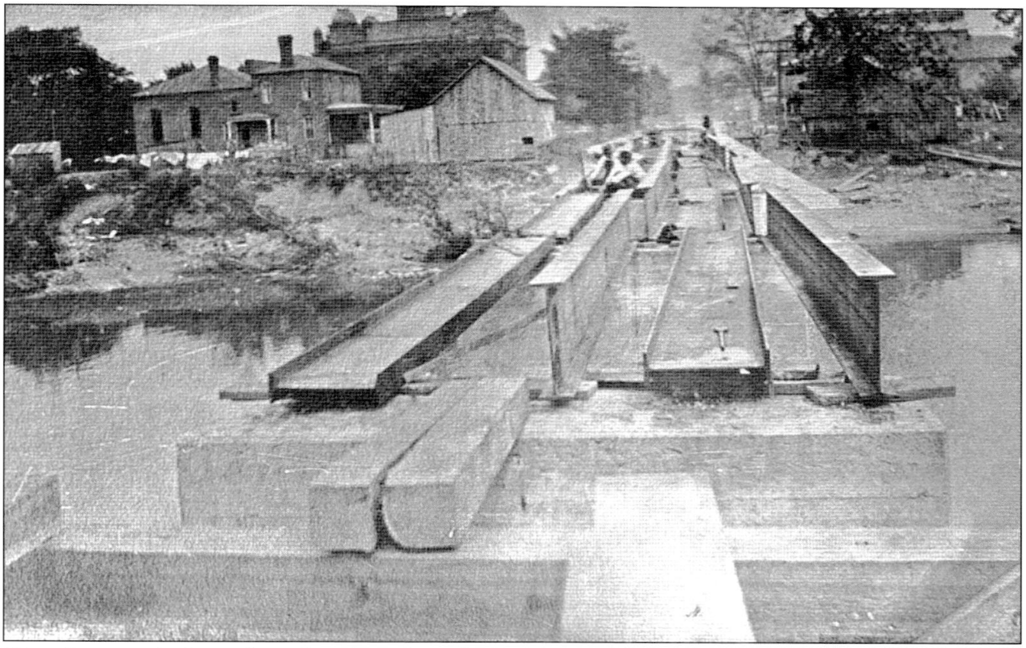

This photograph shows the railroad trestle under construction. The old jail and courthouse can be seen in the distance. (Courtesy of King Family Library History Center, Herbert Lawson Collection.)

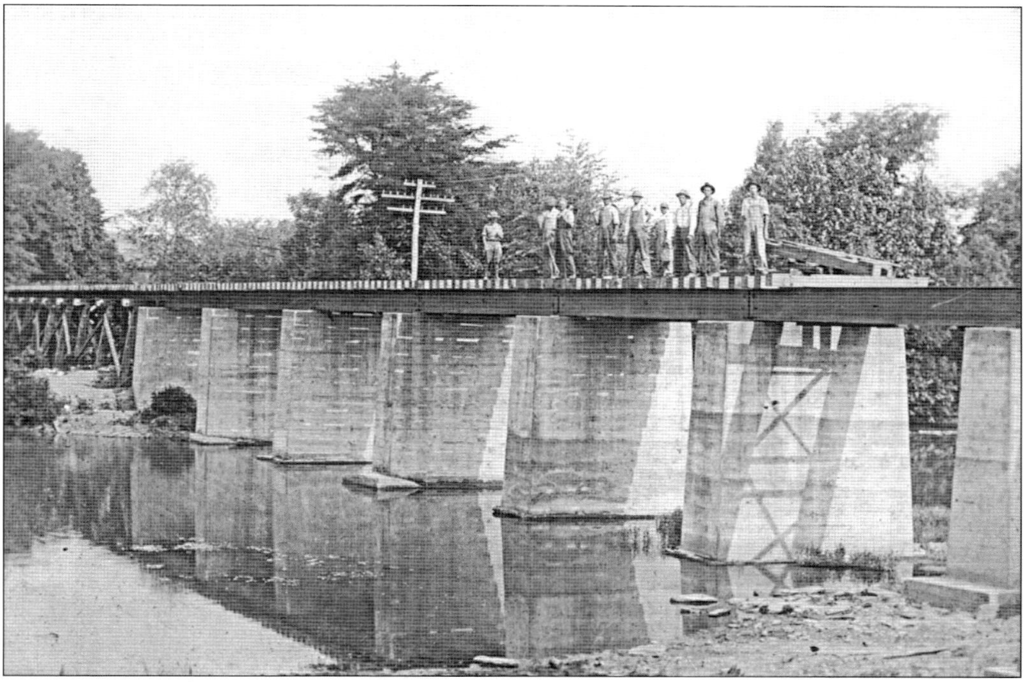

Construction workers pose on the nearly completed trestle. The tracks extended down Bruce Street in Sevierville, through Middle Creek, to the McCookville Station, which was two miles south of Pigeon Forge. (Courtesy of King Family Library History Center, Herbert Lawson Collection.)

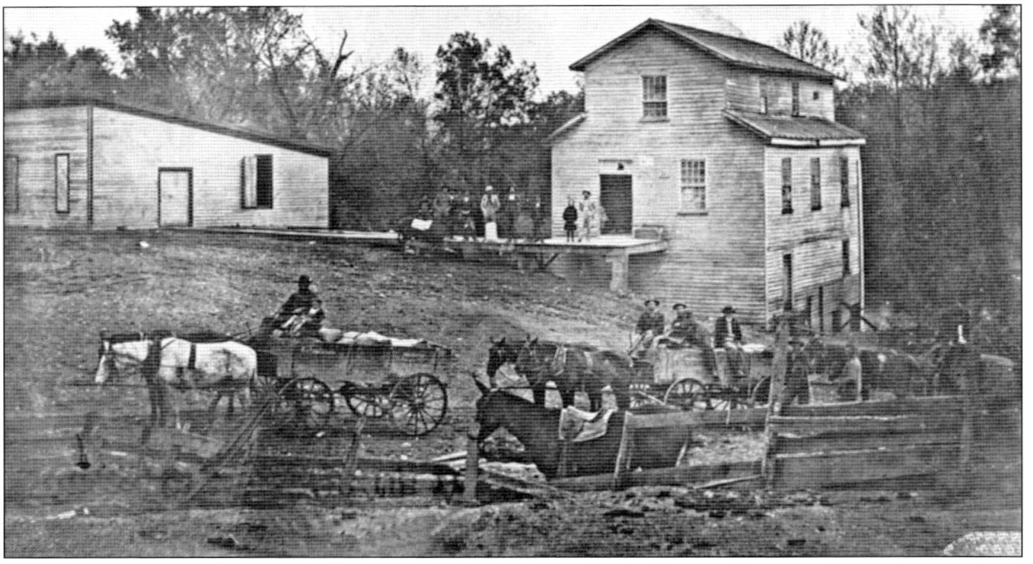

Catlettsburg Mill was located along the banks of the Little Pigeon River, a few miles north of town, and about one mile from the confluence of the Little Pigeon and French Broad Rivers. The mill was commonly called Cobtown Mill. (Courtesy of King Family Library History Center, Herbert Lawson Collection.)

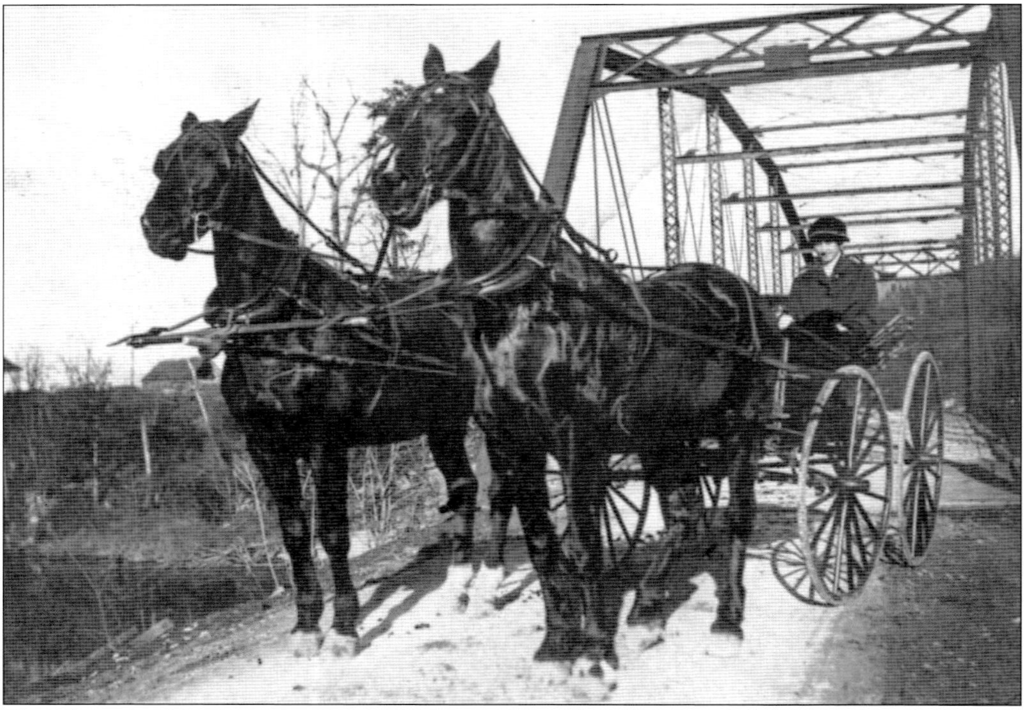

This photograph captures a carriage driver moments after she crossed the old steel bridge leading to Sevierville from the north. Completed in 1893, the bridge was extremely beneficial to residents living on the north side of the river. (Courtesy of King Family Library History Center, Waters Family Collection.)

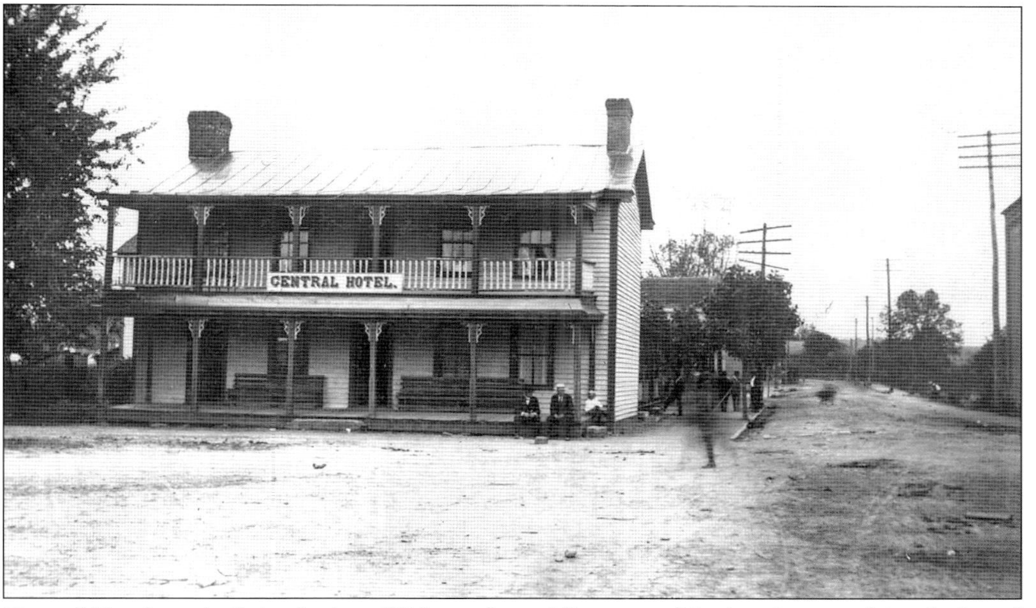

Central Hotel was built in the late 1800s on the public square. The hotel was a white clapboard structure with a large double-stacked porch on the front. There was no running water and the rooms were heated by coal-burning fireplaces. The original frame building burned to the ground in 1923. (Courtesy of King Family Library History Center, Herbert Lawson Collection.)

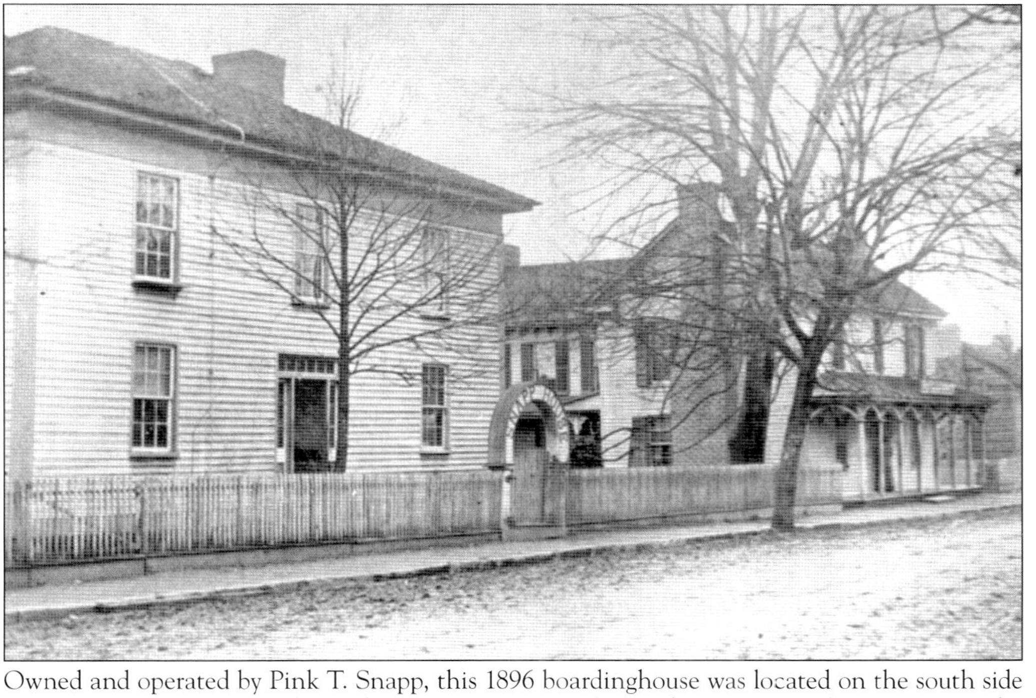

Owned and operated by Pink T. Snapp, this 1896 boardinghouse was located on the south side of Main Street. Bertie Hardin took over as proprietor after Pink Snapp passed away in 1921.The house was moved to a nearby lot and ultimately demolished in 1974. (Courtesy of King Family Library History Center, Herbert Lawson Collection.)

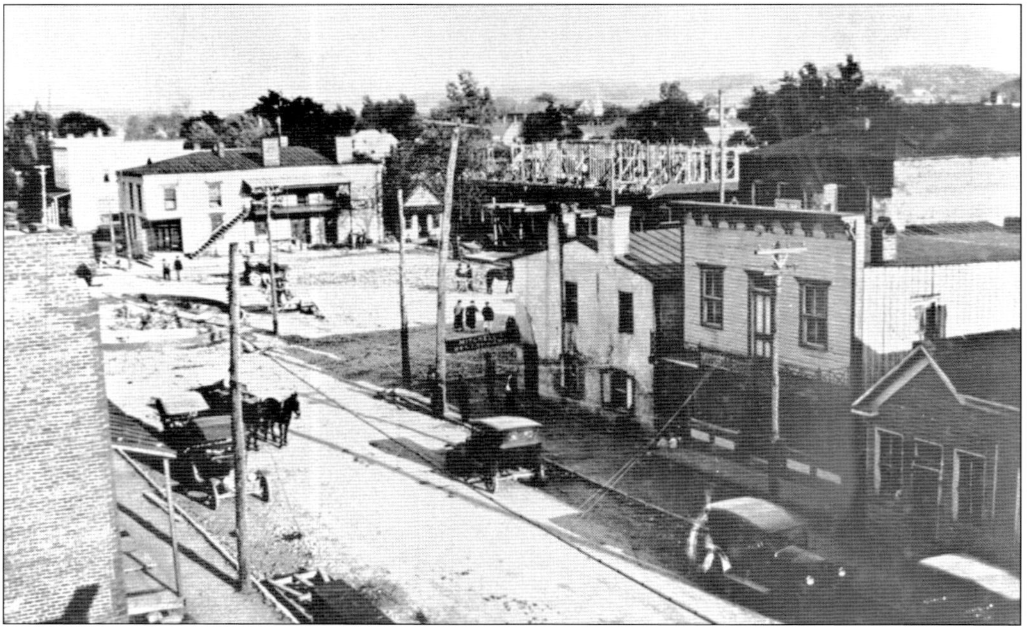

This image of the public square was captured during the construction of the Central Hotel. The Emert Brick Building was located east of the construction site, and the Mitchell Hotel was on the west side. (Courtesy of King Family Library History Center, Herbert Lawson Collection.)

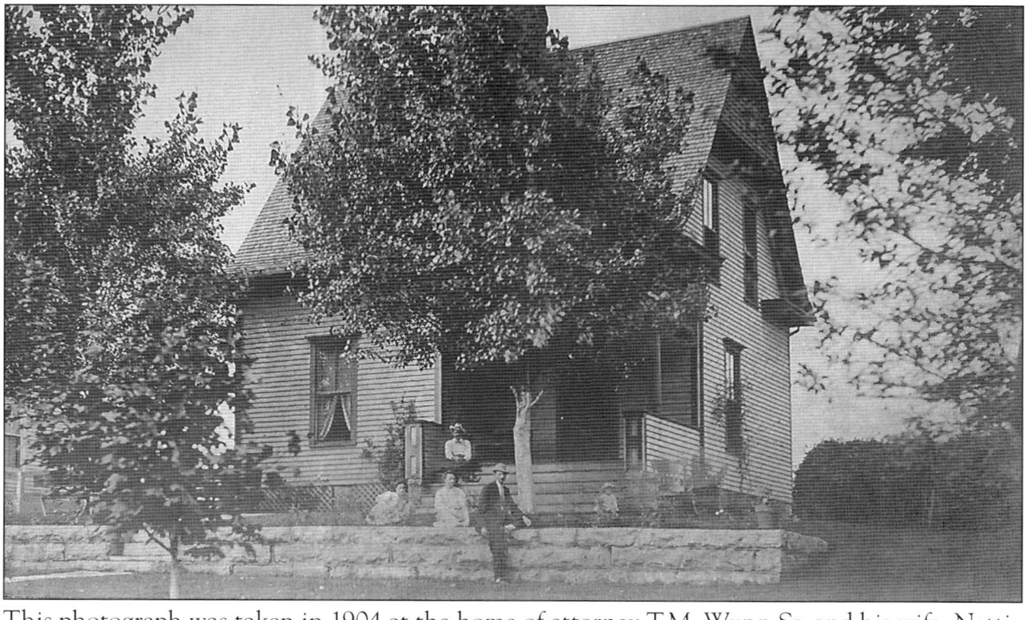

This photograph was taken in 1904 at the home of attorney T.M. Wynn Sr. and his wife, Nettie Thomas Wynn, on New Road. Sitting on the steps is T.M. Wynn Sr., with his infant son Zirkle Wynn at the foot of the steps. Seated on the rock wall, from left to right are Nettie Thomas Wynn, Alice Zirkle, and George Zirkle (brother-in-law of T.M. Wynn Sr.). The street is now named Park Road. (Courtesy of Lanning and Becky Wynn.)

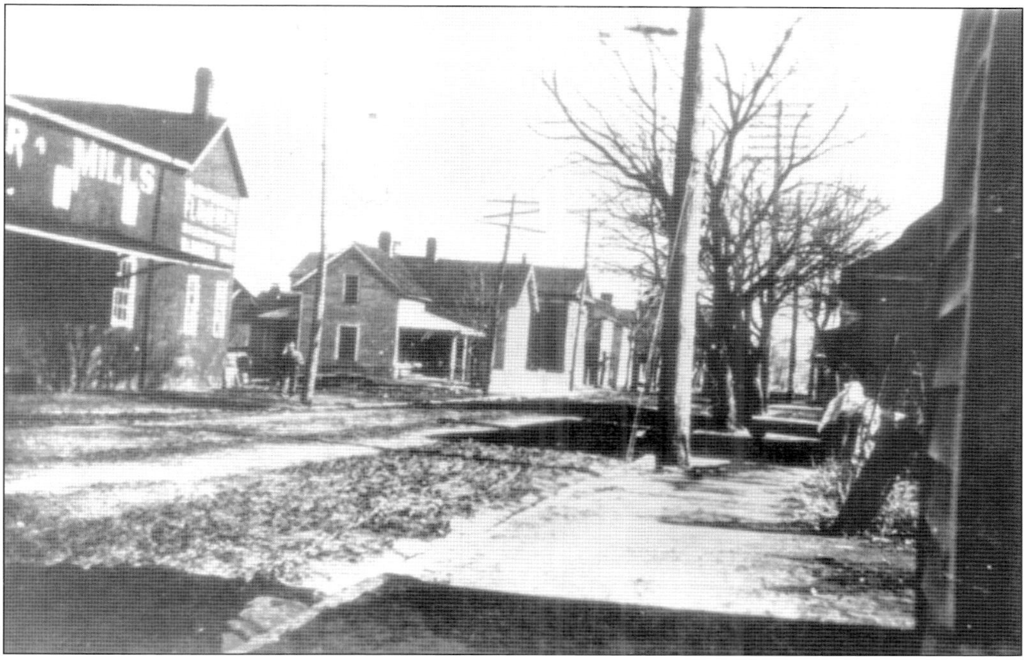

The West Main Street area, shown here with the Sevierville Mill on the left, was sometimes called Chinatown. Over the years, these homes were replaced by commercial buildings. (Courtesy of King Family Library History Center, Herbert Lawson Collection.)

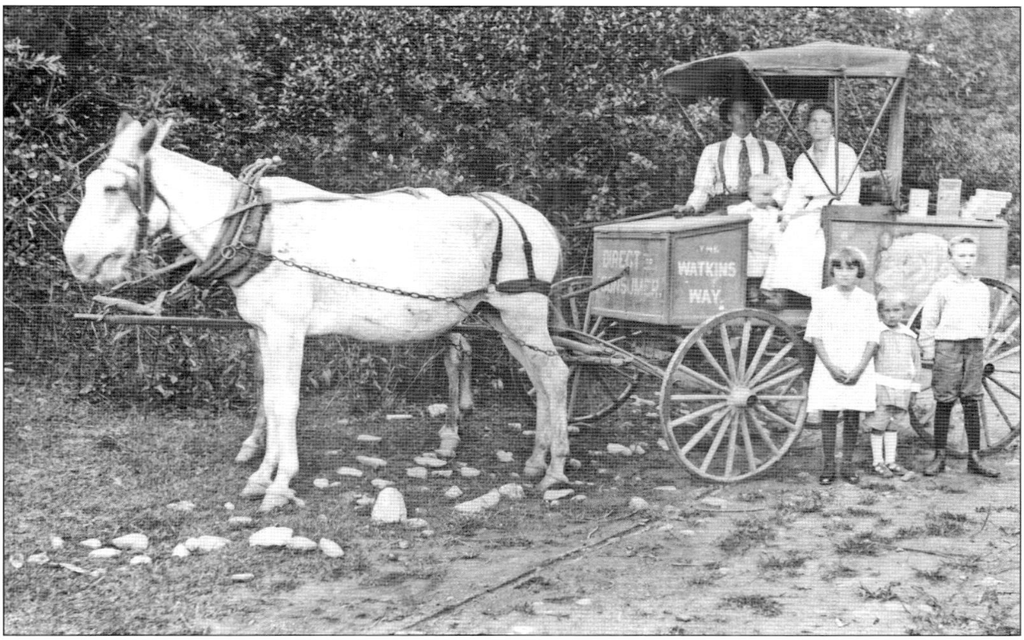

Traveling salesmen, called drummers, made frequent visits to Sevierville in the early 1900s. A salesman for Watkins Co. and his family pose here with his buggy. Local hotels offered special rooms on the ground floor so salesmen could easily display their wares. (Courtesy of King Family Library History Center, Herbert Lawson Collection.)

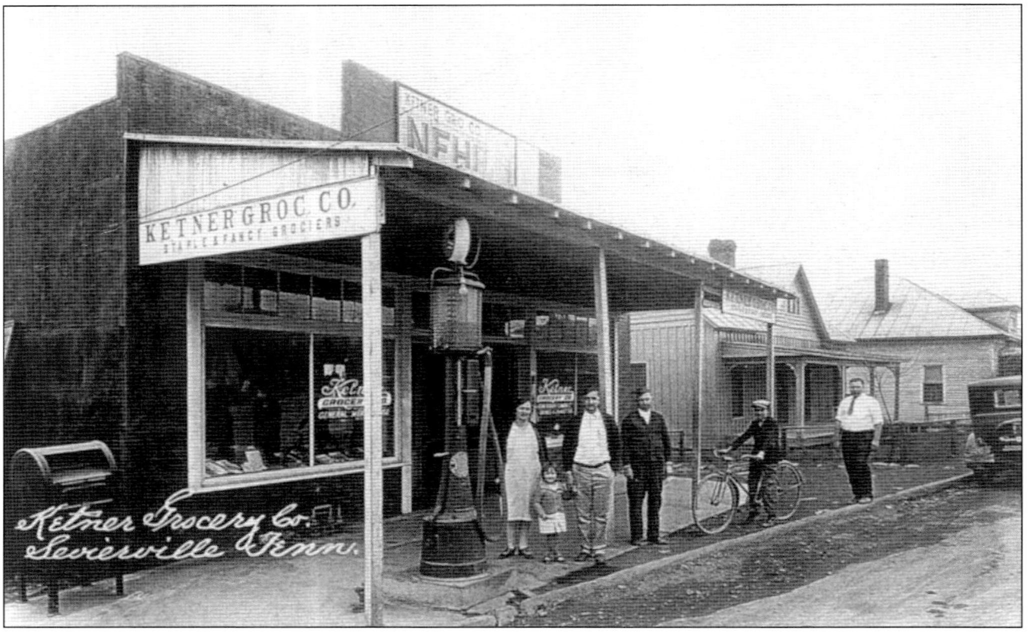

Ketner Grocery Company was located at the intersection of Belle Avenue and New Road (later renamed Park Road). The store also sold delicatessen items, general merchandise, and fuel. (Courtesy of King Family Library History Center, Herbert Lawson Collection.)

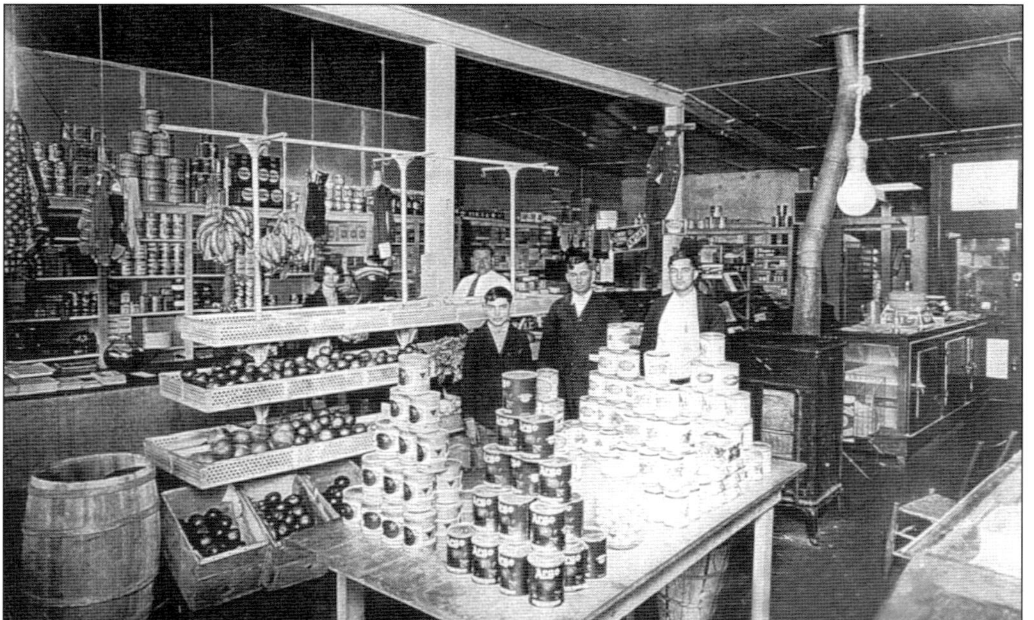

An interior view of the Ketner Grocery shows that fresh produce, hardware products, and clothing were items sold. Similar stores were located in the commercial district and among various residential areas surrounding downtown. (Courtesy of King Family Library History Center, Herbert Lawson Collection.)

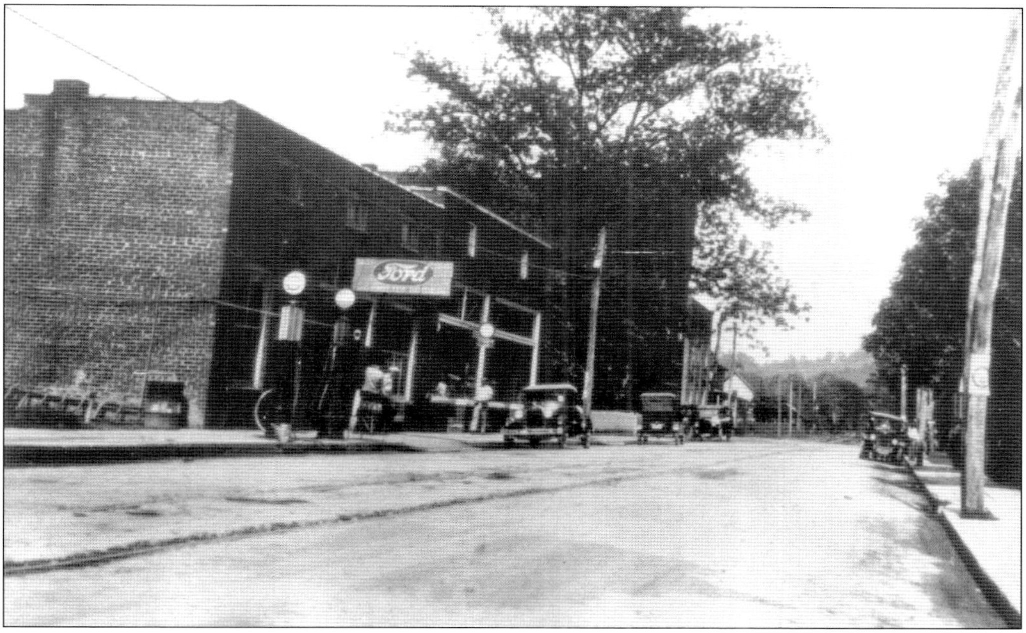

Bruce Street is photographed in 1916 shortly after train tracks were placed down the middle of the street. The train was a fixture on Bruce Street until the mid-1960s. (Courtesy of King Family Library History Center, Herbert Lawson Collection.)

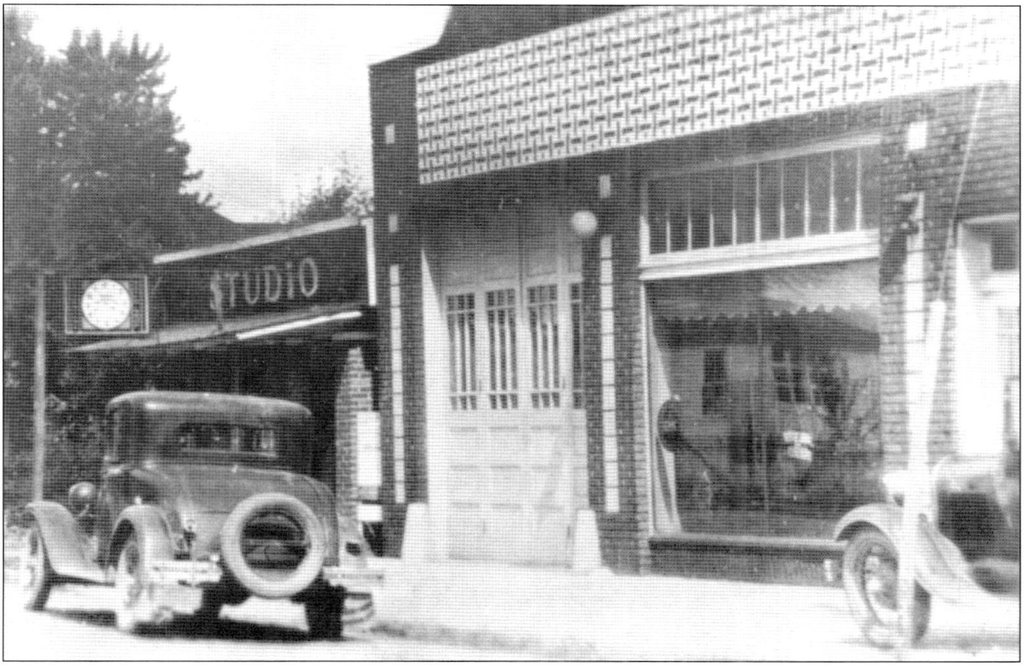

John B. Waters Sr. constructed a large brick garage on the southwest corner of Court Avenue and Joy Street. The first occupant was Watson Motor Company. Patterson's Photography Studio is visible in the section of the building that later became Bashors' Florist. The garage was later converted into the Pines Theatre. (Courtesy of King Family Library, Waters Family Collection.)

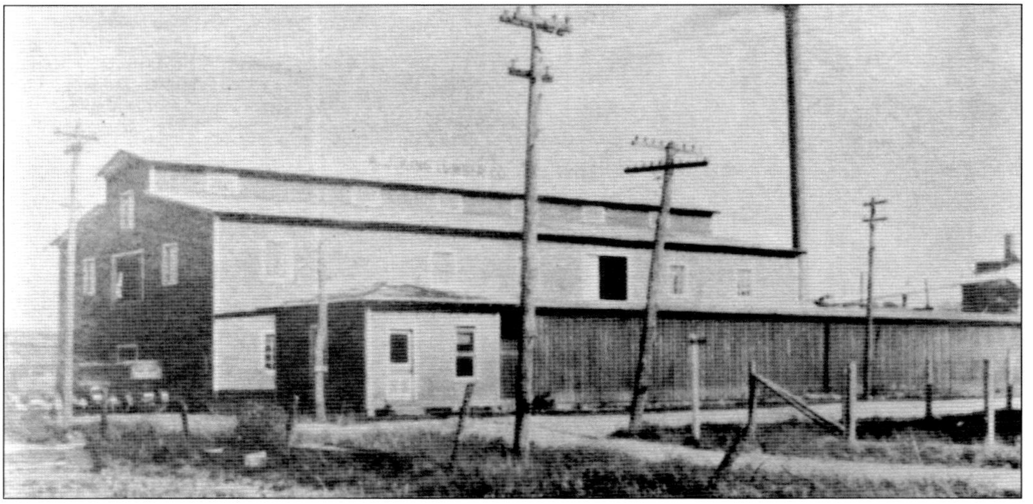

The A.J. King Lumber Company was established in 1919. A. J. King Sr. and Miles B. McMahan Sr. operated the business together until 1924, when they divided the business. King kept the business at the corner of High and Railroad Streets, and McMahan took 700 acres of timberland in Walden's Creek. (Courtesy of King Family Library History Center, Herbert Lawson Collection.)

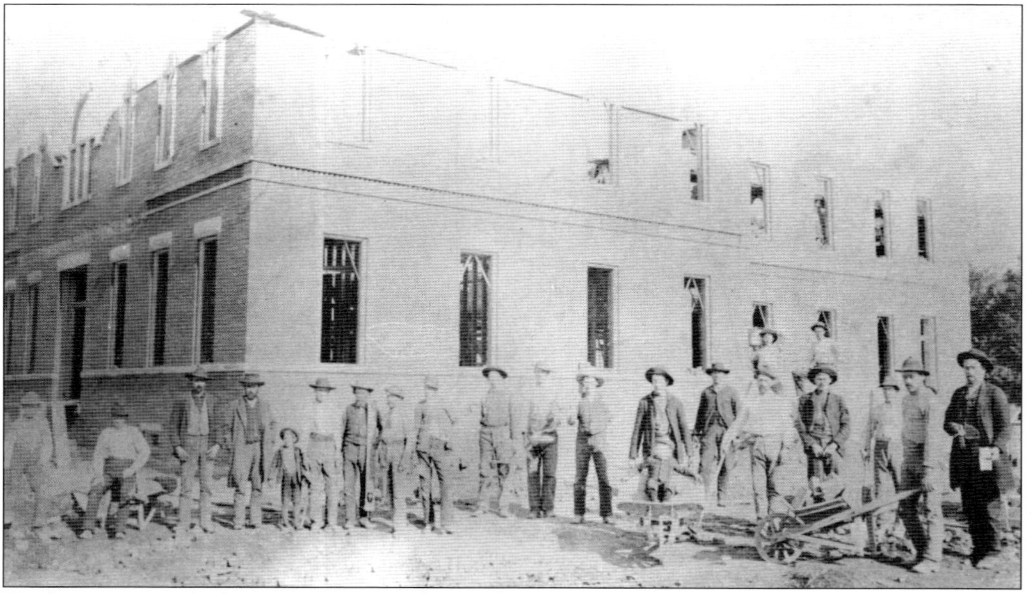

Workers pose on Cedar Street in 1890, during the construction of Murphy College. The building is one of the oldest brick structures still standing in Sevierville. Currently, the Sevier County Board of Education operates from the building. (Courtesy of King Family Library History Center, Herbert Lawson Collection.)

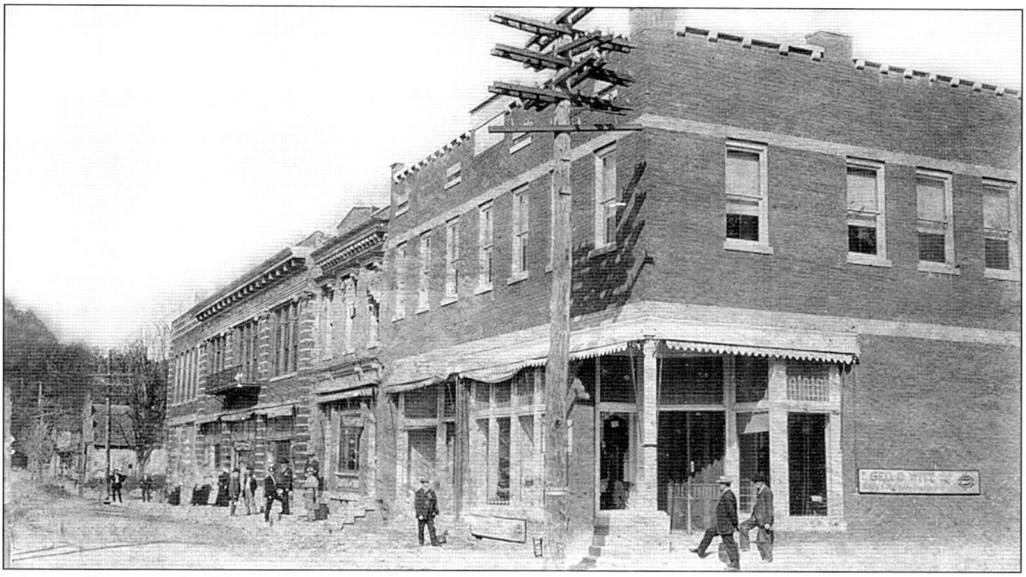

The Miller Yett building was constructed on the northeast corner of Court Avenue and Bruce Street in 1907. The building later became the Corner Store. In 1910, sidewalks were made of wood. (Courtesy of King Family Library History Center, Herbert Lawson Collection.)

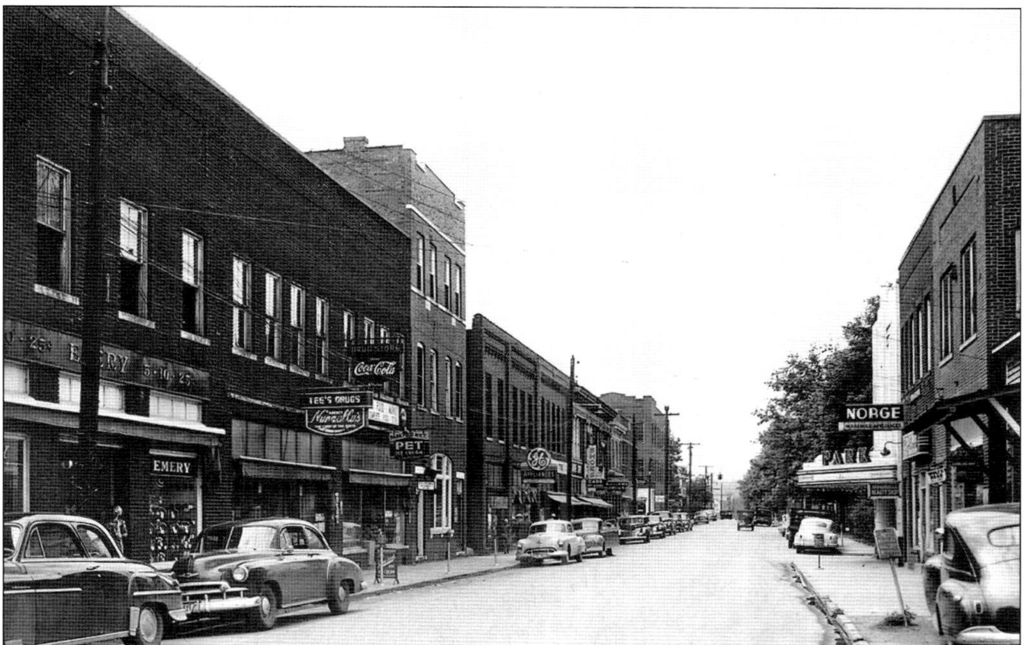

This 1940 view of Court Avenue facing south shows the Park Theatre marquee on the right. The Park Theatre was constructed in 1929 and originally called the Palace. The name changed after Willie Kate Murphy took over operations in 1931. Eddie Patterson operated the projector for many years. (Courtesy of Sevierville Chamber of Commerce.)

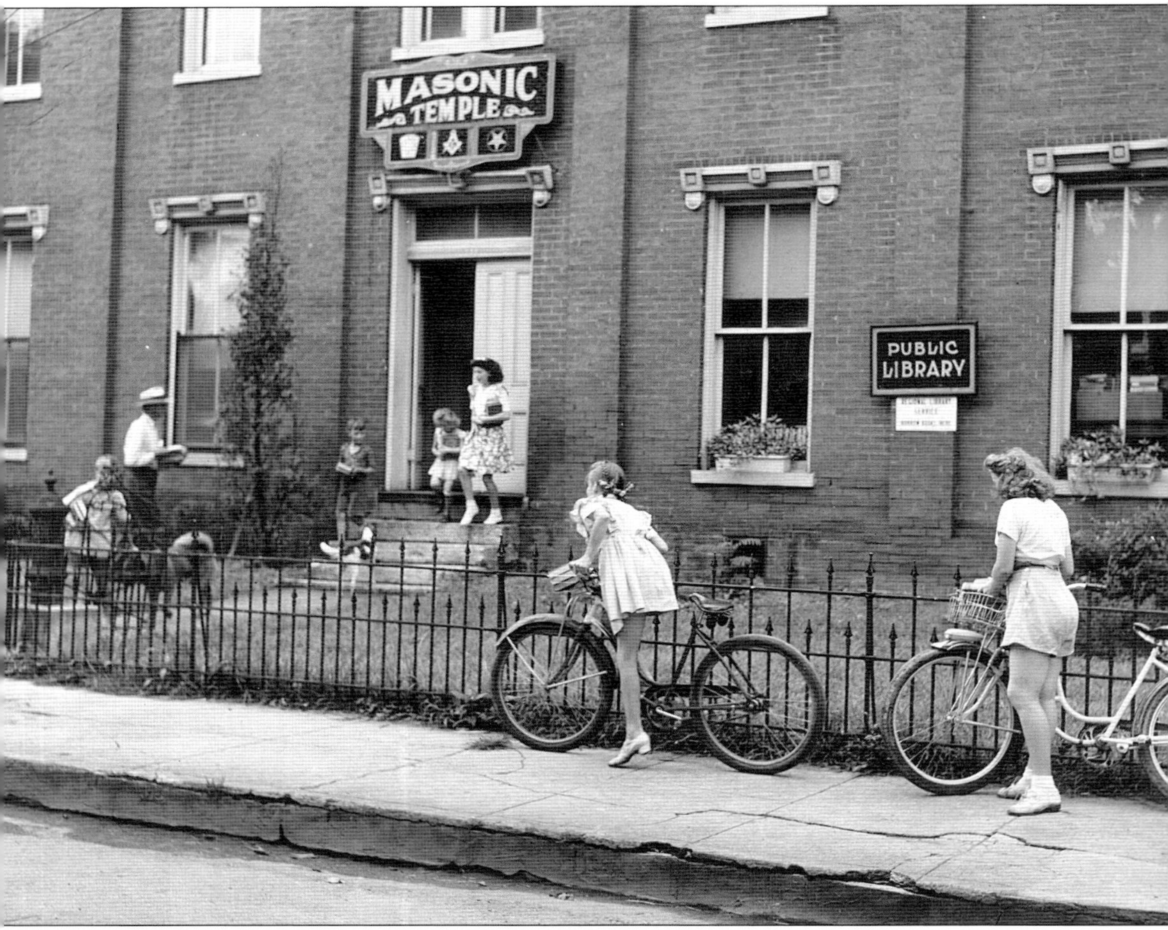

Mountain Star Lodge No. 197 was constructed in 1894 on Main Street. The Masons invited the Sevier County Public Library to use part of the building from 1920 until 1967. The Mountain Star chapter was organized on June 4, 1850. Before the Masons moved to Main Street, they used the old Nancy Academy building and the Southern Methodist Church. (Courtesy of the King Family Library History Center, Manthano Club Collection.)

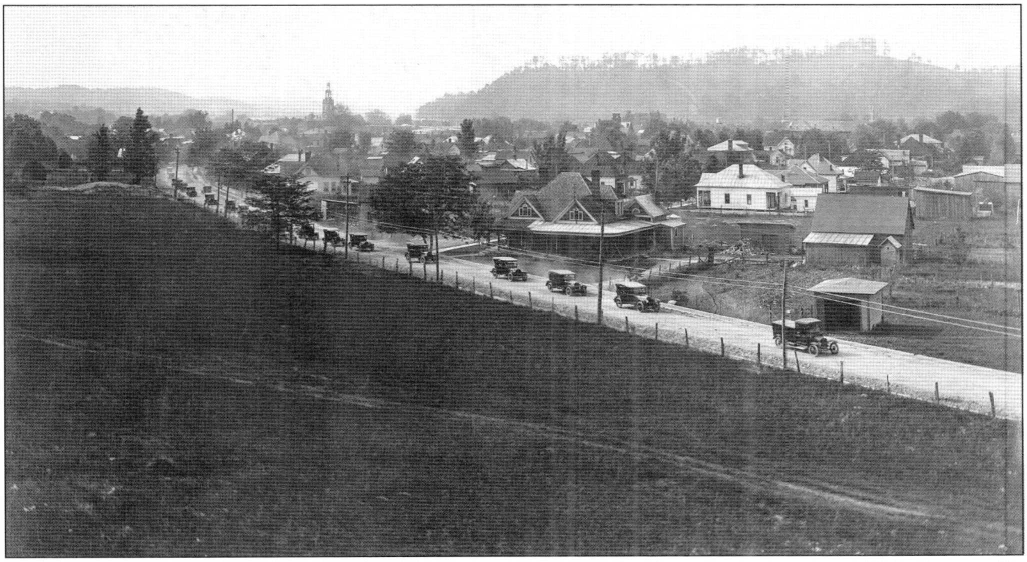

The funeral procession of Dr. Zachary Massey moves south along Park Road in 1923. Originally called New Road, Park Road was the main road connecting Sevierville to Pigeon Forge and Gatlinburg. This picture was taken from the top of Thomas Hill, where the Smoky Mountain Children's Home is currently located. (Courtesy of the *Mountain Press.*)

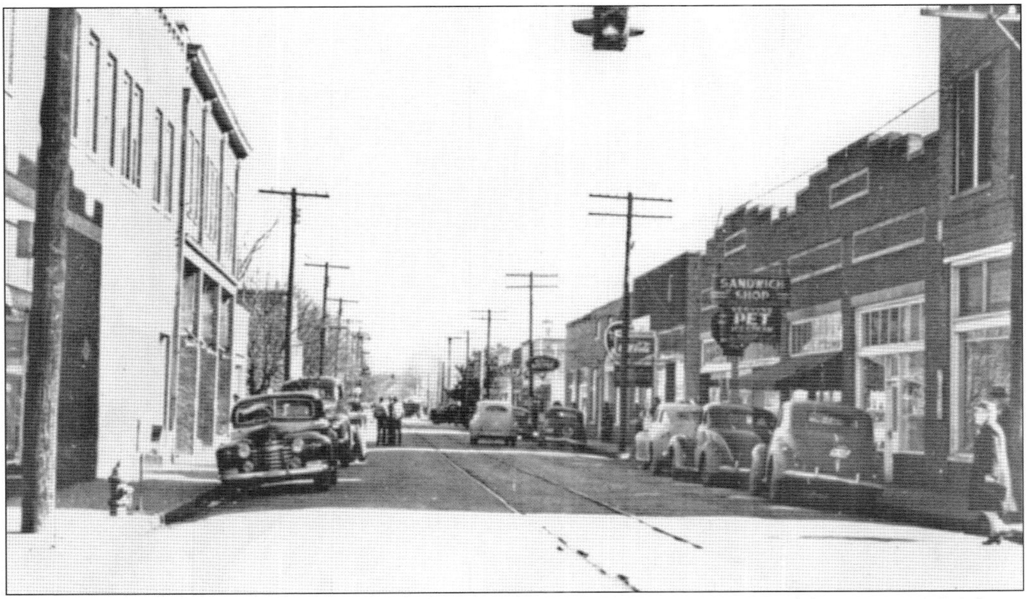

By the 1930s, Bruce Street was rife with businesses. Bruce Street was named for Bruce McMahan, whose grandfather James McMahan (who donated the original 25-acre tract for the town) and father, Wellington McMahan, had lived on the property. Bruce sold it off in lots in 1919. (Courtesy of the *Mountain Press.*)

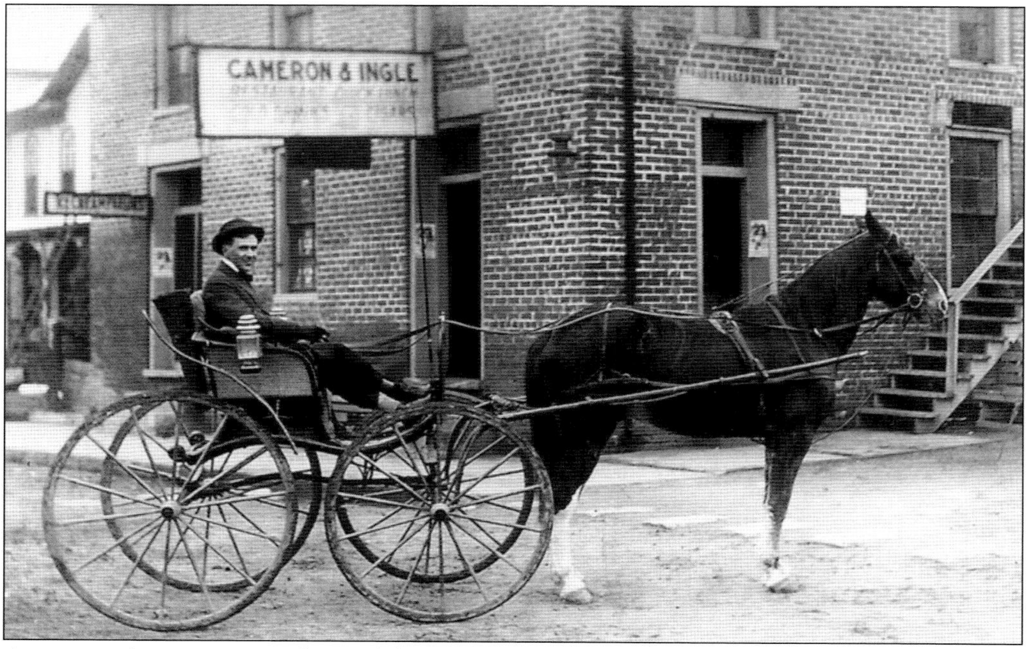

A carriage driver pauses in front of the Cameron-Ingle Restaurant in Sevierville. The sign over the front entrance advertised quick lunches and cigars. The eatery was popular, particularly with local businessmen and court officials. (Courtesy of King Family Library History Center, Herbert Lawson Collection.)

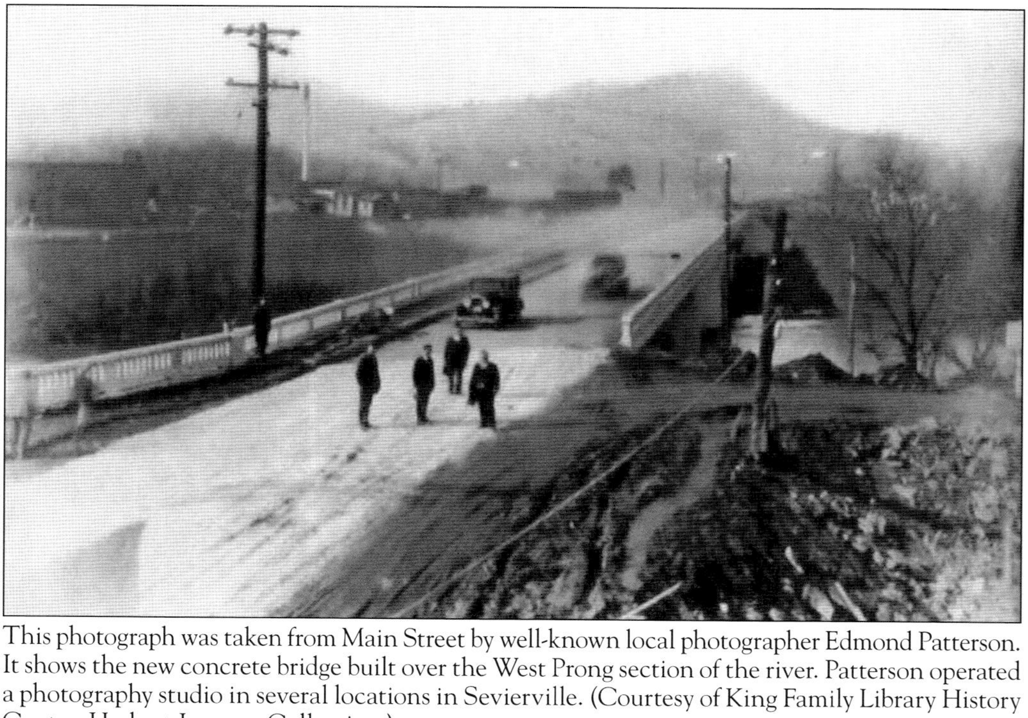

This photograph was taken from Main Street by well-known local photographer Edmond Patterson. It shows the new concrete bridge built over the West Prong section of the river. Patterson operated a photography studio in several locations in Sevierville. (Courtesy of King Family Library History Center, Herbert Lawson Collection.)

Two

Faces and Places

One faces the future with one's past.

—Pearl S. Buck

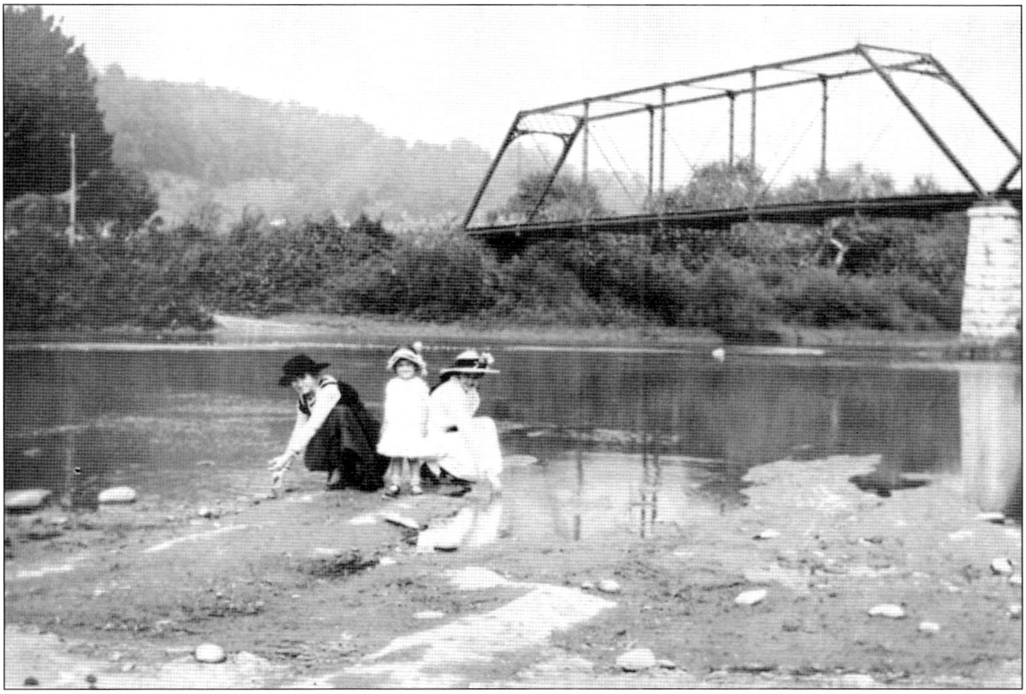

A young girl and two women pose in their Sunday best near the steel bridge built in 1893 over the East Prong section of the river. Seen across the river is the old road leading to the ford that was used before the bridge was built. (Courtesy of King Family Library History Center, Waters Family Collection.)

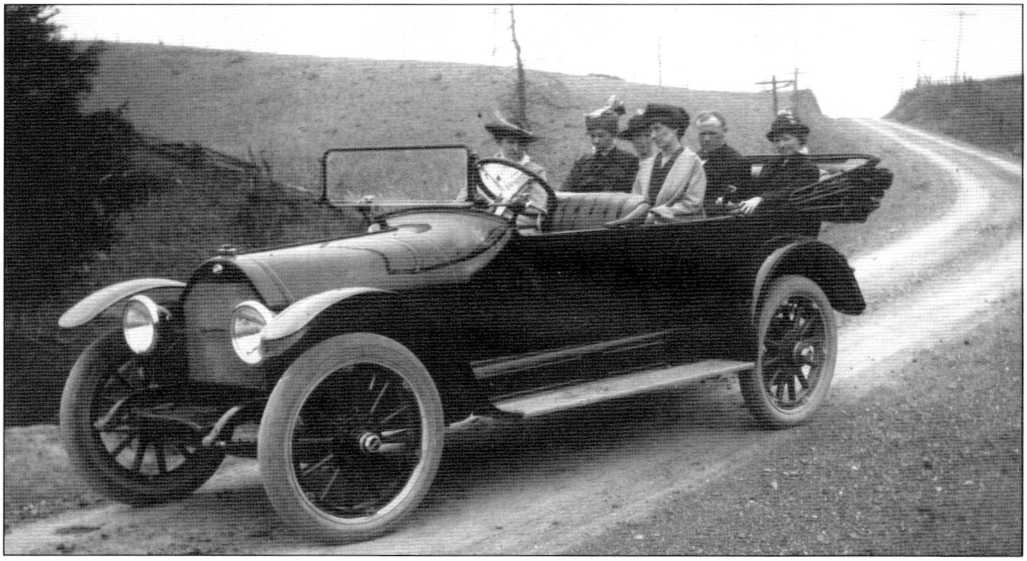

John B. Waters Sr. got out of the car he was driving to snap this photograph of his passengers. A Sunday afternoon drive was a favorite pastime for Sevierville residents after the automobile became prevalent. (Courtesy of King Family Library History Center, Waters Family Collection.)

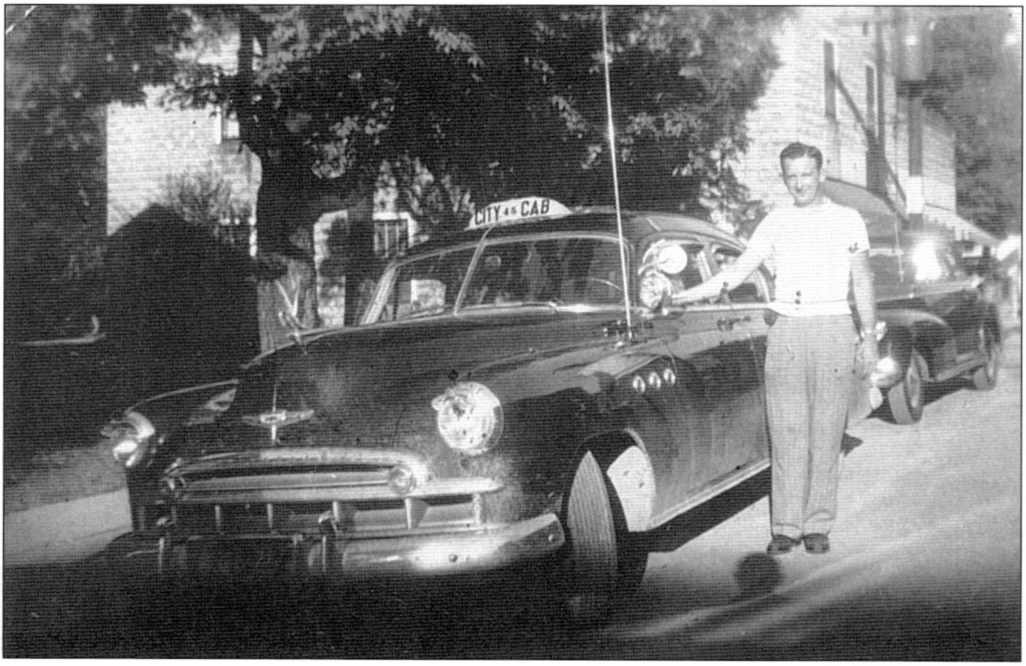

Alfred Newman is pictured standing by his taxicab in 1948. Along with his brother, John, Alfred originally operated a taxi business in Sevierville for several years. Later, they bought a café that became a popular venue for over 30 years. (Courtesy of Johnnie Faye McClure.)

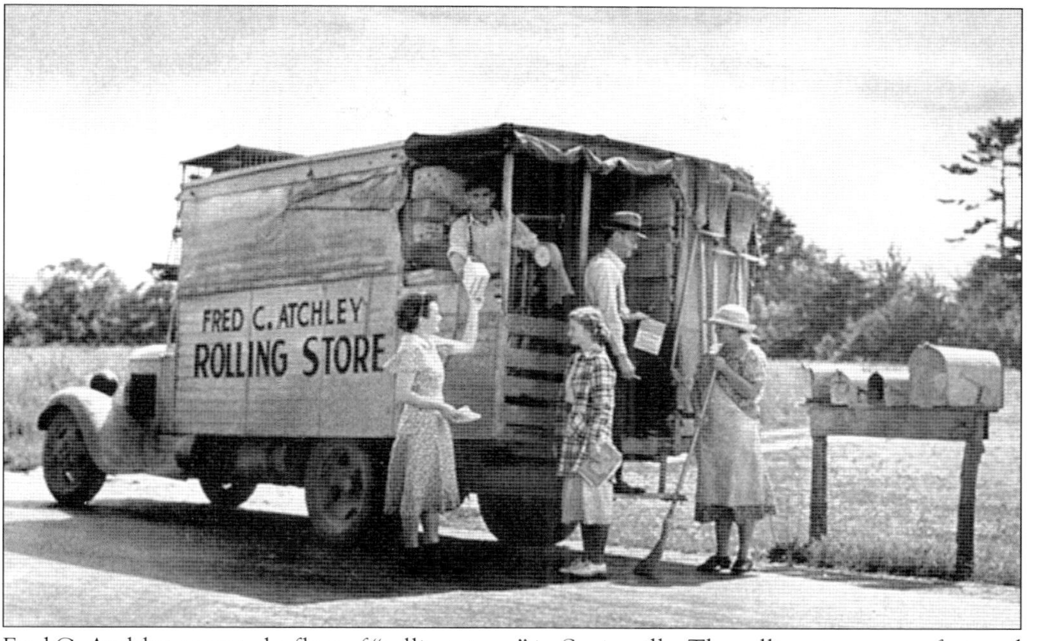

Fred C. Atchley operated a fleet of "rolling stores" in Sevierville. The rolling stores were featured at one point in *National Geographic Magazine*. He also opened Sevierville's first supermarket on Main Street. Fred Atchley was also partners with Earnest Conner in a local automobile dealership for many years. (Courtesy of Sevierville Chamber of Commerce.)

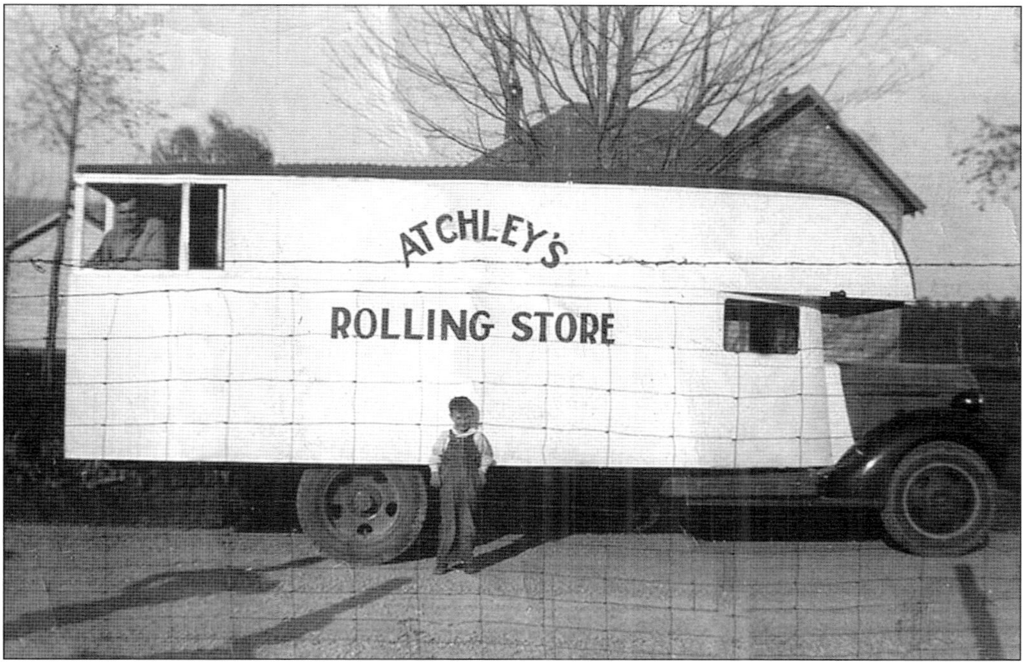

With his son Richard standing in front, Gene Atchley looks out the window of his rolling store. Rolling stores were extremely popular with rural residents who did not have transportation to drive to town for groceries and household items. (Courtesy of Richard Atchley, Jr.)

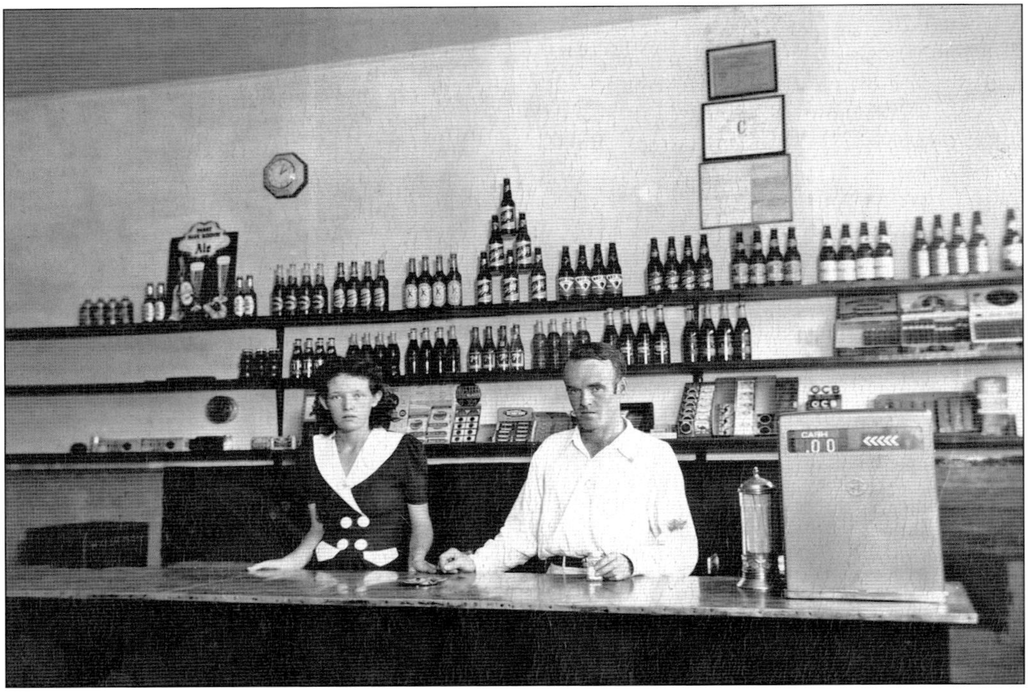

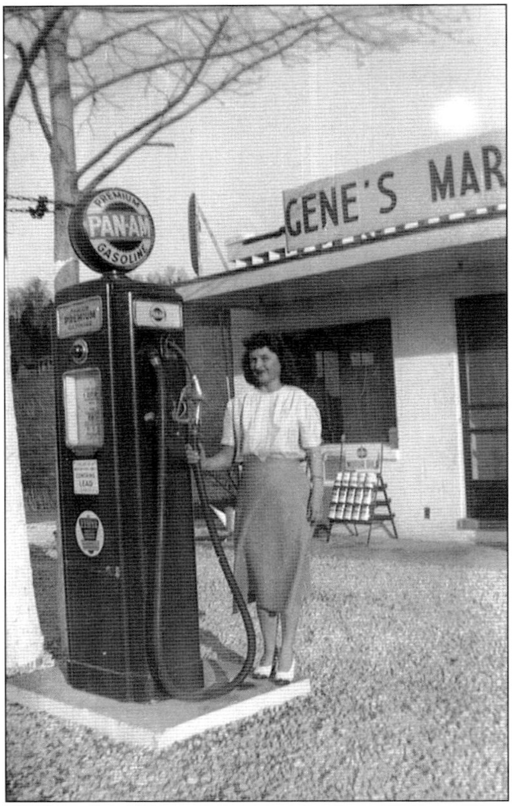

Paul "Red" Clevenger and his wife, Lois, stand behind the counter of the Rainbow Inn, located on Chapman Highway. The Rainbow Inn was a popular restaurant and dance hall. Later, the Clevengers leased a small building on Bruce Street to operate a restaurant that became renowned for their delicious hamburgers. (Courtesy of Marie Clevenger Cameron.)

Marjorie (Coffelt) Atchley stands ready to pump gas in front of Gene's Market on Chapman Highway. Atchley and her husband, Gene, operated the market until Gene and his brother-in-law, Gene Coffelt, opened a body repair shop on Jenkins Hill. (Courtesy of Richard Atchley Jr.)

The Pines Theatre was located on the southeast corner of Joy Street and Court Avenue. The converted garage started showing films in 1944. Operated by Myrtle Paine Waters, the theatre seated 700. Waters lived next-door to the theatre. Western films were a popular Saturday feature. (Courtesy of John B. Water Jr.)

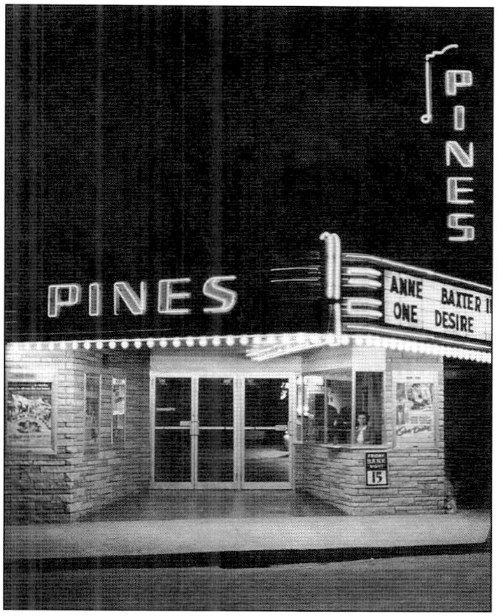

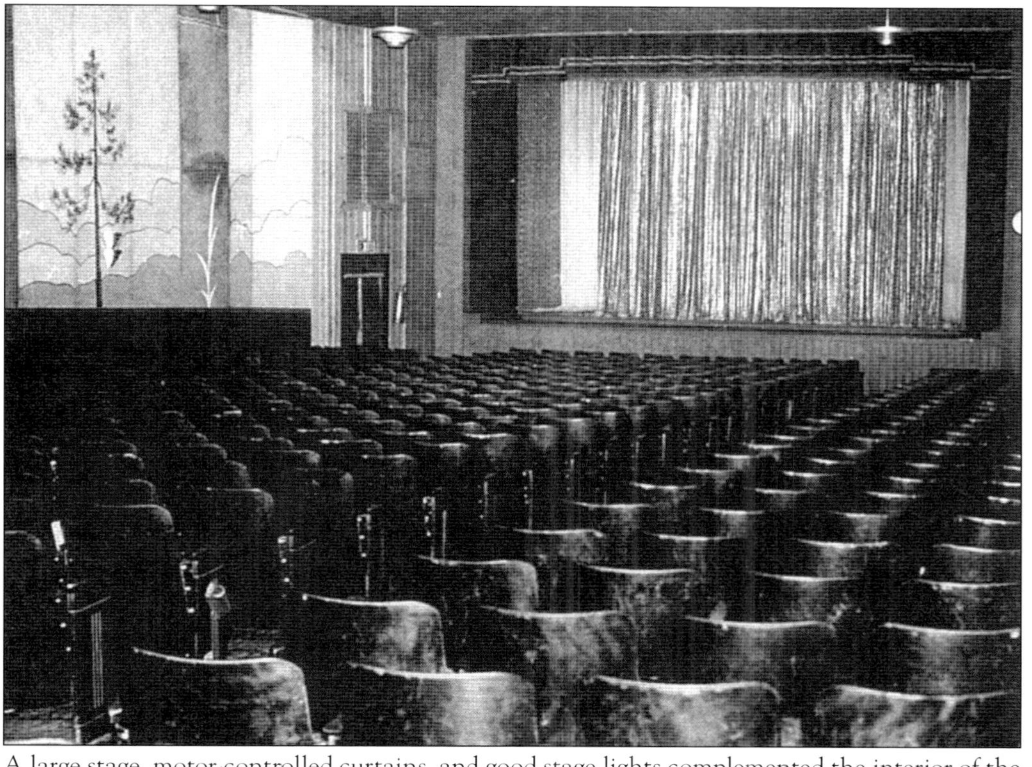

A large stage, motor-controlled curtains, and good stage lights complemented the interior of the Pines Theatre. Along with motion pictures, the Pines offered live stage shows featuring country-western artists, such as the Carter Family, Don Gibson, Sons of the Pioneers, Pee Wee King, and Chet Atkins. The first time Dolly Parton performed for a paying audience was on the stage of the Pines during one of Cas Walker's Amateur Hours. (Courtesy of John B. Waters Jr.)

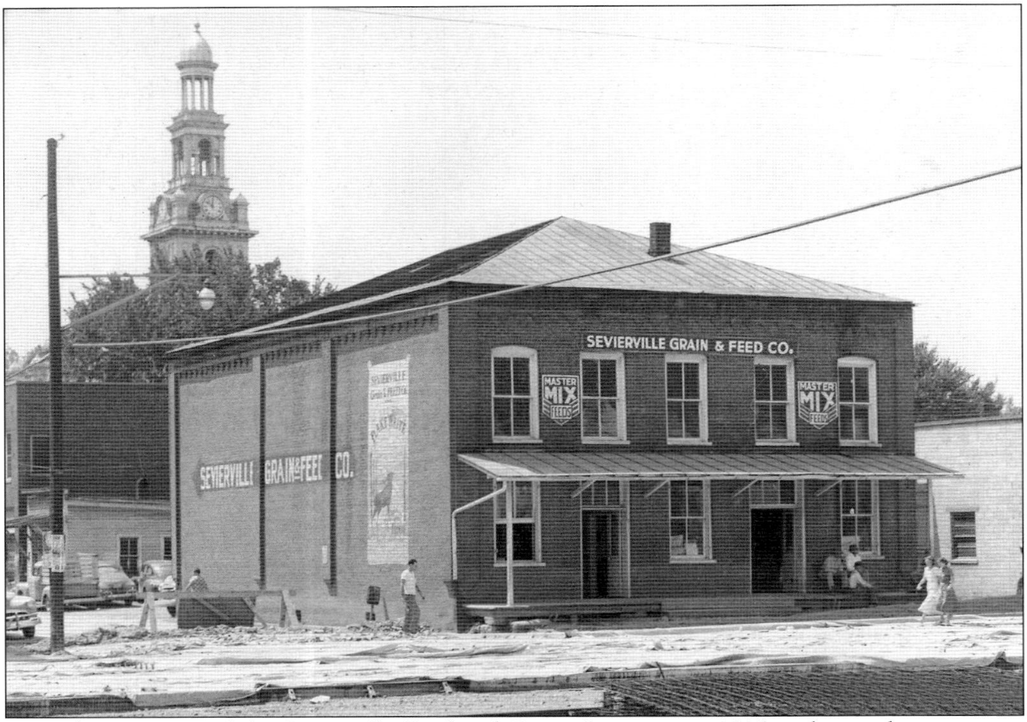

J.S. Adams organized the Sevierville Feed and Grain Company in 1915 at the southwest corner of Main Street and Court Avenue. In 1918, Adams purchased the old Catlettsburg Mill and the merger was named Sevierville Grain and Feed, Inc. The building was saved during a devastating fire in 1925 by dousing the flames with large barrels and tubs of water. In 1957, the old building could not be saved when another fire completely destroyed the building. (Courtesy of King Family library History Center, Herbert Lawson Collection.)

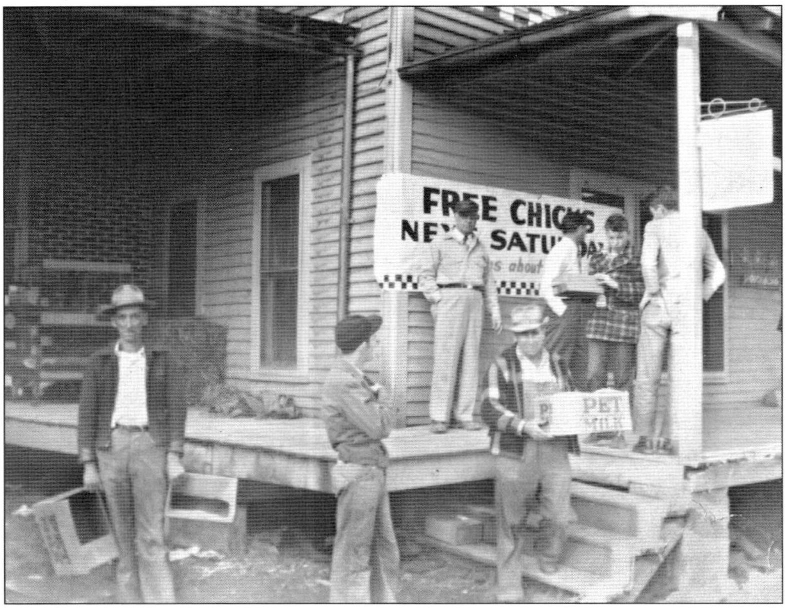

Farmers pick up free baby chickens at Temple Milling Company in the mid-1950s. The Temple family gave away the free chickens around Easter each year. The little chickens were dyed in a variety of pastel colors, and children were delighted to receive them. (Courtesy of James and Marie Temple.)

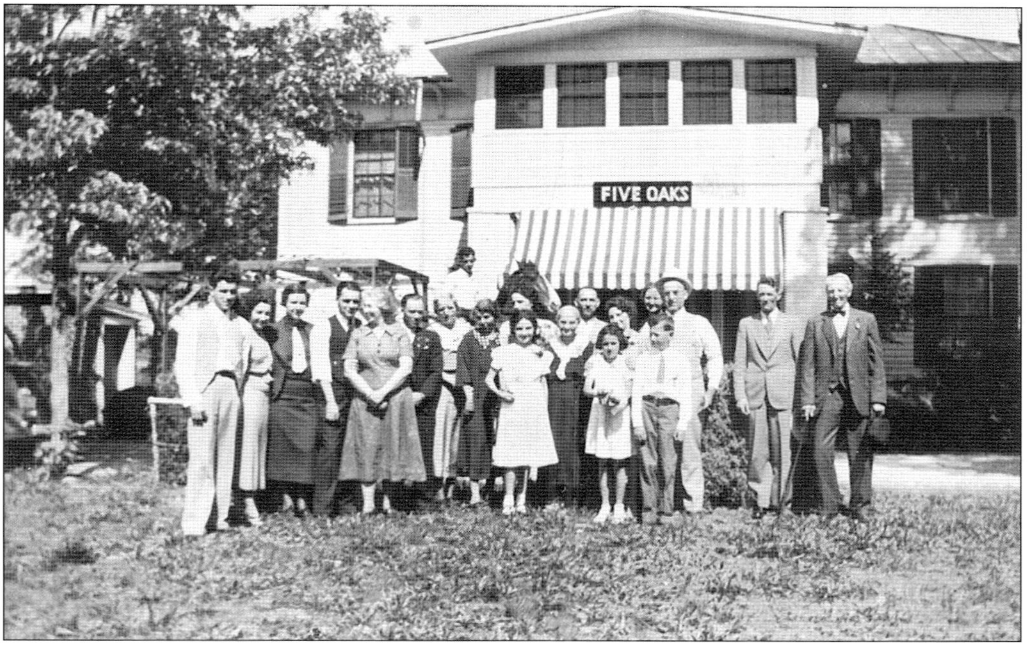

In this picture, the family of Dr. John Ogle gathered to celebrate Mother's Day at Five Oaks Farm. Today, while the old house is still standing, most of the farm is encompassed in the Five Oaks Tanger Outlet Mall on the Parkway in Sevierville. (Courtesy of King Family Library History Center, Tim Fisher Collection.)

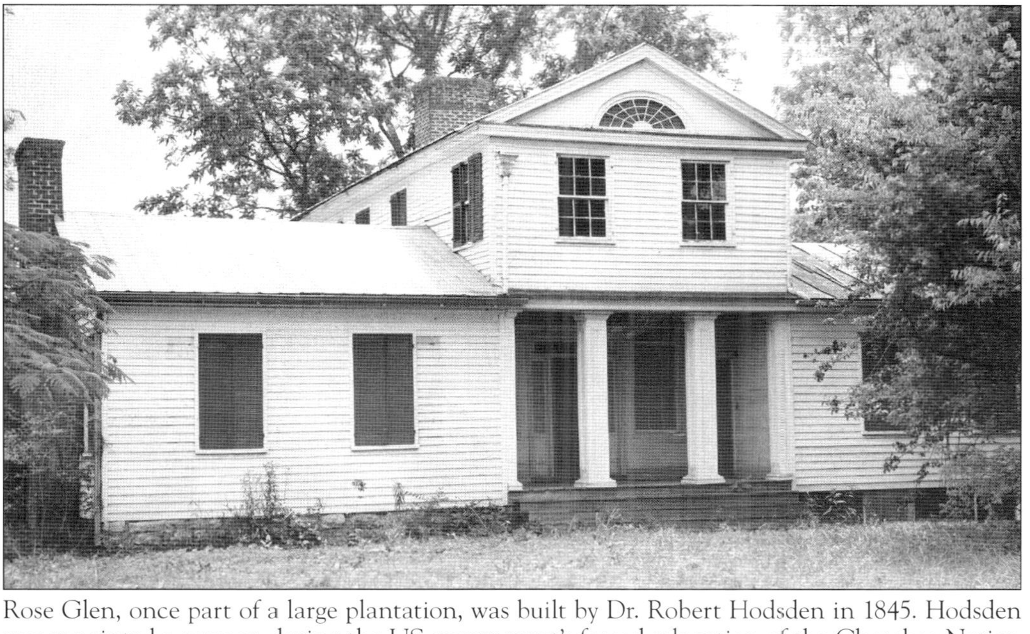

Rose Glen, once part of a large plantation, was built by Dr. Robert Hodsden in 1845. Hodsden was appointed a surgeon during the US government's forced relocation of the Cherokee Nation into the West. He made two trips on the infamous Trail of Tears. The house is across the street from the Sevier County Campus of Walters State Community College on property donated by Hodsden's heirs. (Courtesy of Reece Ripattii.)

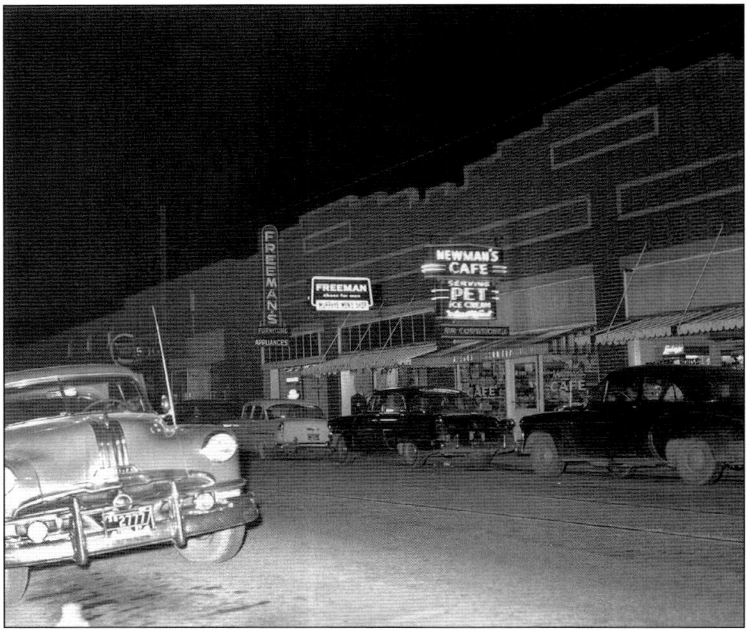

Shown here in 1957 is Bruce Street at night, with Newman's Cafe, Freeman's Furniture, and the Treasure House Jewelry Store open late for Christmas shoppers. Customarily, downtown merchants were closed in the evening hours, Sundays, and holidays. Exceptions were made, such as election night, when most of the restaurants stayed opened until after the votes were counted and announced. (Courtesy of Johnnie Faye McClure.)

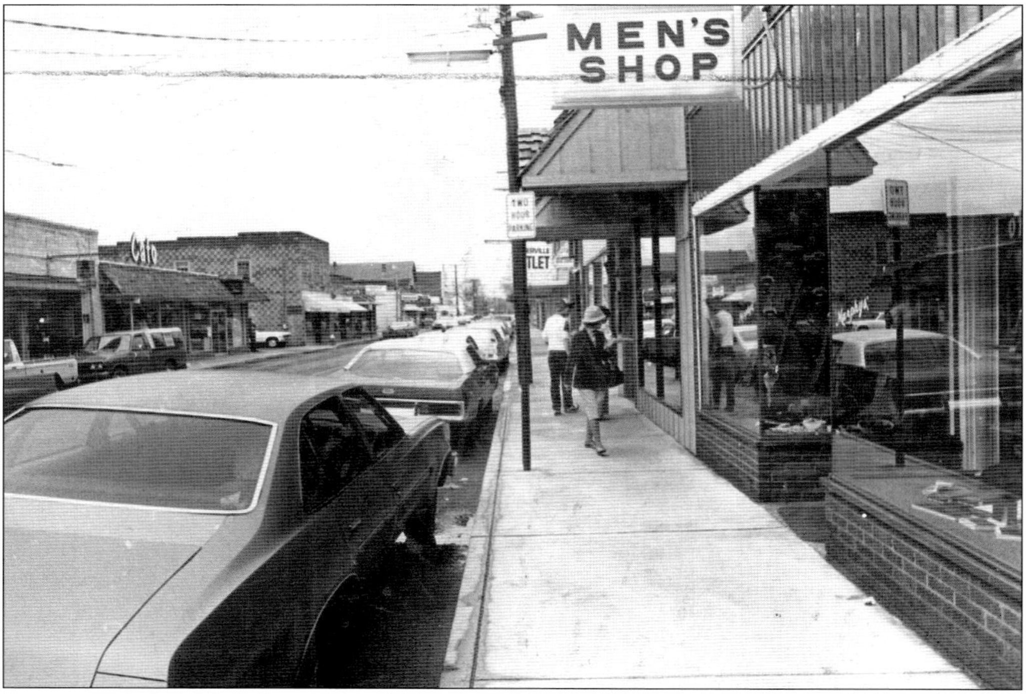

On a normal weekday, the streets of downtown Sevierville were not very crowded. In this early 1960s photograph, only a few shoppers can be seen on Bruce Street. The streets were brimming with activity on Saturdays. (Courtesy of King Family Library History Center, Herbert Lawson Collection.)

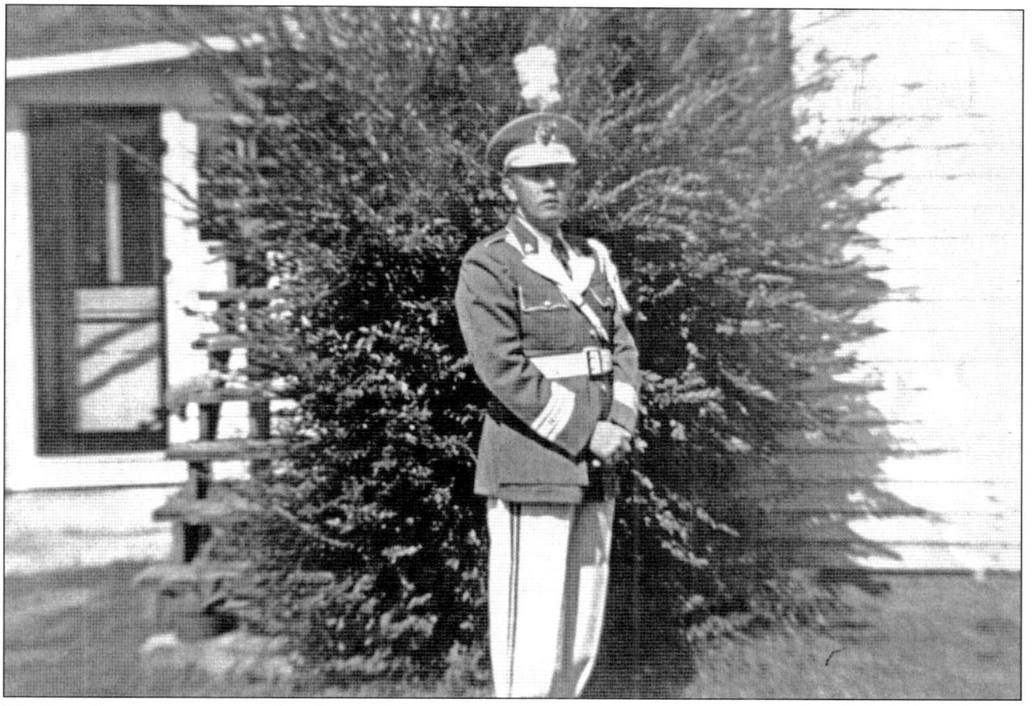

Herbert Lawson poses in his Sevier County High School band uniform in 1951. After he graduated from college, Lawson returned to Sevierville and became a successful businessman, volunteer fireman, and politician. He served as a town alderman and mayor. He was also an avid collector of local history memorabilia. (Courtesy of King Family Library History Center, Herbert Lawson Collection.)

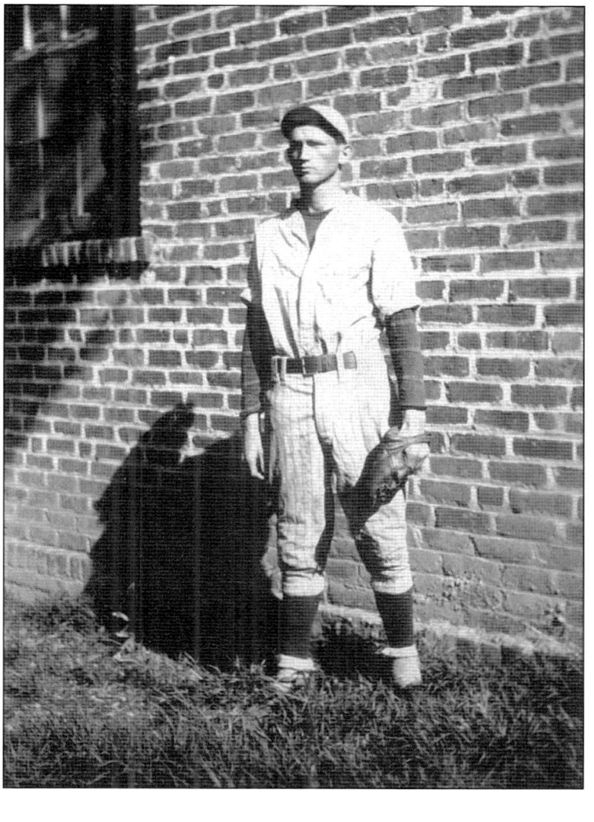

J. Clifford Davis, photographed here in his Murphy College baseball uniform was a lifelong sports enthusiast. After he became a successful businessman and served as a Sevierville mayor, Davis laid the groundwork for a new city park, which provided much-needed space for children to participle in sports events. (Courtesy of Jane Davis Rader.)

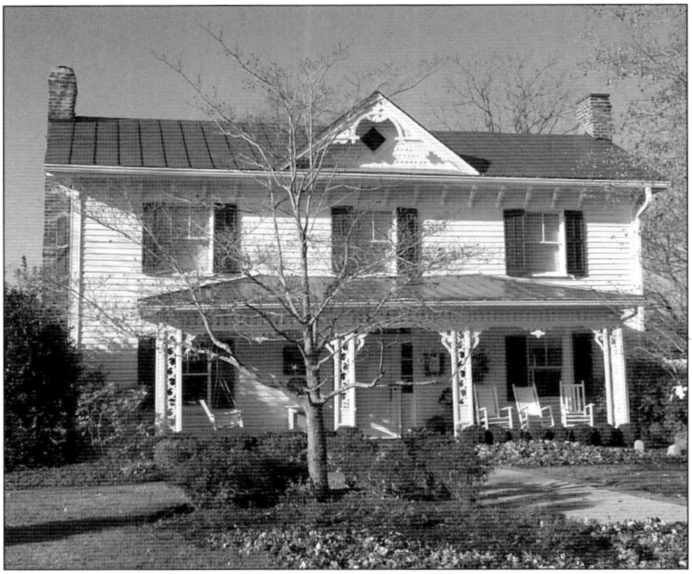

Around 1890, renowned African American craftsman Lewis Buchner was hired to embellish the Riley H. Andes house, which had been built just before the Civil War. The exterior of the house contains both Italianate and Queen Anne vernacular, a trademark of Buckner's style. The structure is located on 812 Old Douglas Dam Road. It was purchased by the John Denton family in the 1940s and is currently the Robert A. Tino Gallery. (Courtesy of Sevierville Chamber of Commerce.)

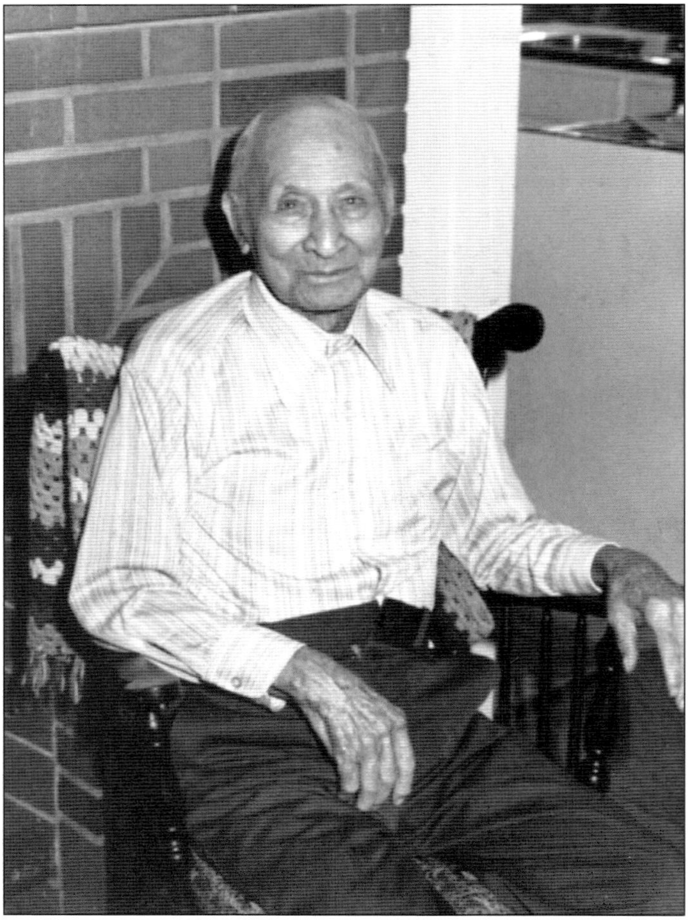

Stewart Burden was a local building contractor and millwork carpenter. He built several well-known Sevierville buildings, including the Central Hotel. He was also known for moving buildings, and most of the structures ever moved in the area were done so by Burden. He also operated a grocery store on Newport Highway. (Courtesy of Martha Burden Bowden.)

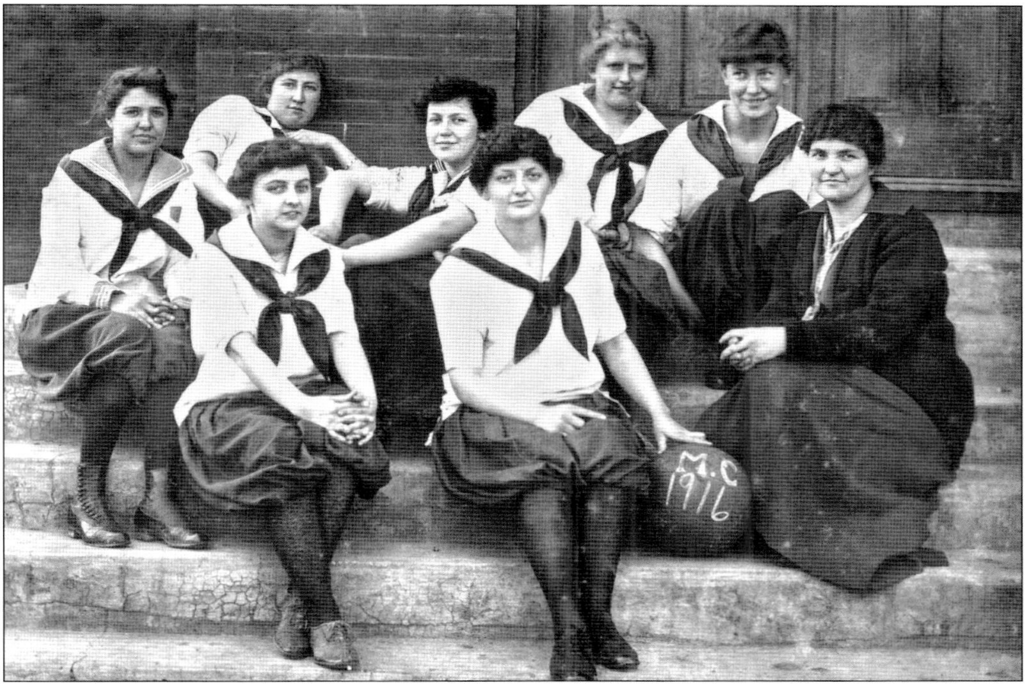

Members of the 1916 Murphy College women's basketball team are pictured on the steps of the school. The female students were given equal opportunity to participate in competitive sports. (Courtesy of King Family Library History Center, Herbert Lawson Collection.)

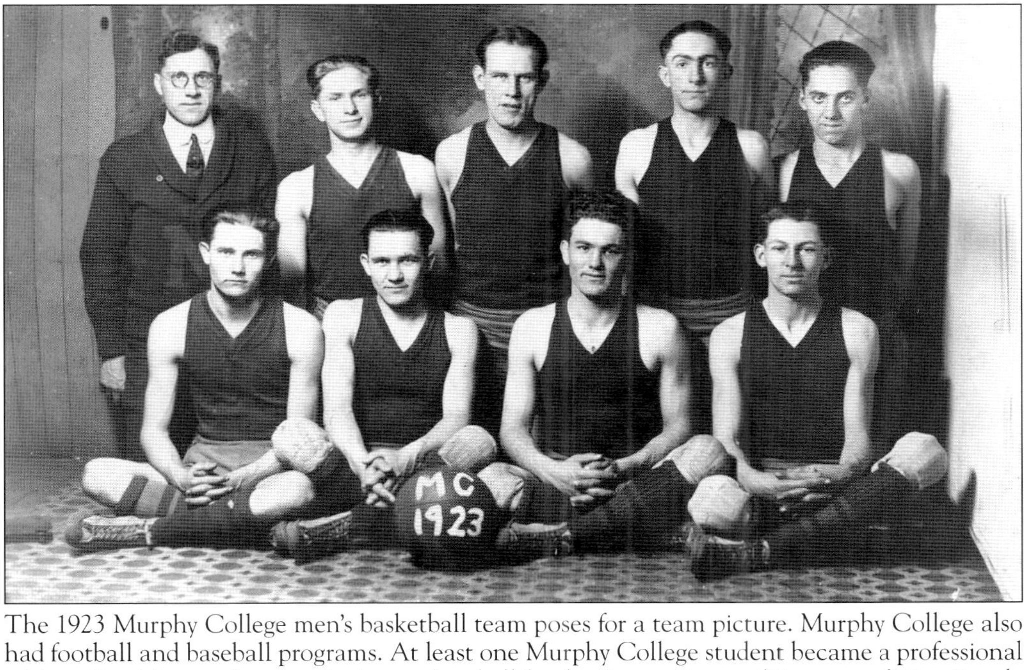

The 1923 Murphy College men's basketball team poses for a team picture. Murphy College also had football and baseball programs. At least one Murphy College student became a professional athlete. Roy Massey played major league baseball for the Boston Braves. (Courtesy of King Family Library History Center, Herbert Lawson Collection.)

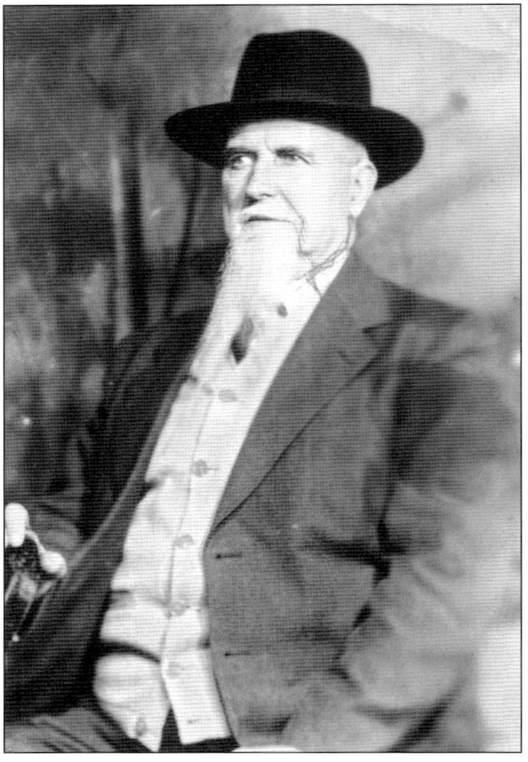

John Hatcher was a fixture in downtown Sevierville during his lifetime. He operated a barbershop for many years in the old Central Hotel and was known for his long white beard. Hatcher was among the first citizens to own a motorcycle in Sevierville. (Courtesy of Ruby Hatcher Maples.)

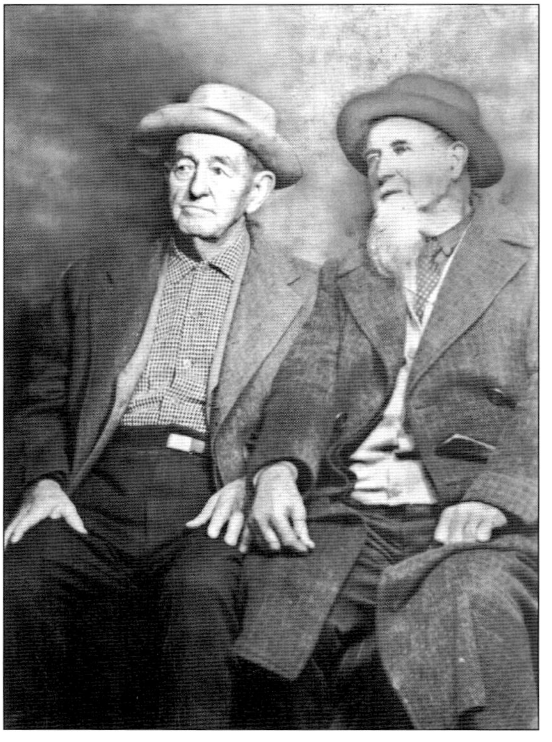

Arthur McCroskey (left) and John Hatcher were lifelong friends. McCroskey, an original stockholder in the Sevier County Bank, owned real estate in Boyds Creek and lived in a red brick home at 108 Winfield Dunn Parkway (now Sweetheart Wedding Chapel), on the north side of the Fred C. Atchley Bridge. Hatcher was a barber. (Courtesy of Travis McCroskey.)

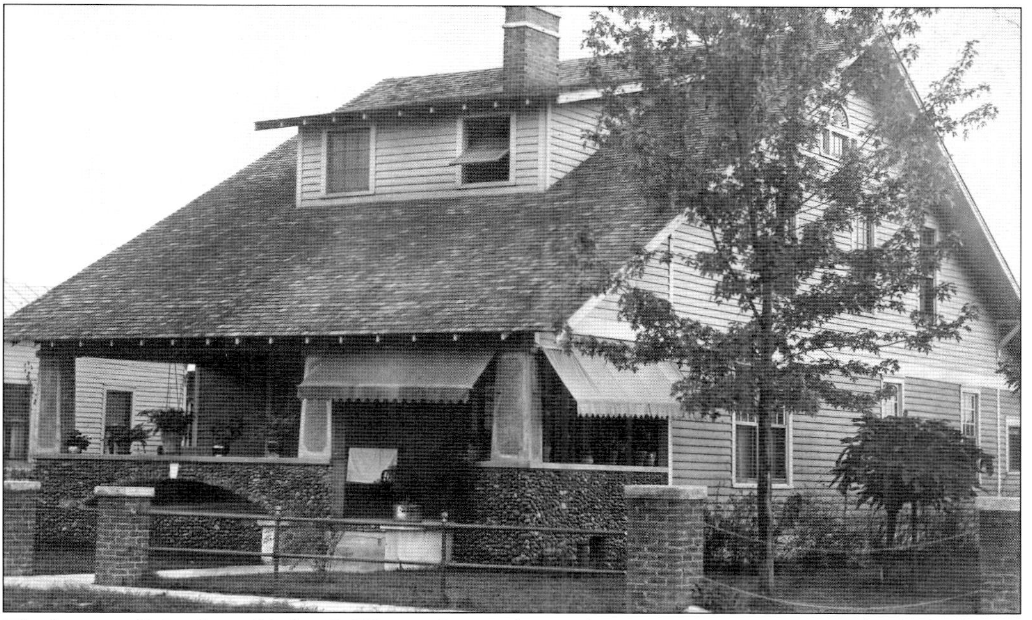

The home of Myrtle and John B. Waters Sr. was located at 107 Joy Street. Waters built the house after he purchased a large section of property, divided it into lots, and sold them to homebuilders. Currently, the house is used as an office for the Waters family. (Courtesy of King Family Library History Center, Waters Family Collection.)

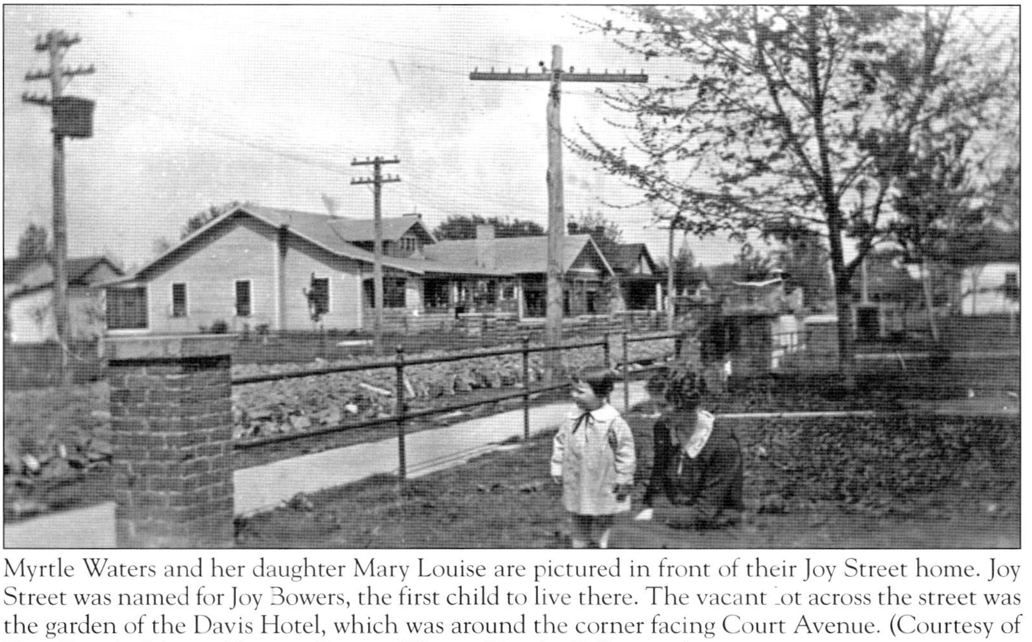

Myrtle Waters and her daughter Mary Louise are pictured in front of their Joy Street home. Joy Street was named for Joy Bowers, the first child to live there. The vacant lot across the street was the garden of the Davis Hotel, which was around the corner facing Court Avenue. (Courtesy of King Family Library History Center, Watters Family Collection.)

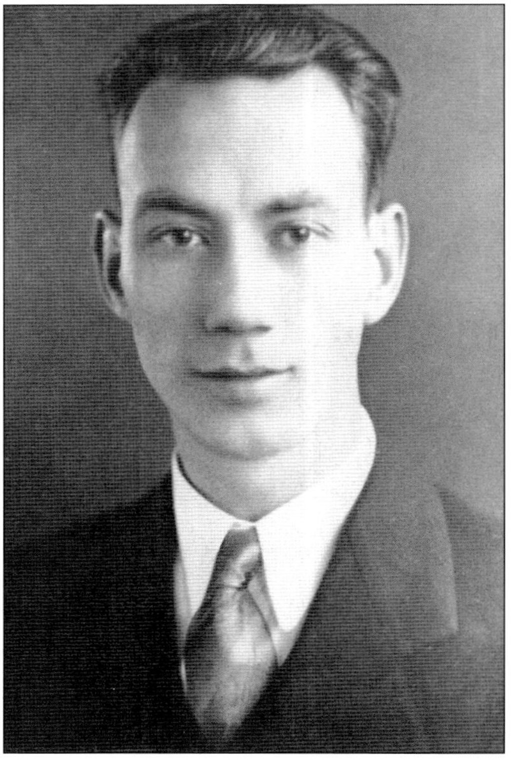

Robert A. Broady, photographed here as a medical student in Pennsylvania, practiced medicine in Sevierville after serving the Presbyterian Church for decade as a medical missionary in China. Before he attended medical school, Broady graduated from Maryville College. (Courtesy of Dr. Joseph Broady.)

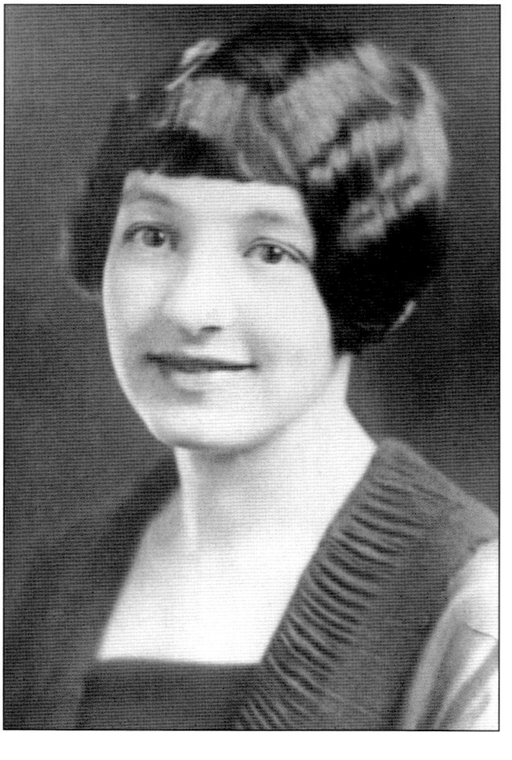

Ellen Cox was a nursing teacher at Philadelphia General Hospital, where she met intern Dr. Robert A. Broady, a friend from Maryville College. They married and worked together in the medical field for the rest of their lives. (Courtesy of Dr. Joseph Broady.)

Fred Matthews, standing beside his mother, Mary Jane (Tarwater) Matthews, was a talented musician who played several musical instruments. Although blind, he authored books and loved to swap knives on the courthouse lawn. He sang and played music in concerts and radio programs across the Southeast. (Courtesy of Jeffery Matthews.)

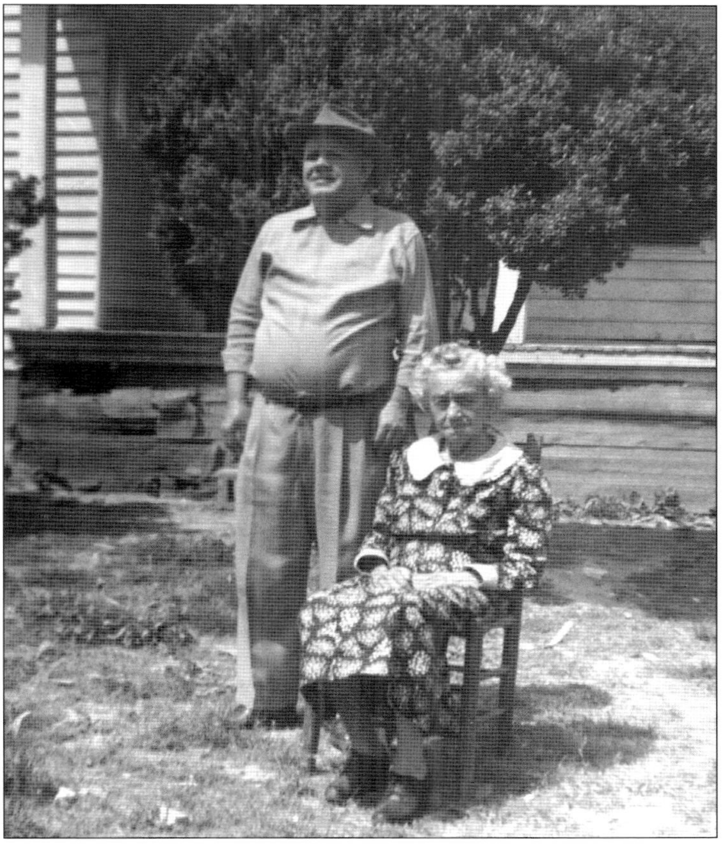

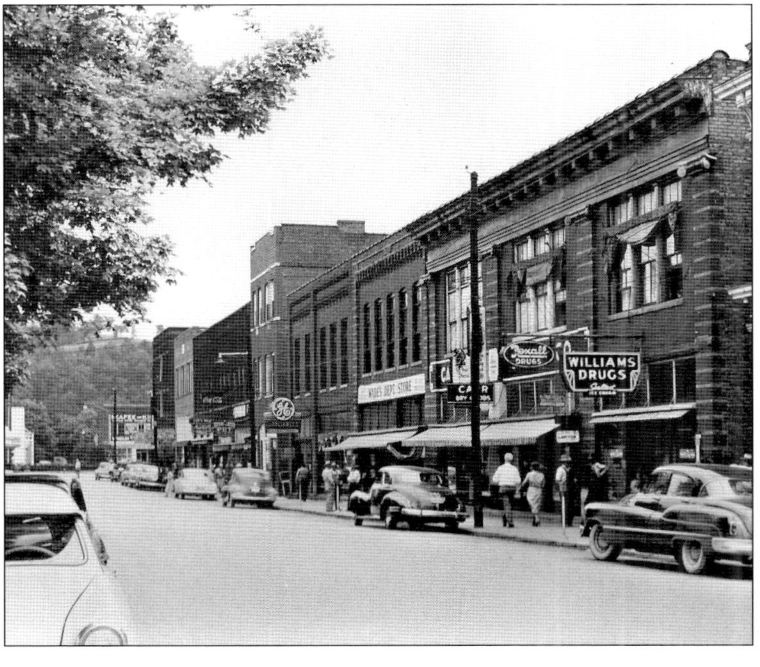

Shown here is Court Avenue facing north in the 1940s. The buildings on the right face the Sevierville County Courthouse. In those days, Sevierville merchants knew most of their customers by name, and a close climate of trust prevailed. Very few residents locked their doors at night. (Courtesy of King Family Library History Center, Herbert Lawson Collection.)

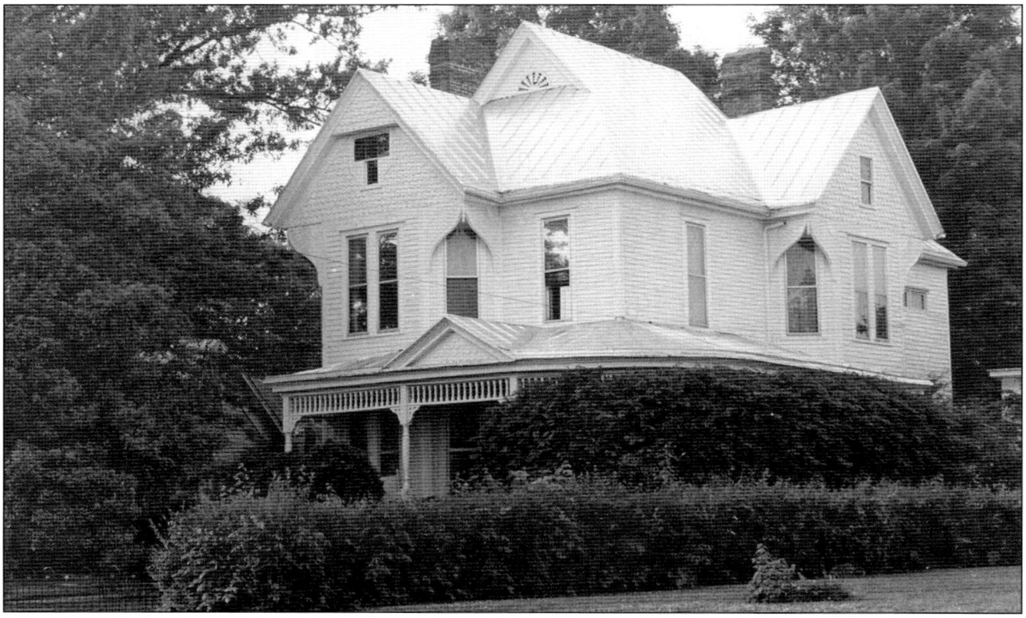

Ashley Wynn Trotter, a prominent dentist, constructed this Queen Anne-Victorian house on the east end of Cedar Street in 1889. Trotter and his wife, Julie Belle (Wynn) Trotter, raised six children here. Carpenter Lewis Buckner carved the house's ornamental woodwork. The house is located across the street from the First United Methodist Church. (Courtesy of King Family Library History Center, Herbert Lawson Collection.)

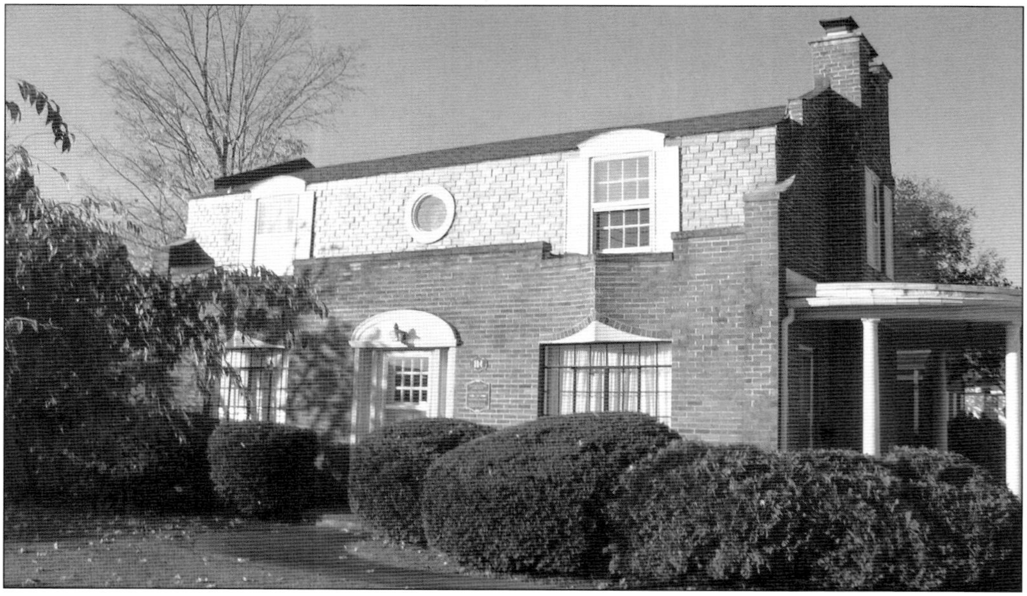

The Dwight Wade, Sr. house located on Joy Street was competed in the fall of 1940. It is a nearly identical replica of the Garden Home at the Town of Tomorrow Exhibit from the 1939 World's Fair in New York. The design was by Vera Cook Salomonsky, one of America's first female architects. Wade and his wife, Kate, discovered the house while on their honeymoon in 1939 and purchased the plans. (Courtesy of the Sevierville Chamber of Commerce.)

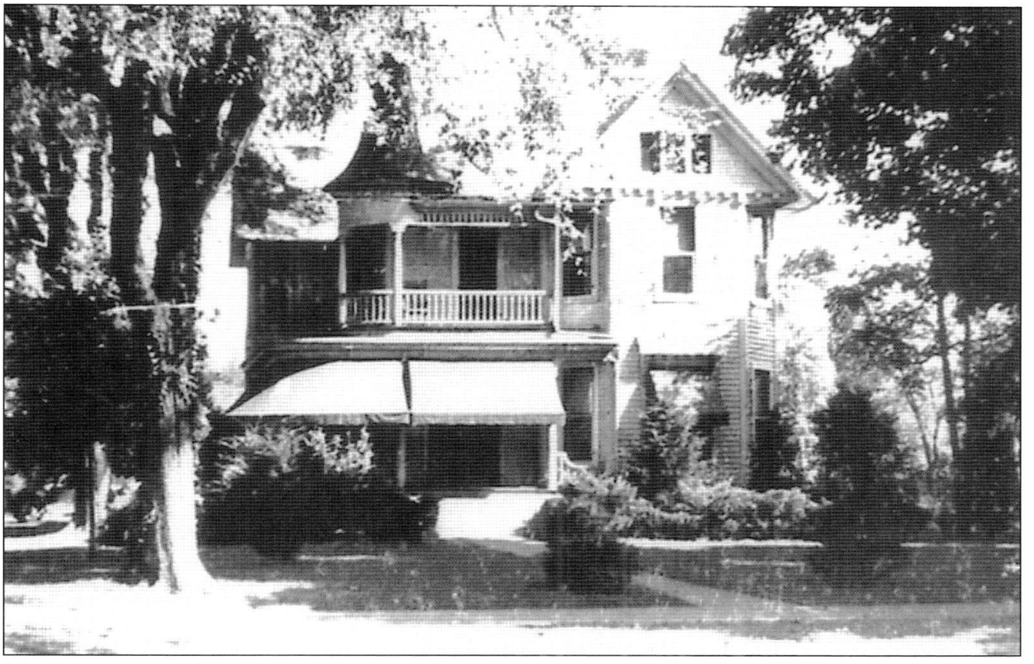

The J.R. Penland house was constructed just before 1900. This photograph dates to 1940, when the home was occupied by Hugh and Robbie Blair. James Atchley purchased the house in 1948 and converted it into the Atchley Funeral Home. Extensive renovations have taken place, but the building is still in use as part of Atchley Funeral Home. (Courtesy of Sevierville Chamber of Commerce.)

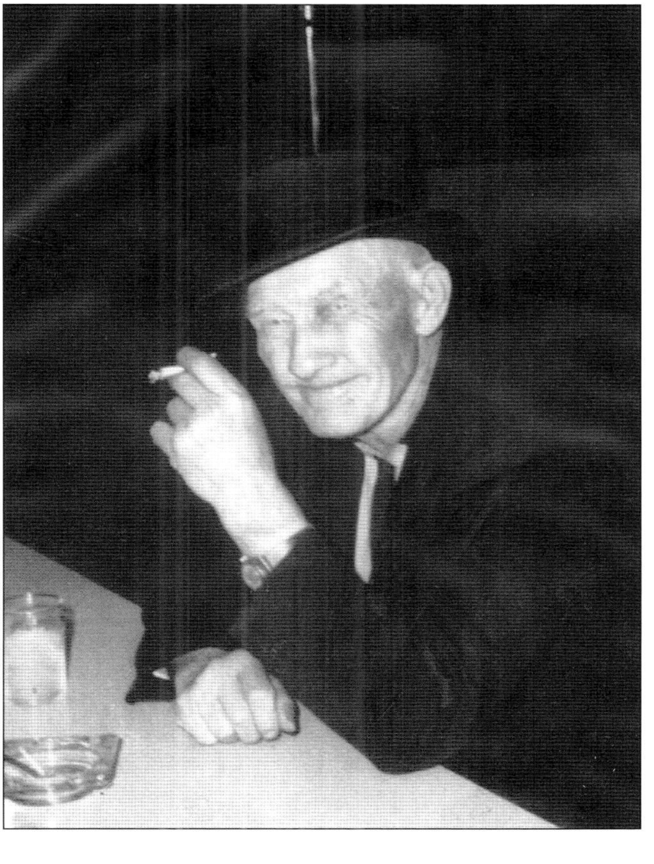

Ollie Wofford was a well-known personality in Sevierville for many years. Known for his loyalty to his friends, he was a bell-ringer at First United Methodist Church. Wofford came to Sevierville with a carnival and never left. He was the victim of many good-natured practical jokes. (Courtesy of King Family Library History Center, Herbert Lawson Collection.)

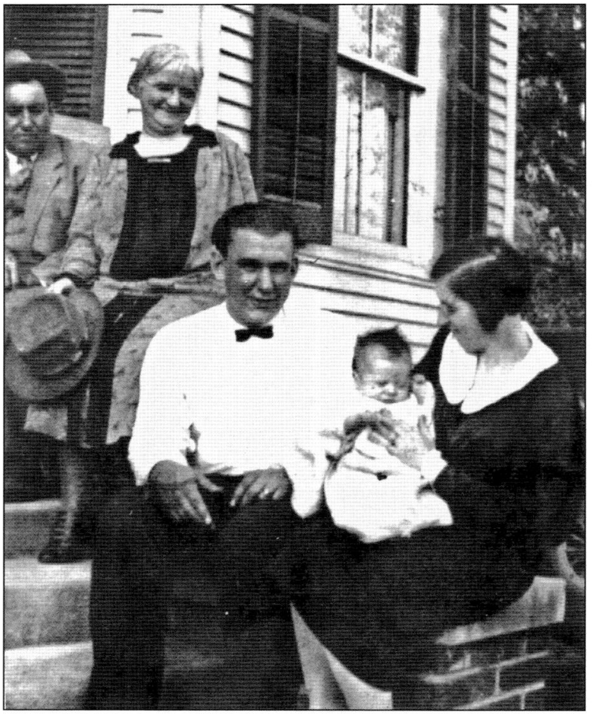

Proud parents George W. and Serena (Bowers) Lawson, pose with their first-born child Fred in 1901. Lawson's brother and sister-in-law, Robert and Sallie (Wynn) Lawson, look on. The Lawson house was formerly located on East Main Street but was taken down to make room for the Highway 448 Bypass. (Courtesy of King Family Library History Center, Herbert Lawson Collection.)

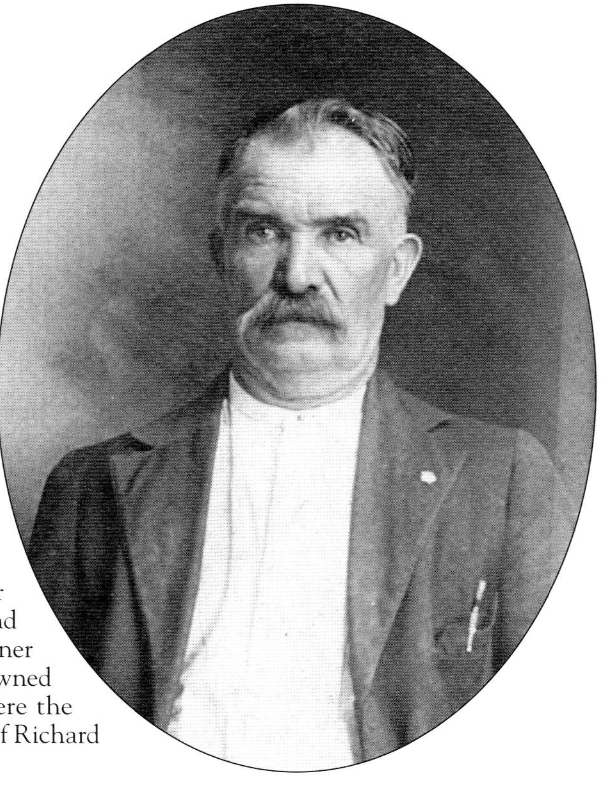

James Coffelt was a local blacksmith who once served on the town board of mayor and aldermen. His blacksmith shop and stables were located at the southeast corner of Bruce Street and Park Road. Coffelt owned a cabin at Seaton Springs Resort, where the family spent their summers. (Courtesy of Richard E. Atchley Jr.)

Here, three schoolgirls leave the Sevier County Public Library after checking out books. The library was located in the Masonic temple on East Main Street from 1920 until 1967. Fred Rawlings first established the library when he returned from active duty in World War I. (Courtesy of King Family Library History Center, Manthano Club Collection.)

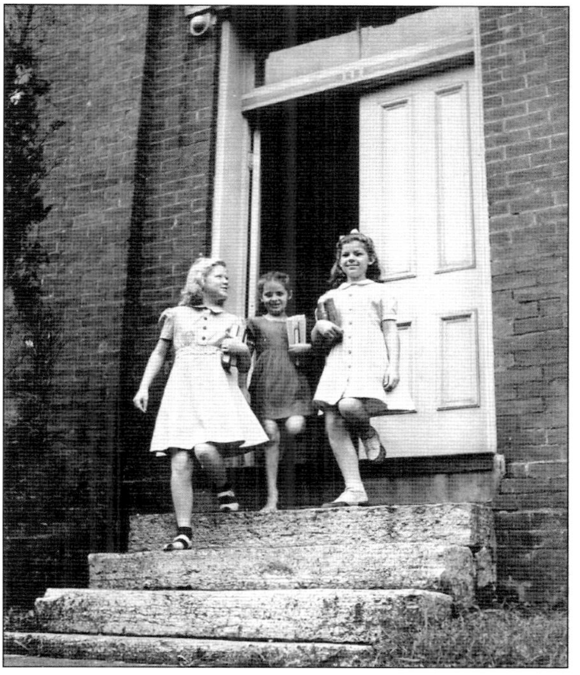

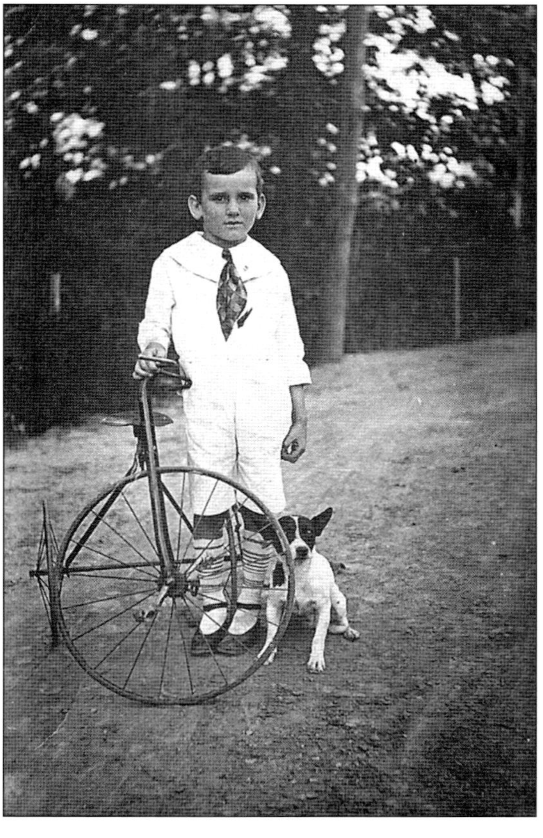

Five-year-old Gene Samuel Atchley poses in 1918 with his tricycle and dog. Atchley was the youngest of six children of a prominent Baptist minister, Rev. Sam Atchley, and his wife, Sarah Ella (Thompson) Atchley. (Courtesy of Richard E. Atchley Jr.)

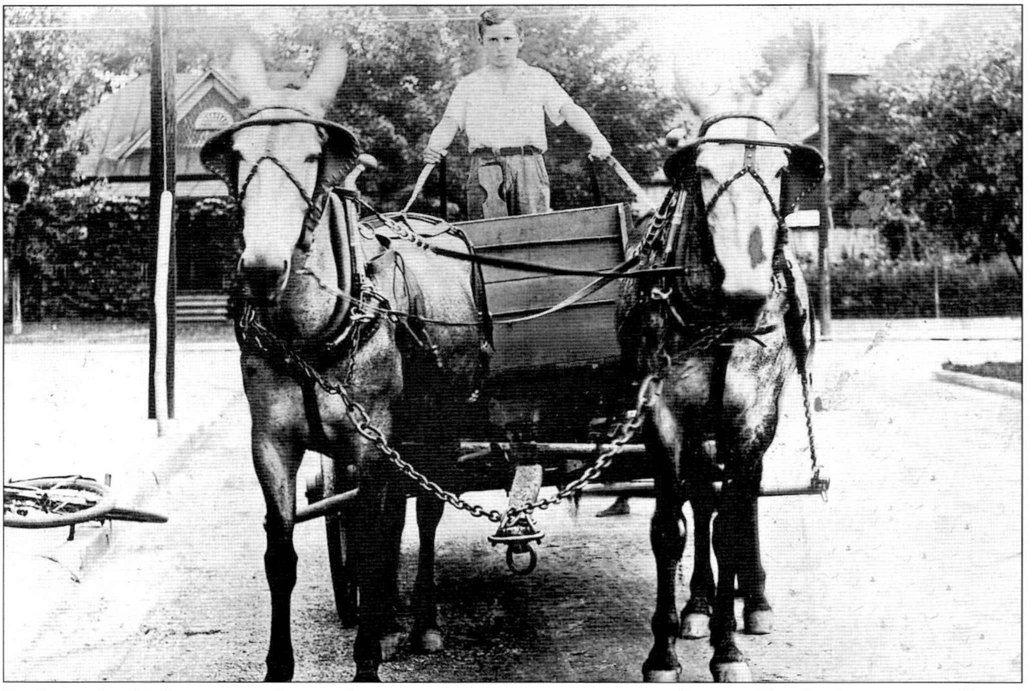

Early in the 20th century, horse-drawn wagons were common in Sevierville. In this picture, David Paine Waters holds the reins. By the time Waters was born in 1925, automobiles were becoming commonplace. (Courtesy of King Family Library History Center, Waters Family Collection.)

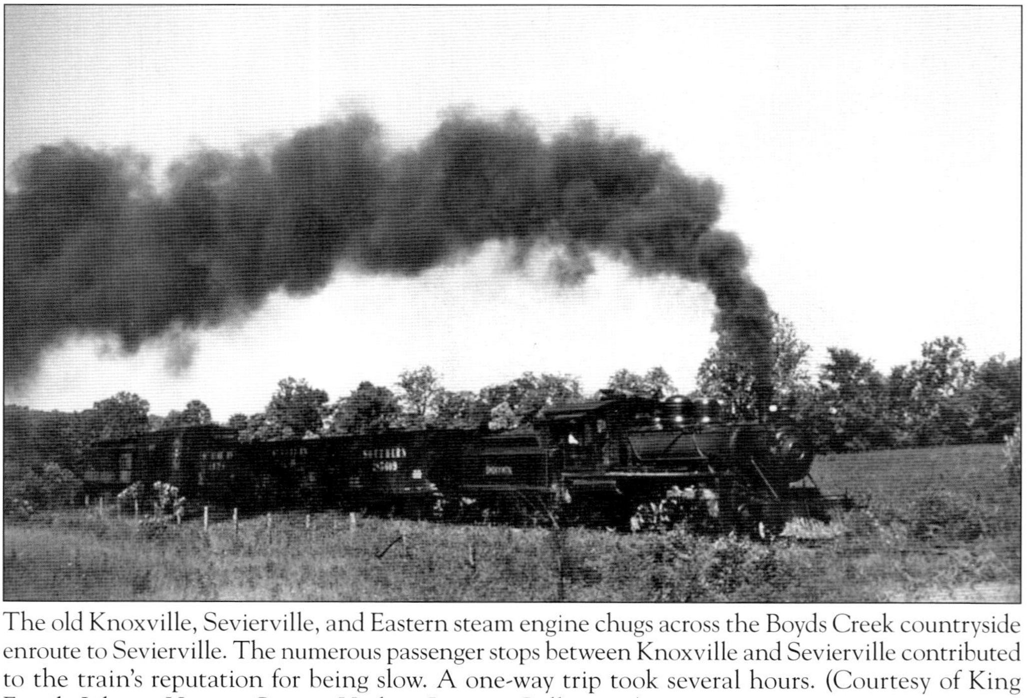

The old Knoxville, Sevierville, and Eastern steam engine chugs across the Boyds Creek countryside enroute to Sevierville. The numerous passenger stops between Knoxville and Sevierville contributed to the train's reputation for being slow. A one-way trip took several hours. (Courtesy of King Family Library History Center, Herbert Lawson Collection.)

John B. Waters Sr. was a Sevierville real estate developer and auctioneer. He first worked with his father-in-law, Judge Ambrose Paine, under the name of Paine and Waters Auction Company. Known to his family and friends as J.B., his slogan was "Your price is mine." (Courtesy of King Family Library History Center, Waters Family Collection.)

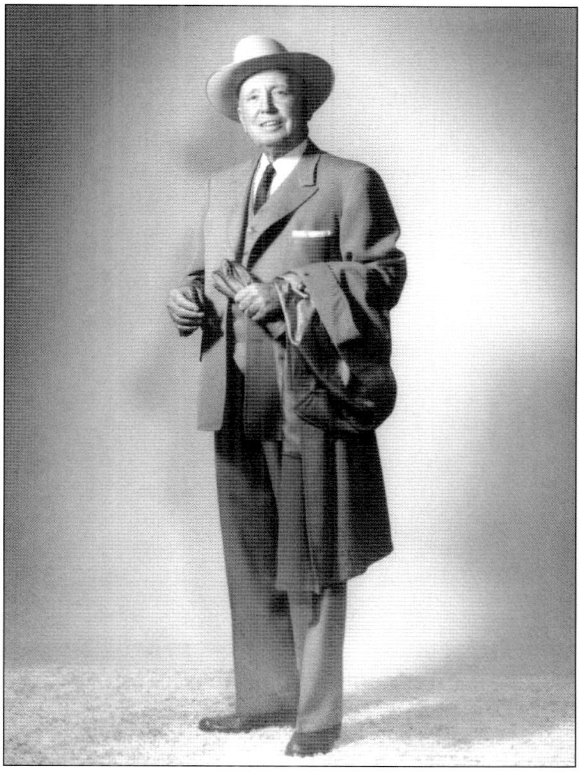

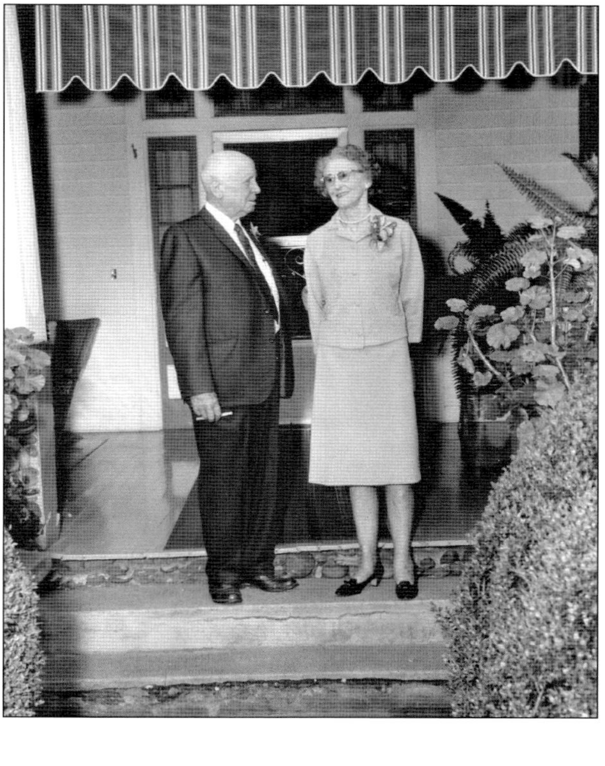

Here, John B. Waters Sr. poses with his wife, Myrtle (Paine) Waters. Myrtle was the only daughter of Judge Ambrose Paine and was the proprietor of the Pines Theater located next to her home on Joy Street. Myrtle's father and husband both served terms as mayor. (Courtesy of King Family Library History Center, Waters Family Collection.)

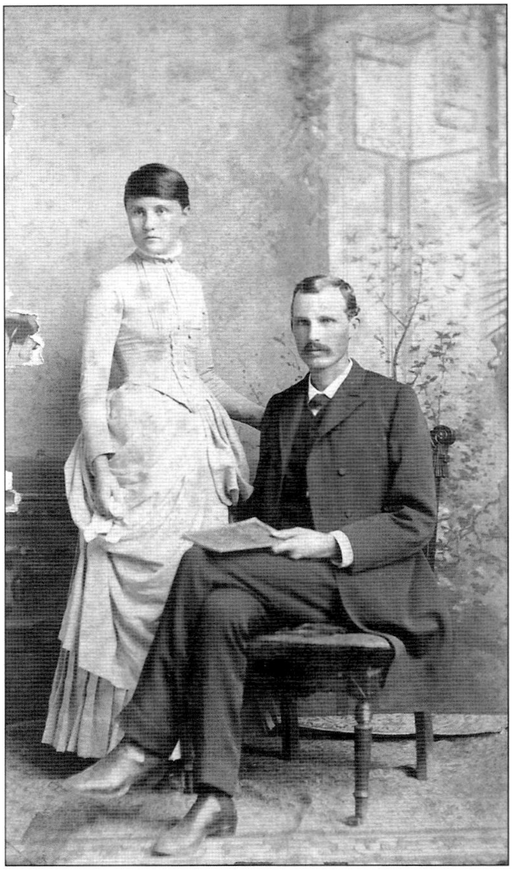

George Zirkle, posing here with his wife, Alice (Thomas) Zirkle, was an attorney and had a long and distinguished career in Sevierville. He served on the board of aldermen for 12 years and represented Sevier County in the Tennessee House of Representatives for two consecutive terms. (Courtesy of Lanning and Becky Wynn.)

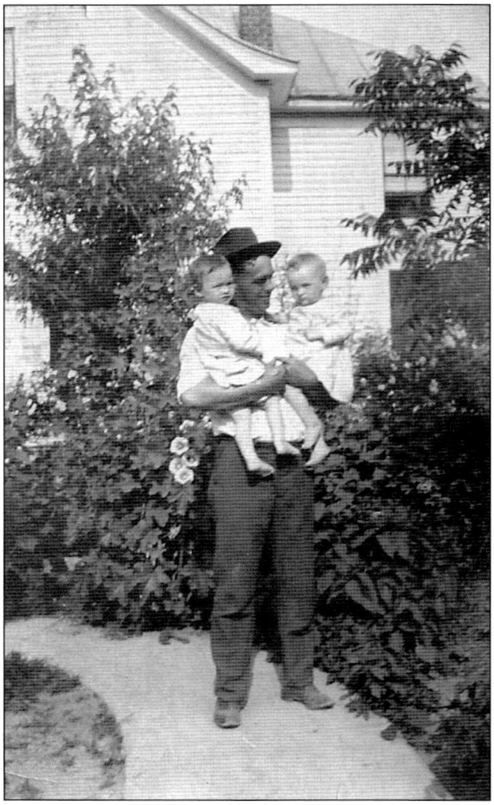

Twins James and Amos are held by their father, Roy Marshall, in this 1919 photograph. Marshall was mayor from 1933 until 1937. His wife was the former Addie Harrison. Twin Amos would one day serve as a Sevierville's aldermen. (Courtesy of Lanning and Becky Wynn.)

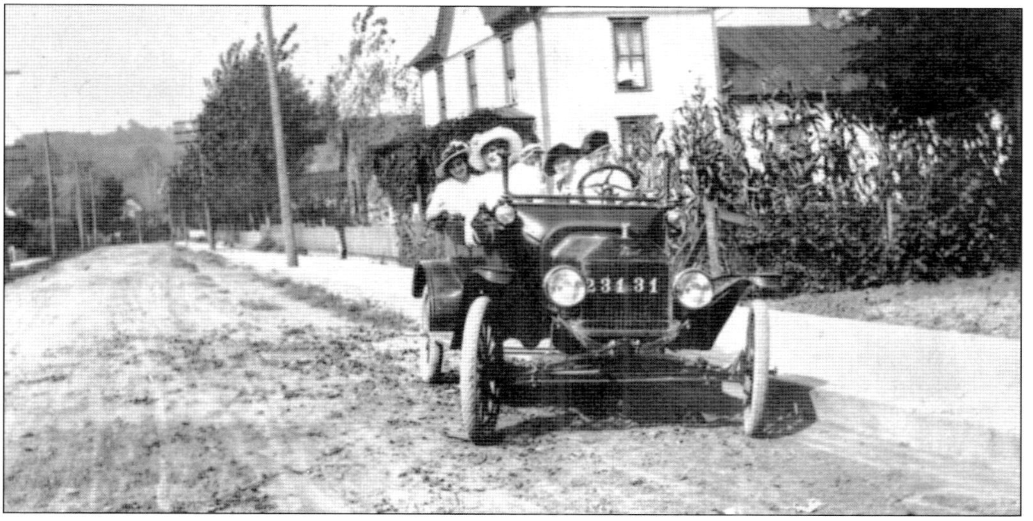

Before the 1920s, women rarely drove, and, small wonder, judging from this particular road. But, these intrepid Sevierville ladies made a nod toward independence this Sunday afternoon. (Courtesy of King Family Library, Waters Family Collection.)

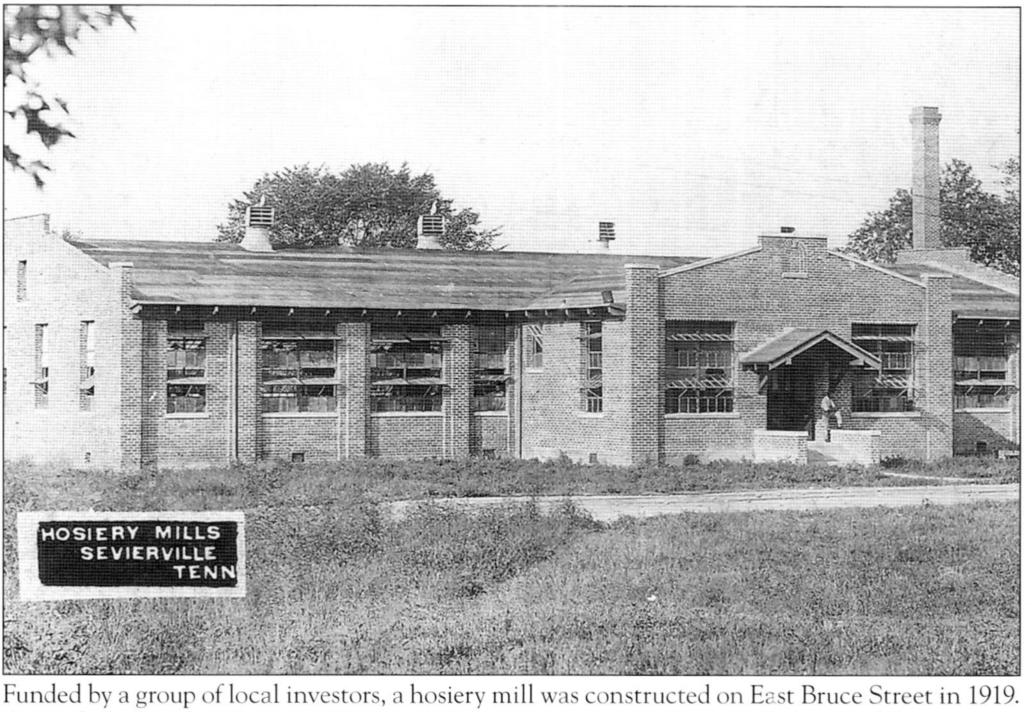

Funded by a group of local investors, a hosiery mill was constructed on East Bruce Street in 1919. A year later, Loudon Hosiery Mill rented the structure to manufacture silk hosiery. The manager was Carmichael Green, and Colonel Beacon was president. Angus Hosiery Mills of North Carolina later operated out of this building. The old building was renovated by the Sevier County Utility District and used for their offices for a number of years. (Courtesy of King Family Library History Center, Herbert Lawson Collection.)

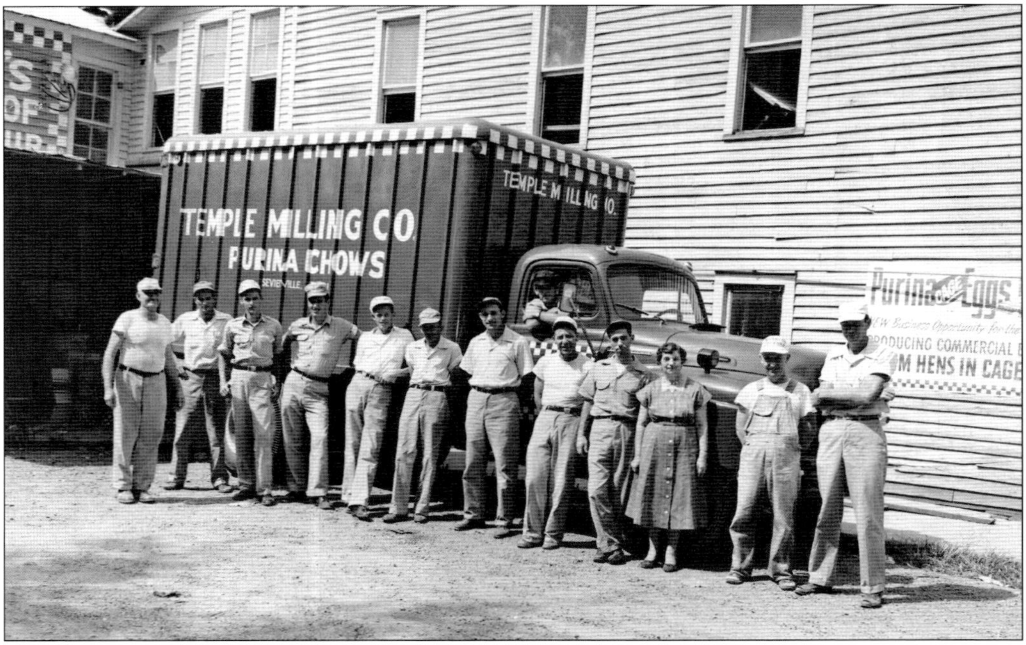

The staff of Temple Milling Company poses in front of their delivery truck in the 1940s. John and Effie Temple (the only woman pictured) began operating the former Walker Milling Company in 1934. (Courtesy of Jimmie and Marie Temple.)

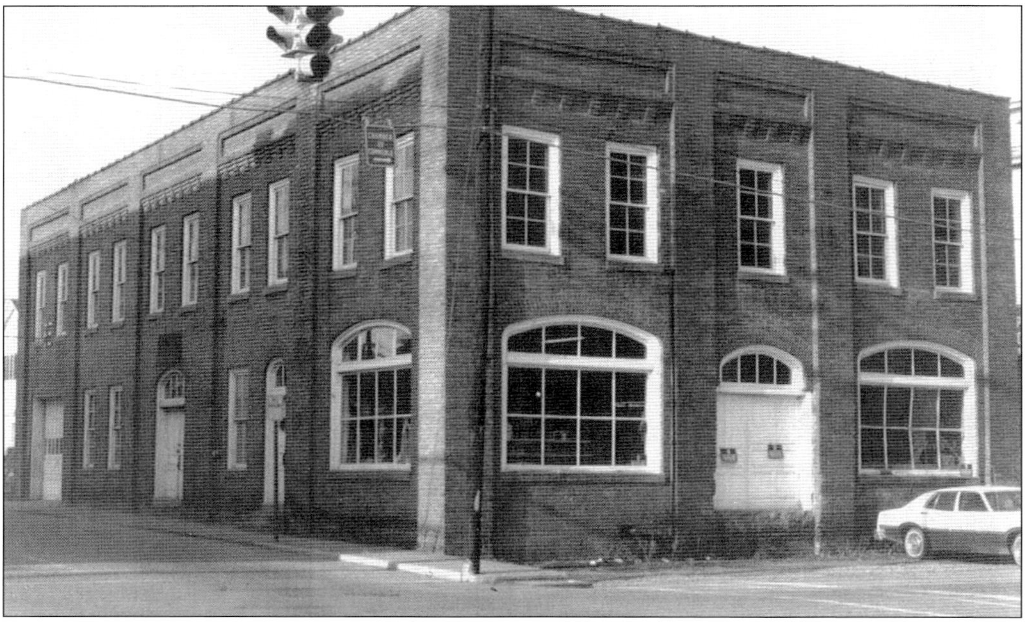

The McAfee-Yett Wholesale Grocery Company building was located on the southwest corner of Bruce Street and Court Avenue. Erskine G. McAfee and John R. Yett, along with several other businessmen, made up the company. The building was later purchased by John E. Temple and used as part of the Temple Milling Company. Today the Sevier County Courthouse parking area is located on the site. (Courtesy of Sevierville Chamber of Commerce.)

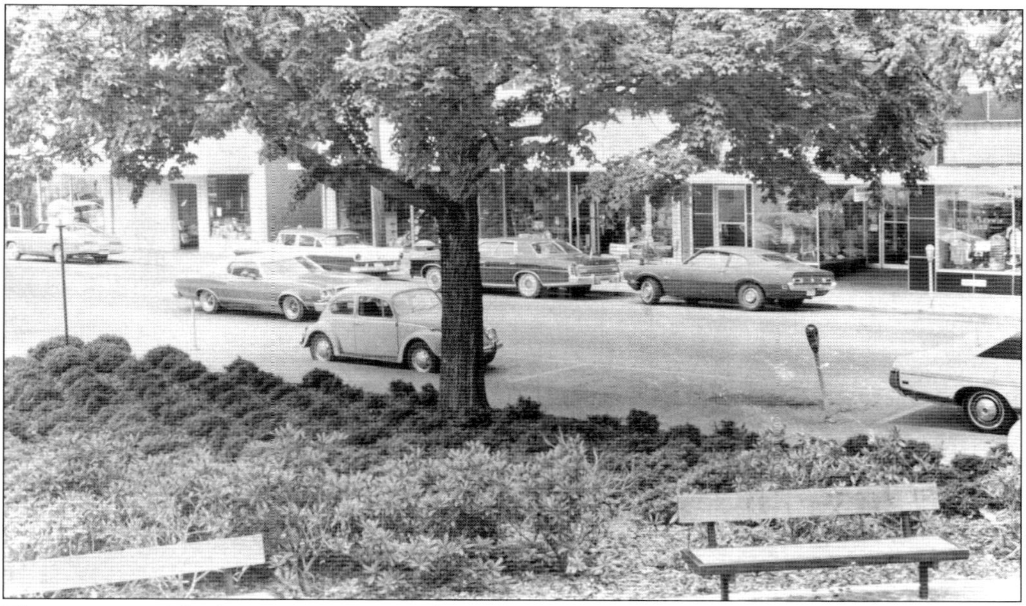

This is a view of the Sevier County Courthouse lawn from the 1970s, after an extensive renovation of the courthouse. It included landscaping an area that had long been a grassy lawn with scrubs and mulch. The unpopular landscaping shown here was replaced because townsfolk preferred the grassy gathering place to upscale landscaping. (Courtesy of the *Mountain Press.*)

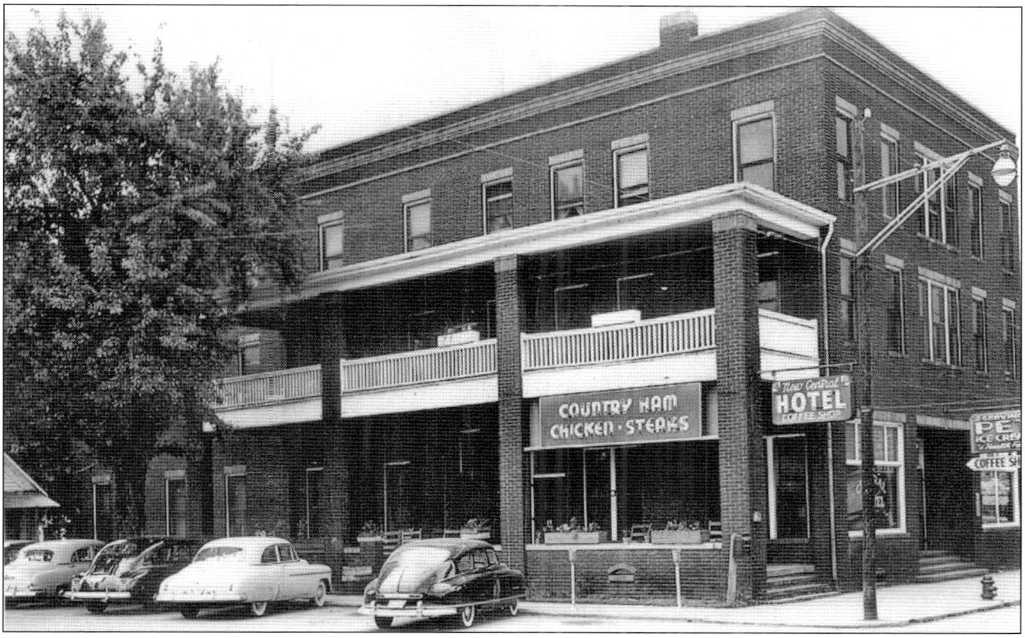

The new Central Hotel opened in 1924. The contractors were Stewart and George Burden. The modern building replaced the original building, which had burned to the ground in 1923. Ralph Murphy was the first manager. Later the name of the hotel was changed to the Hotel Sevier and was operated by Eugene and Mildred Robertson. The building was demolished in 1967 to make way for the new Sevier County Bank building. (Courtesy of Sevierville Chamber of Commerce.)

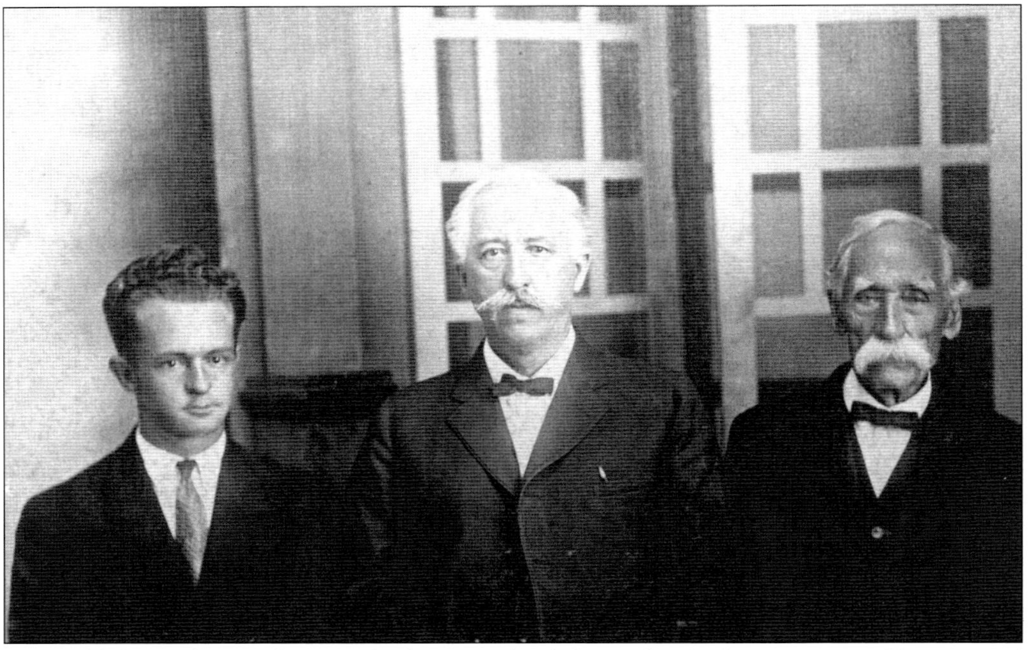

Pictured left to right are Thomas Charles Paine; his father, Judge Ambrose Paine; and his paternal grandfather Rev. Smith Ferguson Paine. Thomas Paine and his father practiced law in Sevierville. Rev. Paine was the founder of the Smoky Mountain Academy. (Courtesy of King Family Library History Center, Waters Family Collection.)

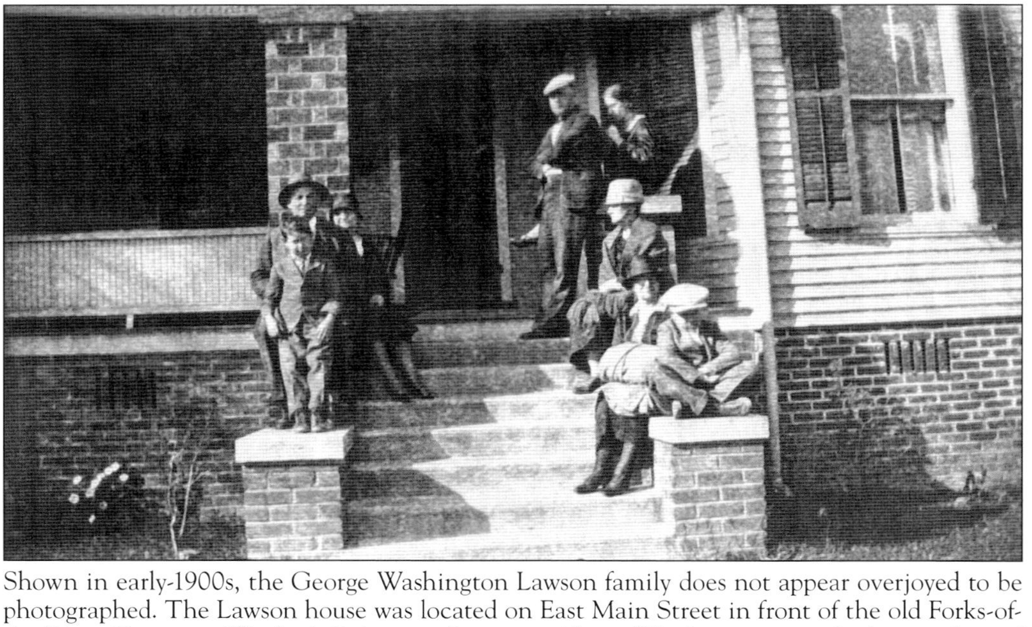

Shown in early-1900s, the George Washington Lawson family does not appear overjoyed to be photographed. The Lawson house was located on East Main Street in front of the old Forks-of-the-River Cemetery. Elizabeth Robertson Lawson, widow of Tip Lawson, was the last resident of the home. (Courtesy of King Family Library History Center, Herbert Lawson Collection.)

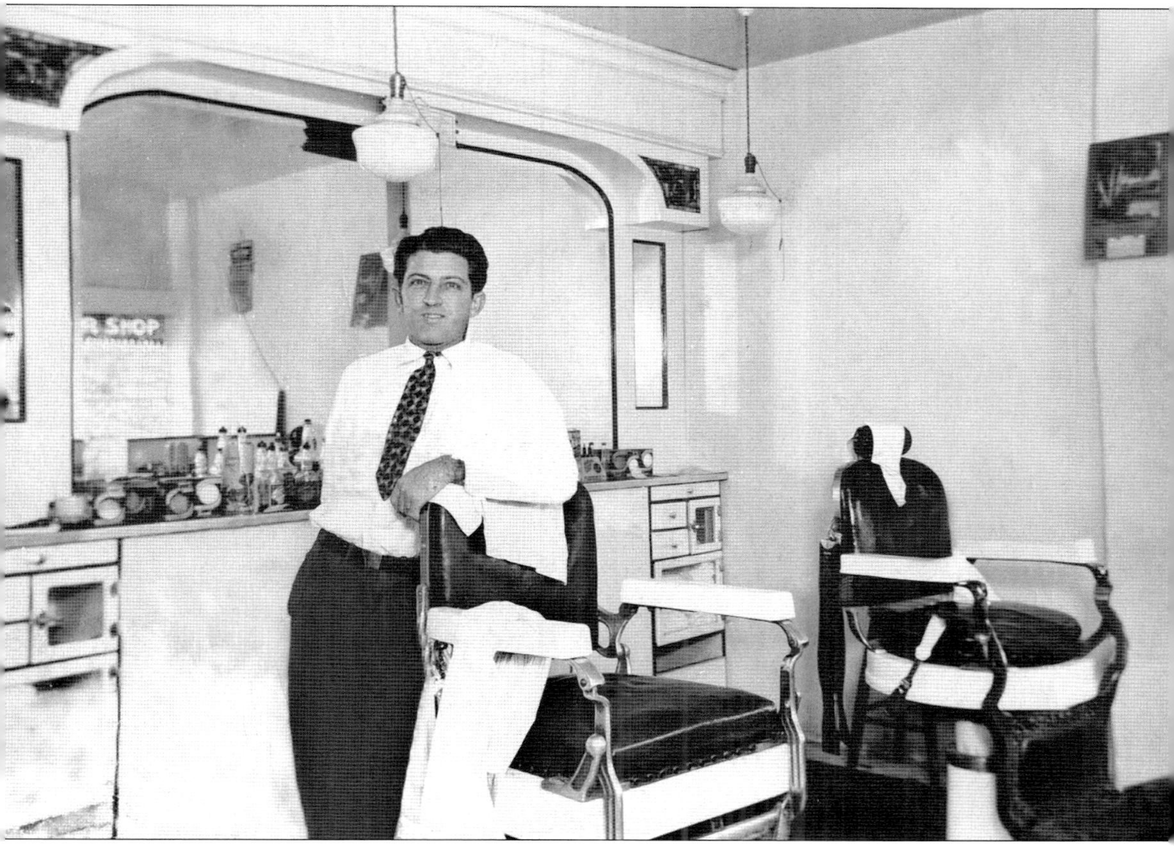

Conley Sims operated a barbershop in downtown Sevierville for four decades. He was later joined by his son Johnny, who continues to operate Sims Barbershop on Bruce Street. Before becoming a barber, Conley Sims was a set-up man for magician Charles Fine. Conley's wife, Lavanna, was Fine's onstage assistant. (Courtesy of Johnny Sims.)

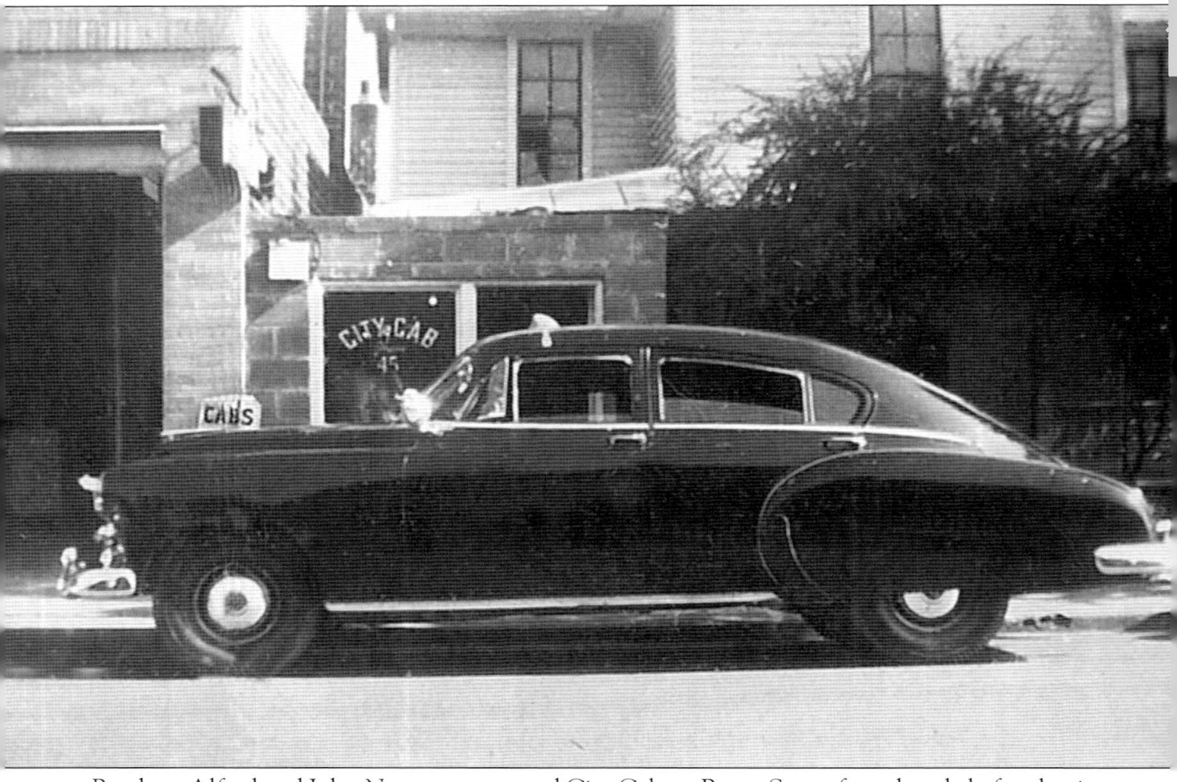

Brothers Alfred and John Newman operated City Cab on Bruce Street for a decade before buying a restaurant across the street in 1956, which they operated as Newman's Cafe for 30 years. By the time this photograph was taken in 1949, City Cab Company consisted of a fleet of five new taxicabs and several drivers. (Courtesy of Alfred Newman.)

Three

FLOODS AND FIRES

Noble souls, through dust and heat, rise from disaster and defeat the stronger.

—Henry Wadsworth Longfellow

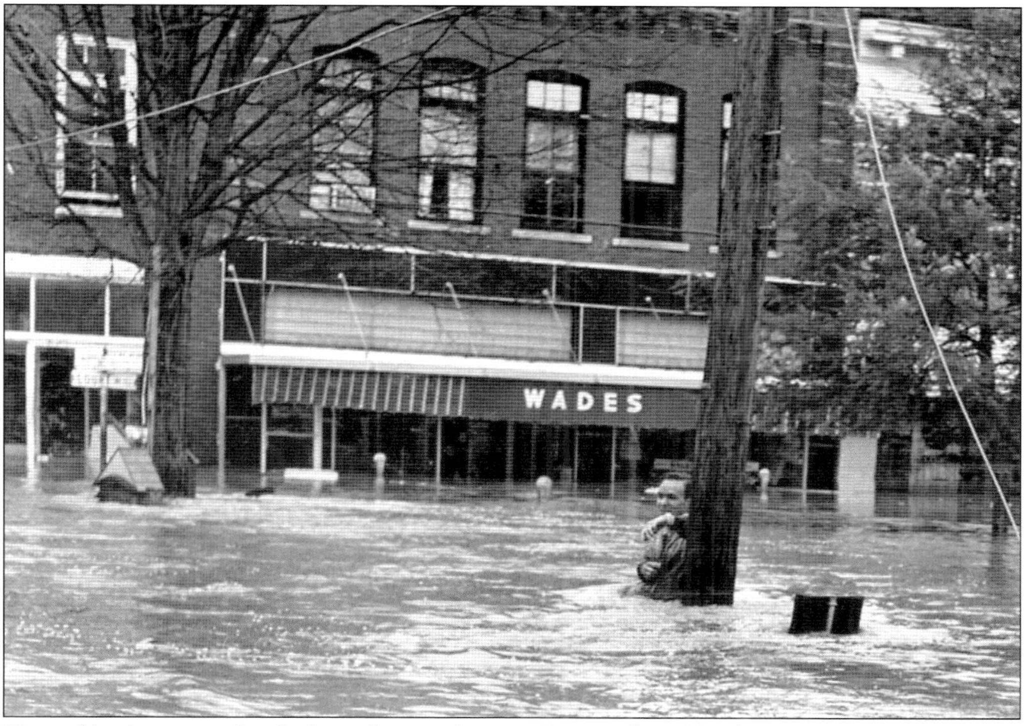

Plagued by disastrous floods throughout its history, Sevierville suffered two major floods in a span of less than two weeks in 1963. This photograph reveals that waters were nearly as high as the parking meters on Court Avenue. Every business in downtown Sevierville was damaged by the two floods. The disaster served as a catalyst for the Tennessee Valley Authority Flood Control Project. (Courtesy of the *Mountain Press*.)

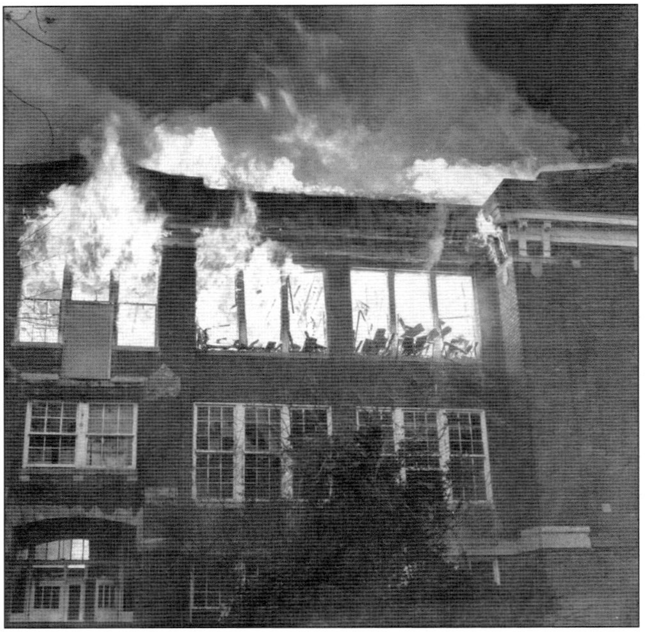

On March 11, 1975, the vacant Sevier County High School building on High Street was destroyed by fire. Flames from the fire could be seen for miles. The school had moved to a new location in 1968. Forty-eight classes graduated from the old school, which was the first public high school in Sevier County. (Courtesy of the *Mountain Press*.)

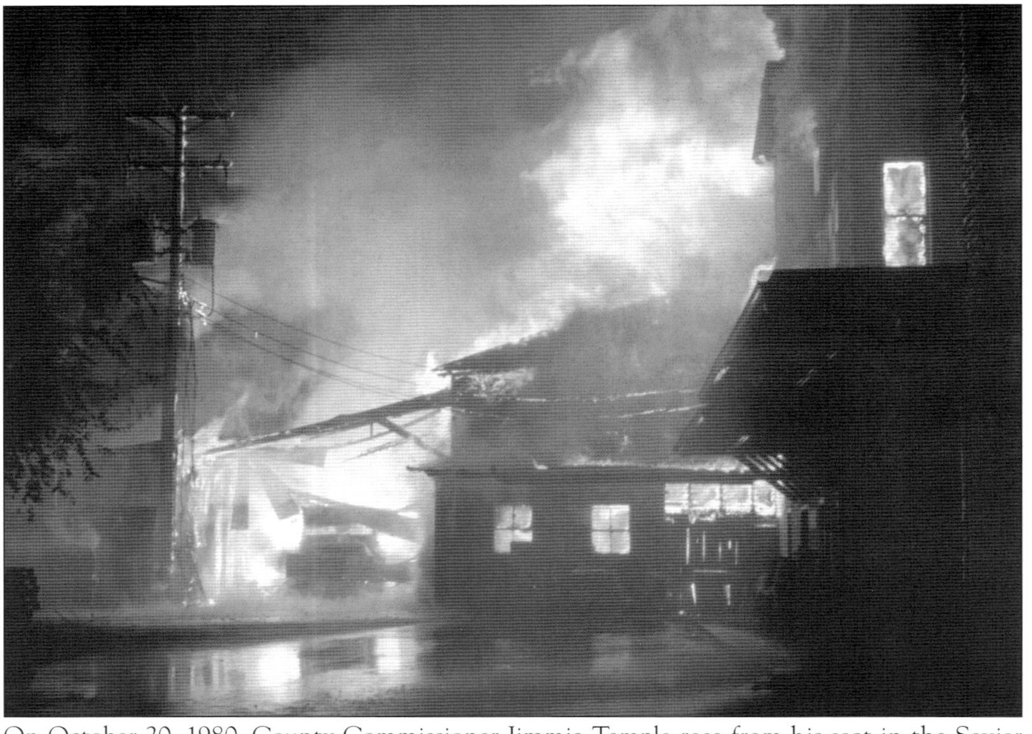

On October 20, 1980, County Commissioner Jimmie Temple rose from his seat in the Sevier County Courthouse, ran to the door, and yelled, "The mill's on fire!" The Temple Milling Company was quickly engulfed in flames, where a large crowd gathered to witness one of the worst fires in years. Units from Pigeon Forge, Walden Creek, Kodak, and Gatlinburg joined in the effort to control the blaze. (Courtesy of Jimmie and Marie Temple.)

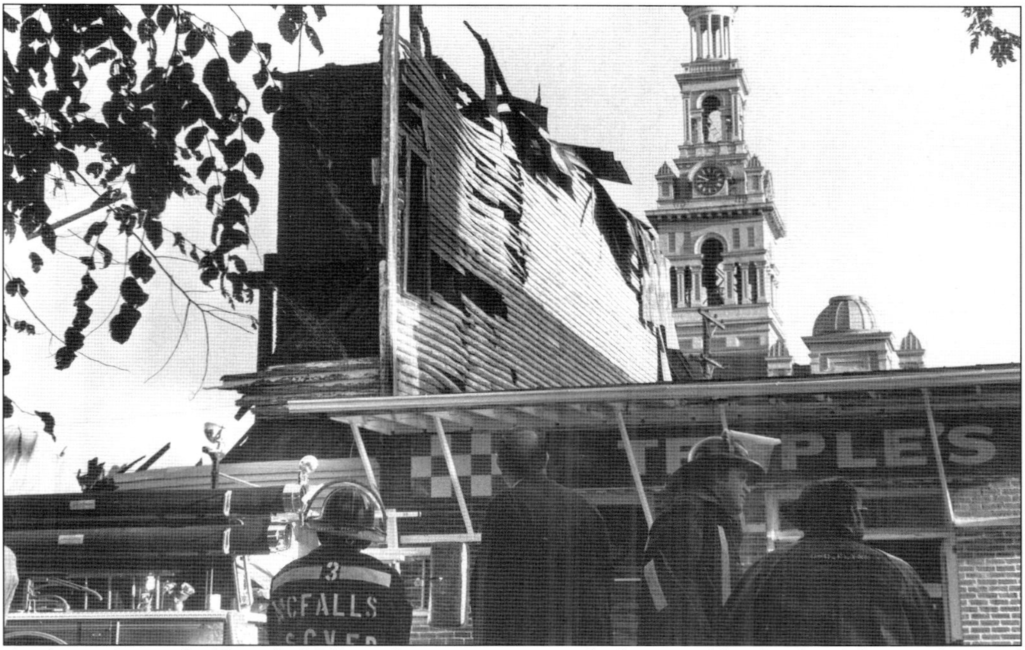

As shown here, the Temple Milling Company was nearly destroyed by the fire. Three exhausted firemen assess damage the following morning. The vintage structure had played a role in the history of Sevierville for nearly a century. (Courtesy of Jimmie and Marie Temple.)

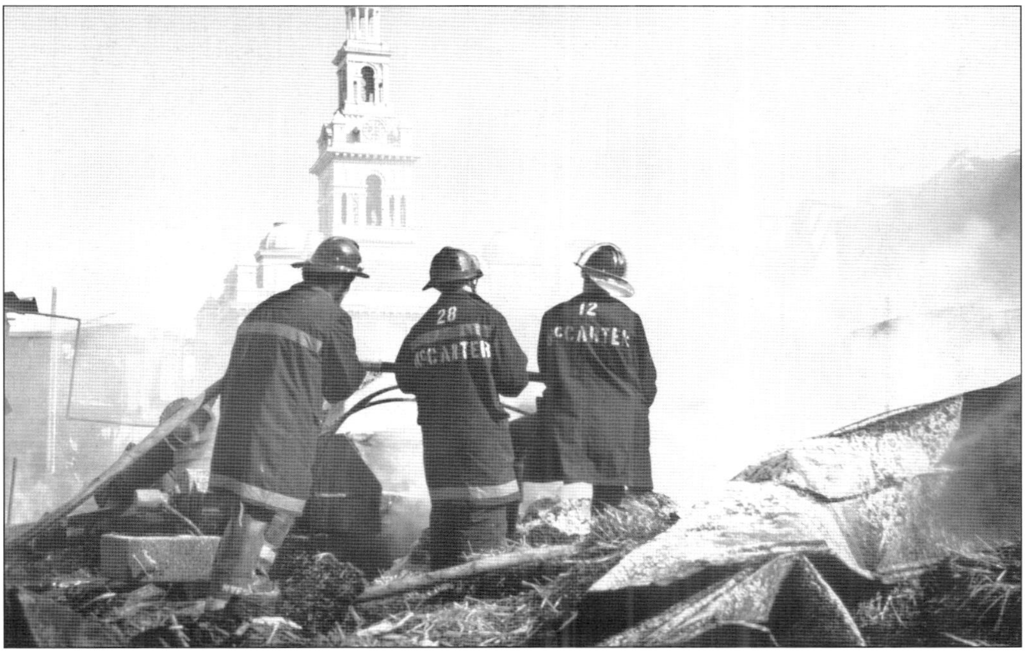

While fighting the Temple Milling Company fire throughout the evening of October 20, 1980, firefighters kept a vigilant eye on surrounding buildings. The roof of the Sevier County Courthouse was of particular concern and was sprayed with water throughout the night, which prevented flames from spreading to the treasured icon. (Courtesy of Jimmie and Marie Temple.)

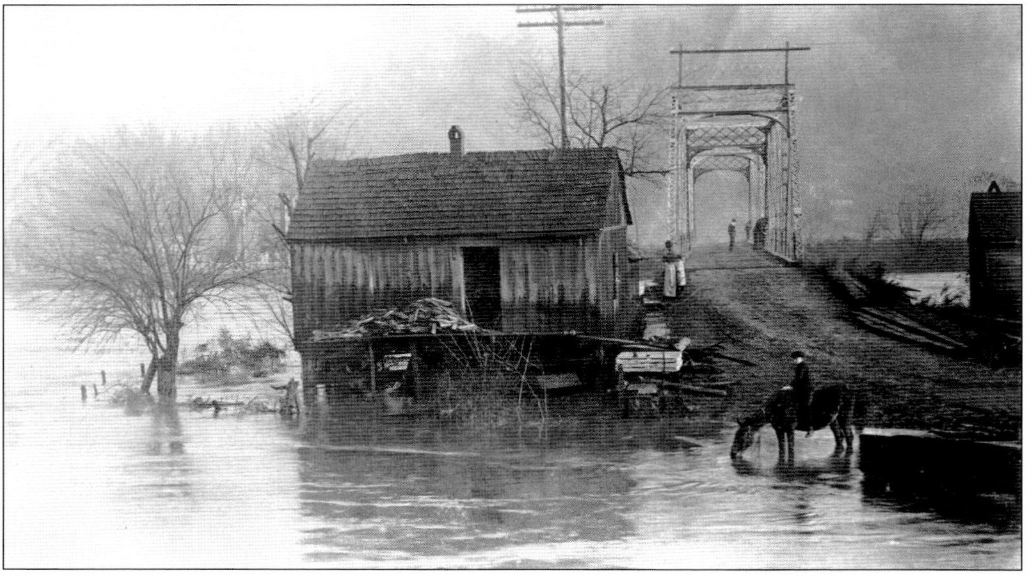

The flood on April 2, 1920, was one of the most disastrous events in town history. After officials started keeping records in 1875, only five floods reached levels higher than the 16 feet reported in 1920. Here, a horse pauses for a drink. (Courtesy of Sevierville Chamber of Commerce.)

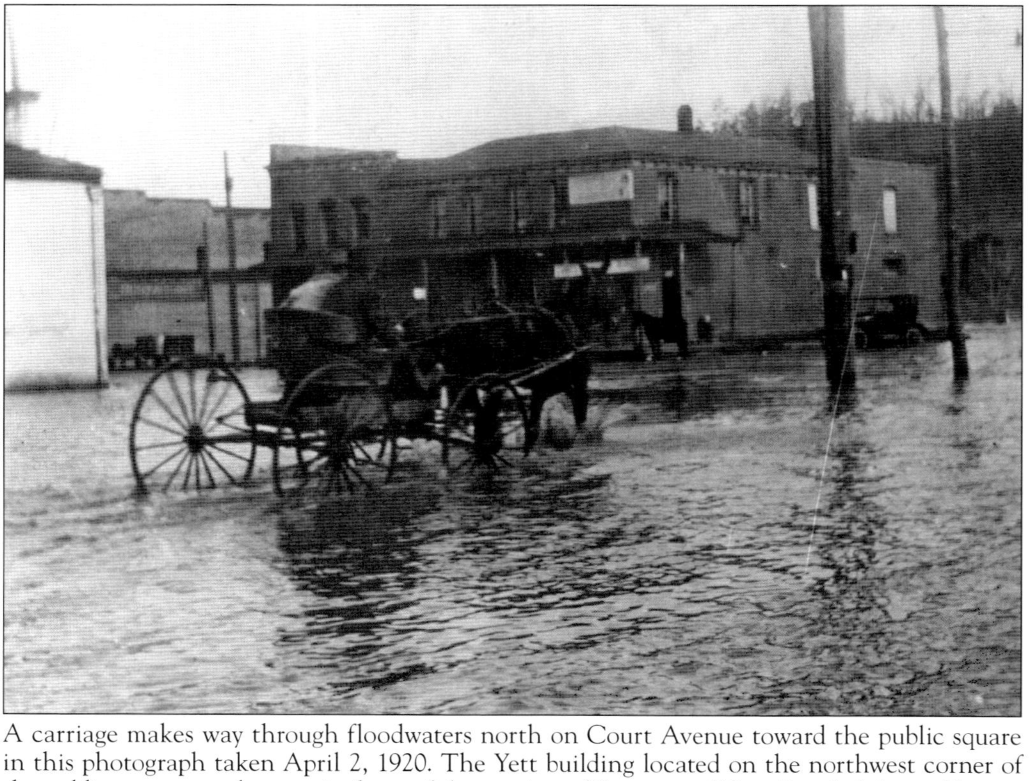

A carriage makes way through floodwaters north on Court Avenue toward the public square in this photograph taken April 2, 1920. The Yett building located on the northwest corner of the public square can be seen in front of the carriage. (Courtesy of King Family Library History Center, Herbert Lawson Collection.)

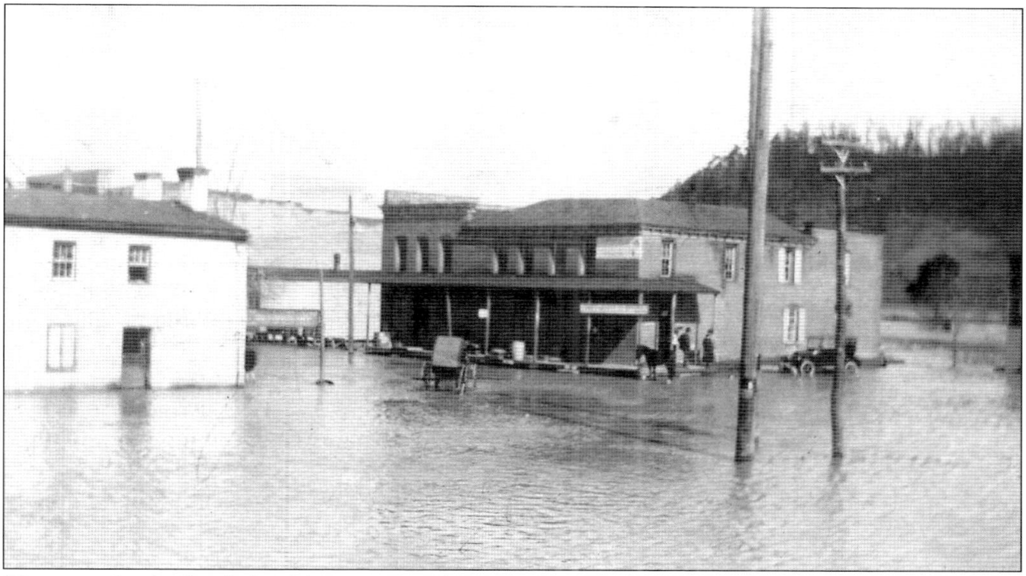

The completely flooded public square is shown in 1920. Although high water did not reach the Yett building, most downtown businesses suffered extensive damage. (Courtesy of King Family Library History Center, Herbert Lawson Collection.)

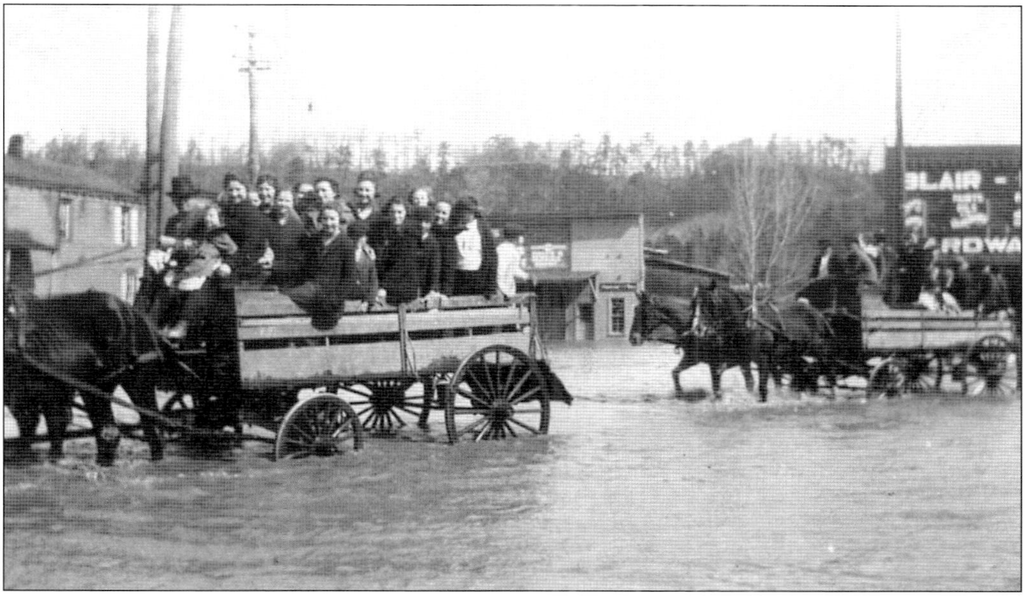

Two wagons of Murphy College students hazard a joyride through the flooded streets of Sevierville in 1920. Located on the higher ground of Cedar Street, floodwater did not reach Murphy College. Here, Blair-Love Hardware Store can be seen in the background. (Courtesy of King Family Library History Center, Herbert Lawson Collection.)

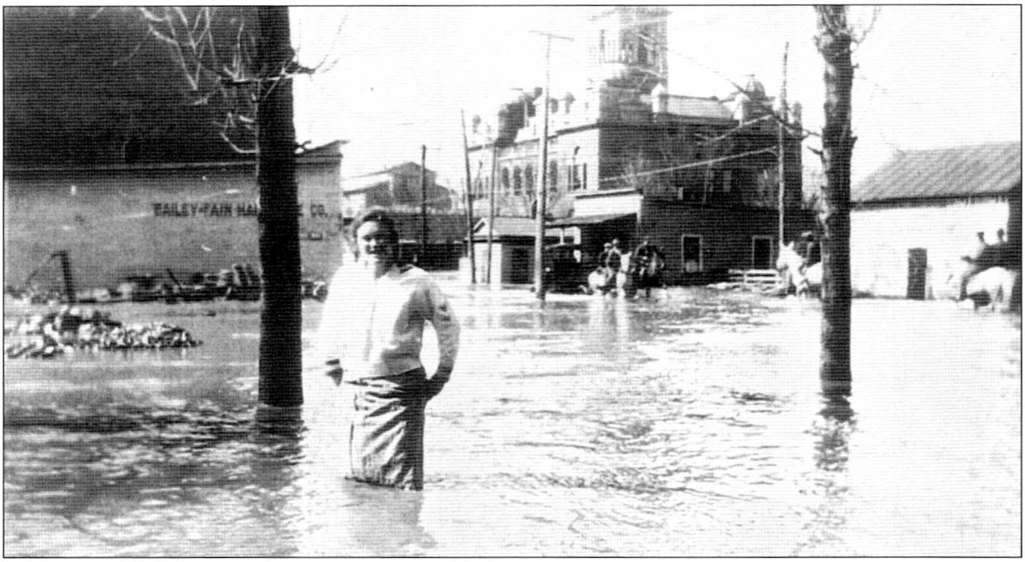

This photograph was taken April 1, 1896, facing south down Court Avenue. The Bailey-Fain Hardware Store is on the left and the courthouse tower is on the right. Walker Milling Company is beyond the courthouse. An unknown individual is standing on the site where the Central Hotel will be built. (Courtesy of King Family Library History Center, Herbert Lawson Collection.)

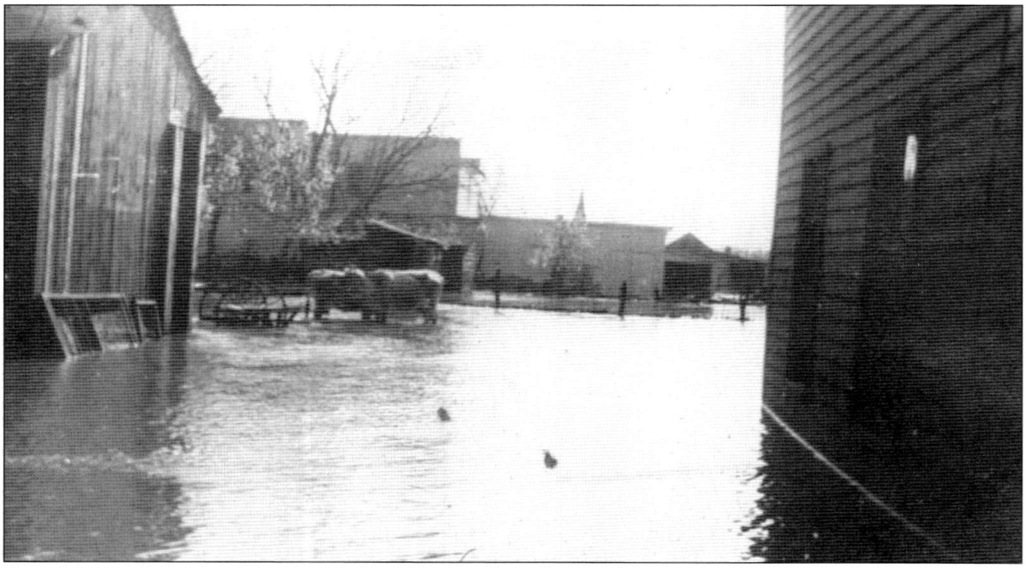

It was not uncommon in those days for Sevierville residents to keep livestock and maintain large vegetable gardens in their yards. The courthouse tower can be seen in the background of this photograph from the 1896 flood. (Courtesy of King Family Library History Center, Herbert Lawson Collection.)

Motorists stranded and seeking high ground are photographed on the Main Street Bridge on March 6, 1963. The spot on the right of the bridge is where Walgreen's is currently located. Residents could not have predicted that another flood would occur only six days later. (Courtesy of the *Mountain Press.*)

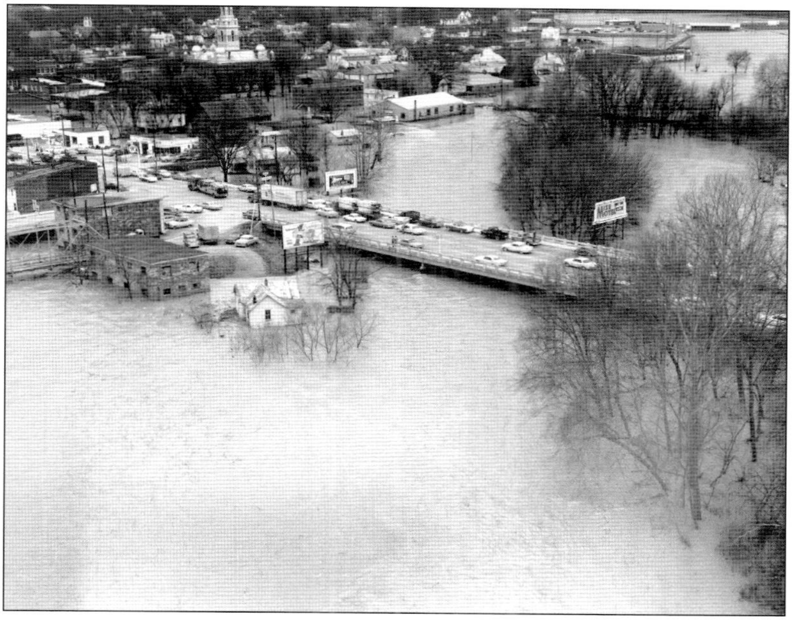

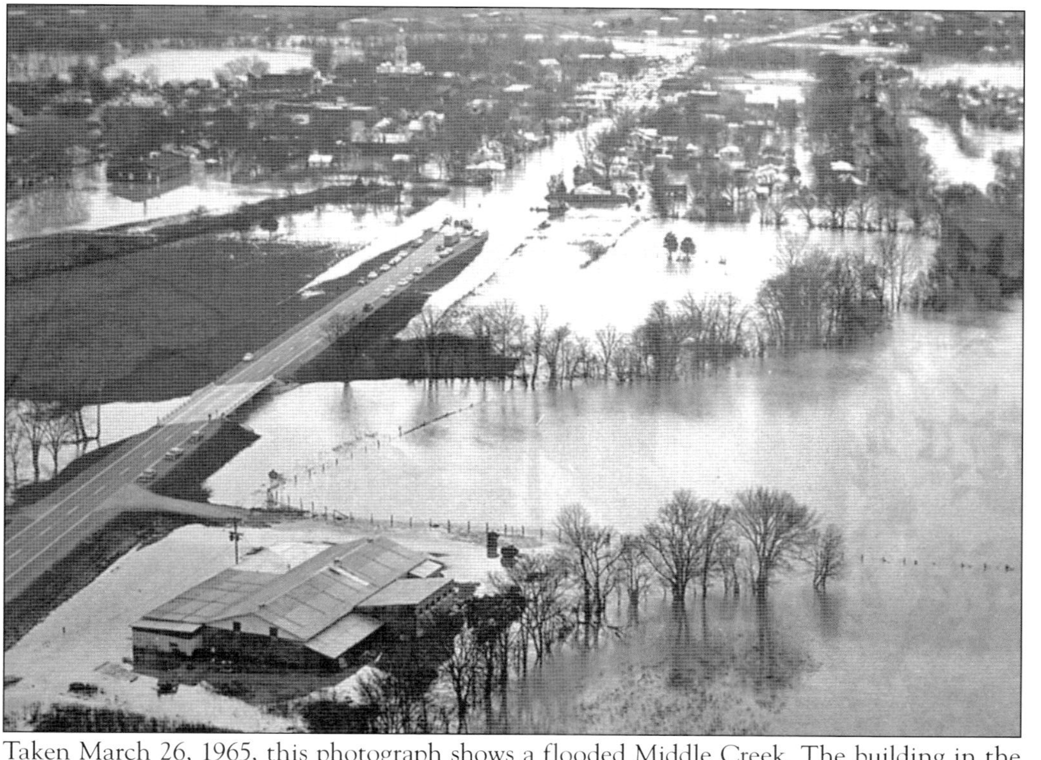

Taken March 26, 1965, this photograph shows a flooded Middle Creek. The building in the foreground is Southern Casting Company. Beyond the swollen creek on the right side of road is the spot where the Sevierville municipal complex is currently located. (Courtesy of the *Mountain Press.*)

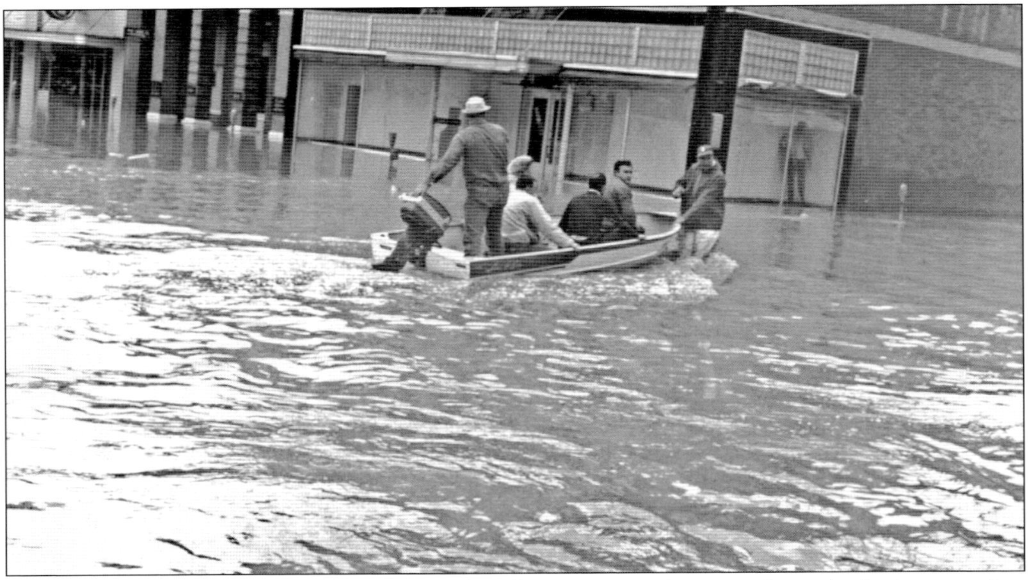

A boat is shown carrying rescue personnel and an evacuated citizen through the intersection of Court Avenue and Bruce Street during the 1963 flood. Downtown business owners and employees remained at work as long as possible hoping to minimize damage to goods. (Courtesy of the *Mountain Press.*)

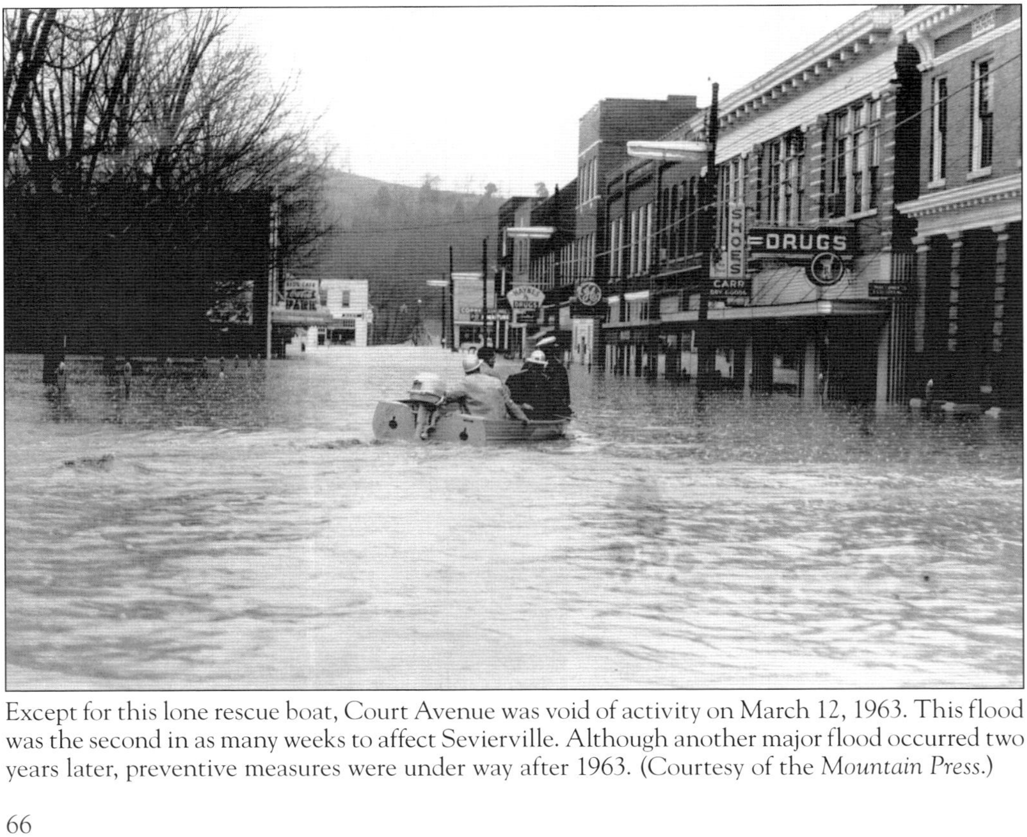

Except for this lone rescue boat, Court Avenue was void of activity on March 12, 1963. This flood was the second in as many weeks to affect Sevierville. Although another major flood occurred two years later, preventive measures were under way after 1963. (Courtesy of the *Mountain Press.*)

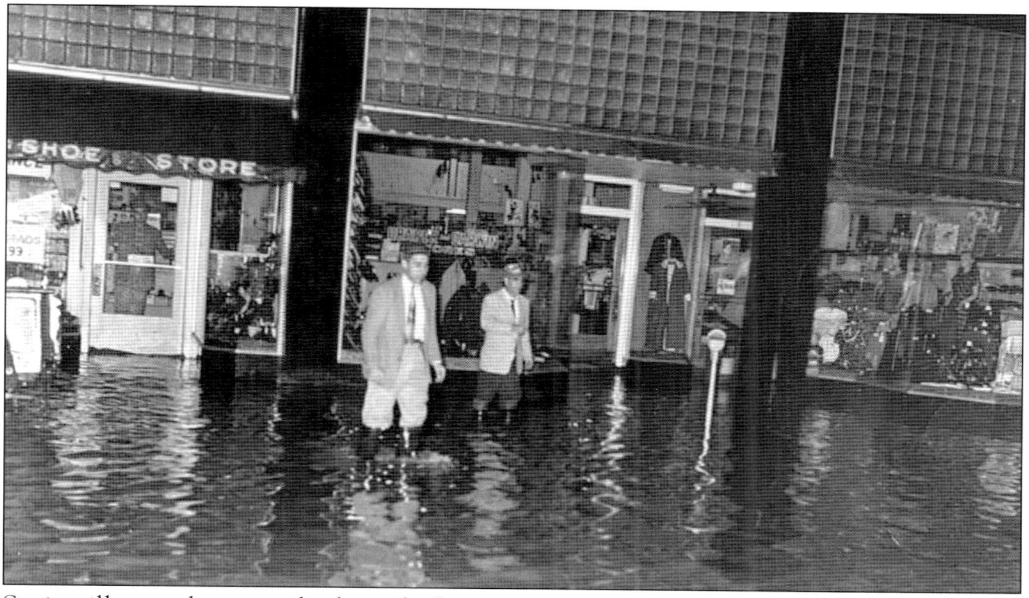

Sevierville merchants wade through the rising waters on Bruce Street on the evening of January 31, 1957. Raymond's Shoe Store and the Draper and Darwin Dry Goods Store can be seen in the background. The river did not crest until the following day. (Courtesy of Johnny Faye McClure.)

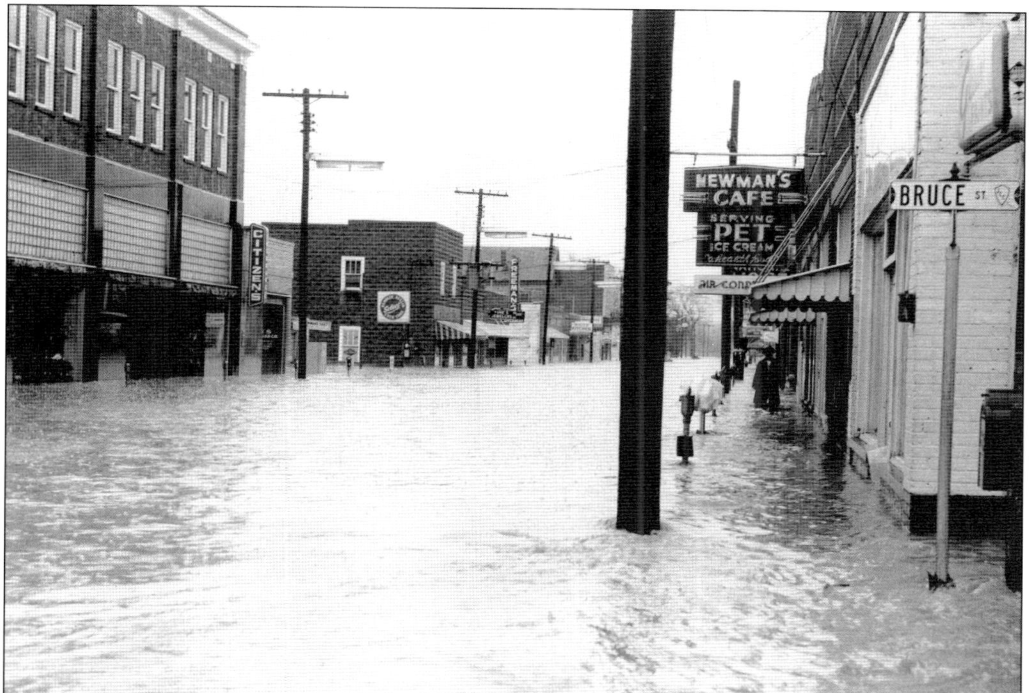

A Sevierville resident walks down Bruce Street in front of Newman's Cafe on February 1, 1957. Floodwater turned the street sign the wrong way. Newman's Cafe had been in business for only a short time when the flood occurred. (Courtesy of Johnny Faye McClure.)

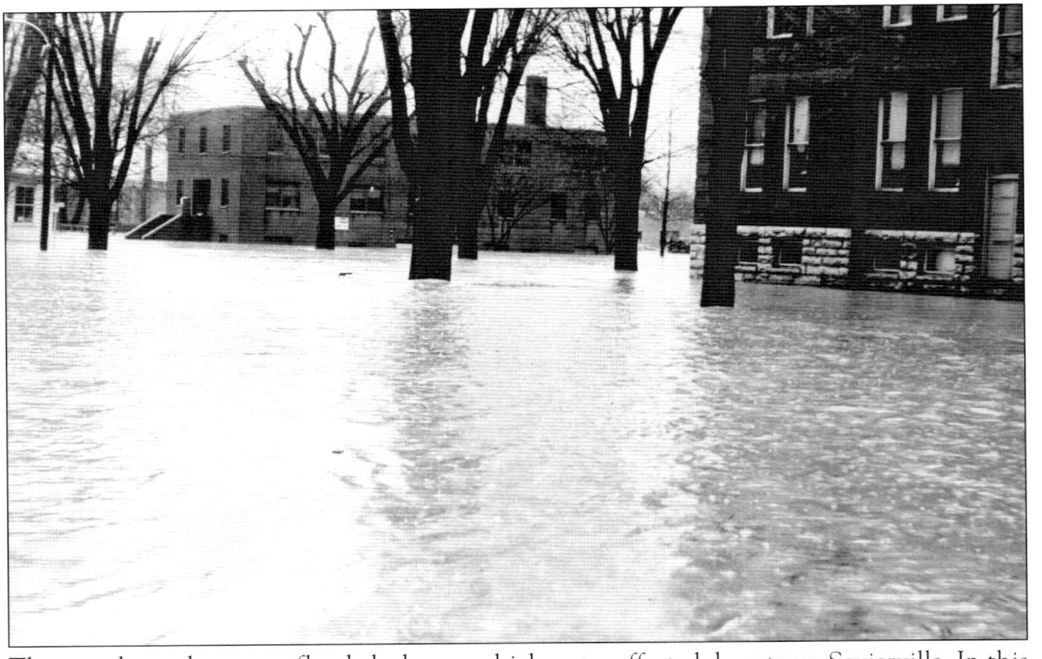

The courthouse basement flooded whenever high water affected downtown Sevierville. In this 1963 photograph, the old jail can be seen directly behind the courthouse. While prisoners were not routinely evacuated, the basement of the jail always flooded. (Courtesy of the *Mountain Press.*)

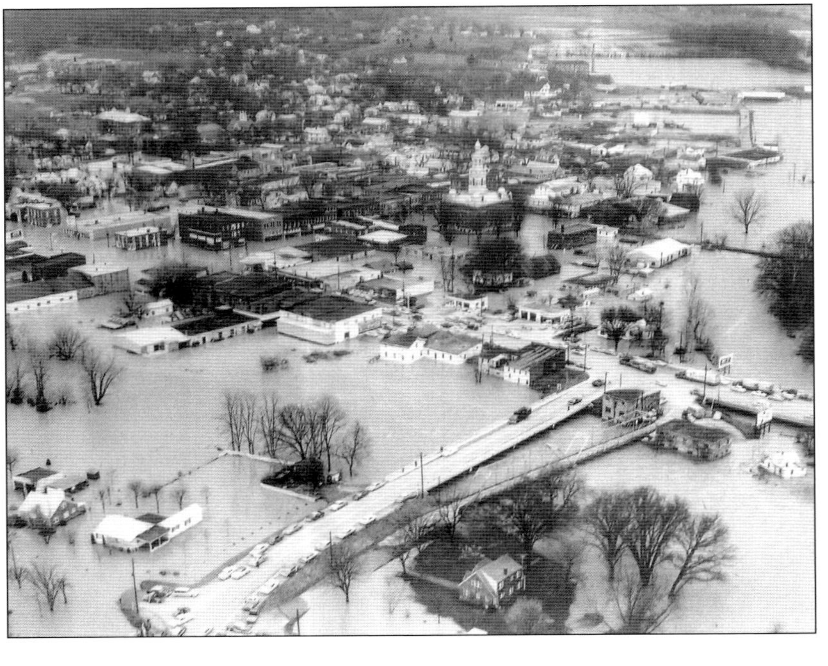

The Fred C. Atchley Bridge and the older steel bridge are seen side-by-side in 1965. The old milldam behind Frost Mills cannot be seen because of the high water level. Parked vehicles line both sides of the road north of the bridge. (Courtesy of the *Mountain Press.*)

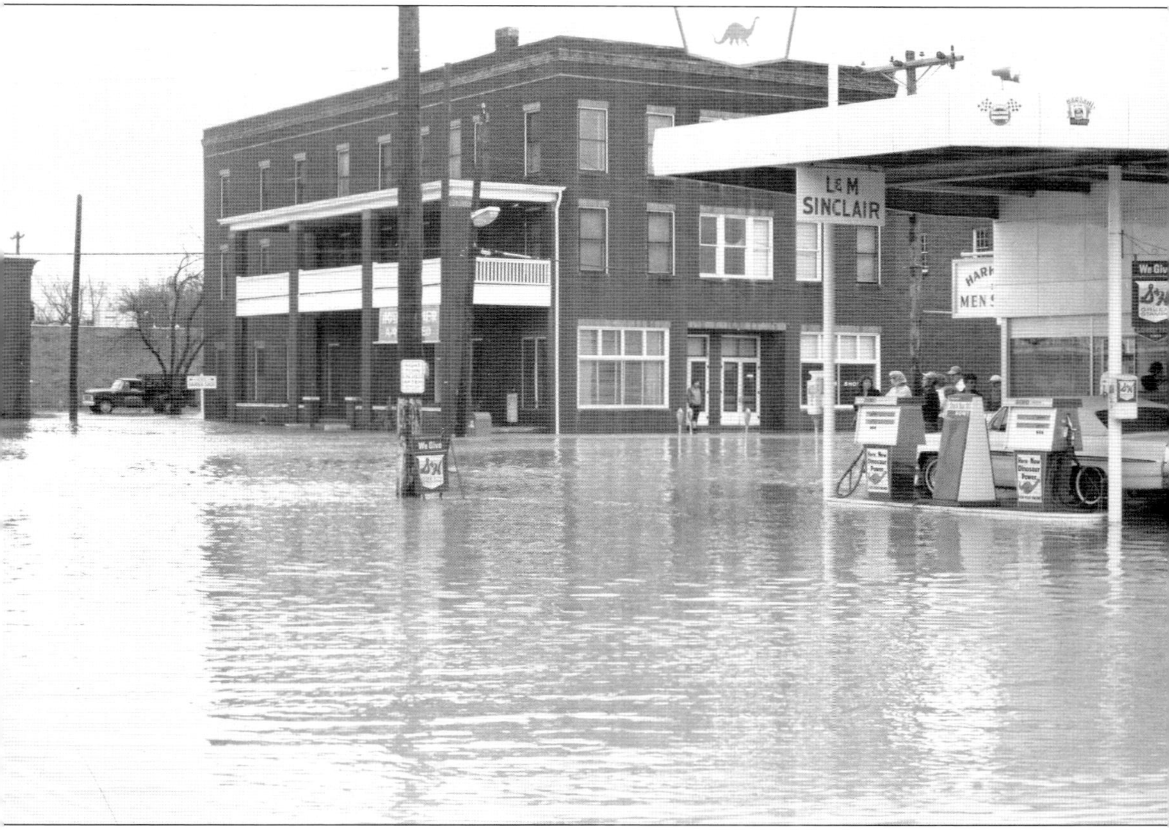

The Hotel Sevier (formally Central Hotel) is engulfed by floodwater in 1963. On the left is the back corner of the old Emert Brick Building. In 1963, the Cloth Shop was located in the building. (Courtesy of the *Mountain Press.*)

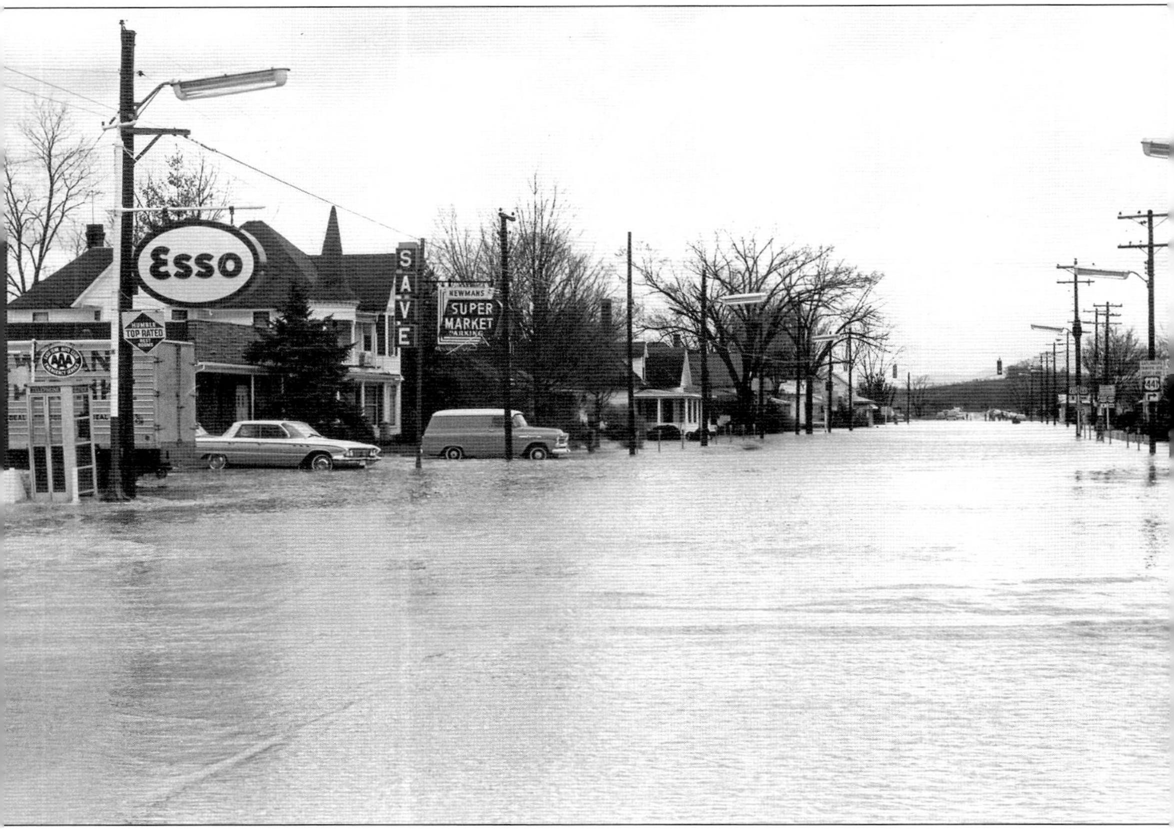

Jim Atchley's Esso Service Station is shown on the left, in front of Newman's Supermarket and the Atchley Funeral Home. Private residences can be seen in the background. (Courtesy of the *Mountain Press*.)

Four

Serving the Community

A different world cannot be built by indifferent people.

—Peter Marshall

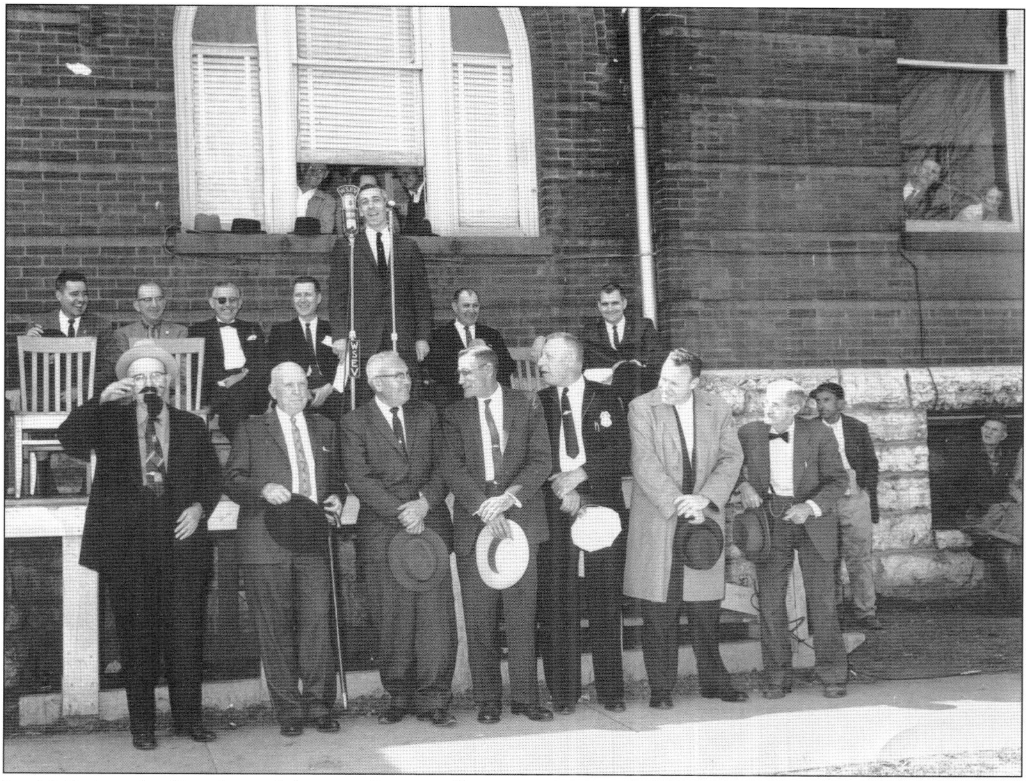

In 1961, local officials and former Sevierville mayors attend the 60th anniversary celebration of the town's incorporation. Shown here, standing before the microphone, Mayor Jimmie Temple addresses the crowd gathered on the courthouse lawn after the parade through town. (Courtesy of the *Mountain Press*.)

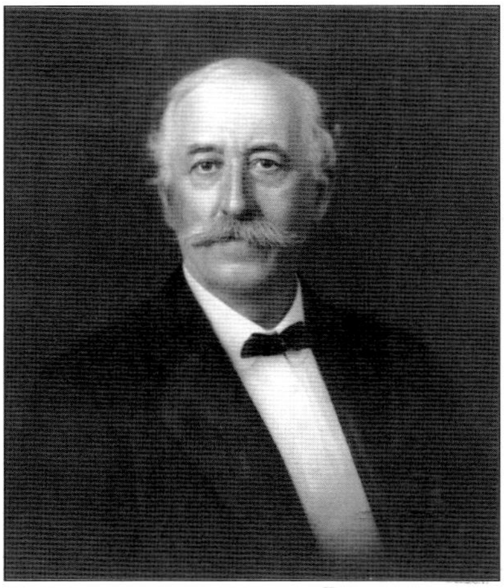

Judge Ambrose Paine was the mayor of Sevierville from 1901 until 1904. When Paine died in 1947, newspaper editor H.O. Eckel wrote the following tribute: "Judge Paine was a colorful figure in the history of Sevier County. He practiced law in all the courts of Sevier County and adjoining counties. Gov. Tom Rye appointed him circuit judge to fill out the term of Judge Henderson who had died. This is where Paine got the title of judge, and it stuck to him through all these years." (Courtesy of John B. Waters Jr.)

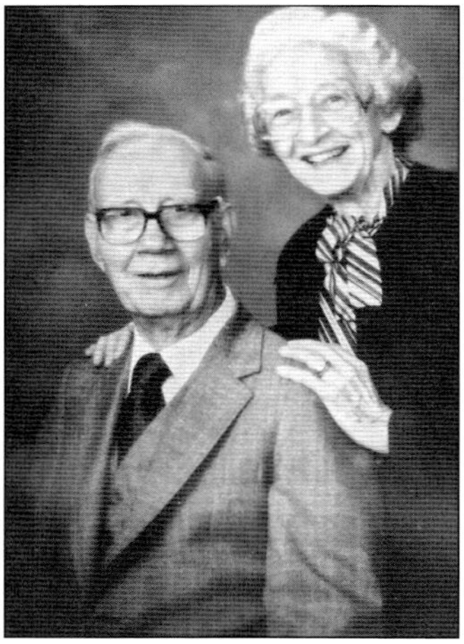

Physician Robert A. Broady and his wife, Ellen (Cox) Broady, moved to Sevierville in 1937 from China, where they had worked for five years as medical missionaries for the Presbyterian Church. Their first office was located on the floor above Wade's Department Store on Court Avenue. They delivered over 7,000 babies while practicing in Sevierville. (Courtesy of Dr. Joseph Broady.)

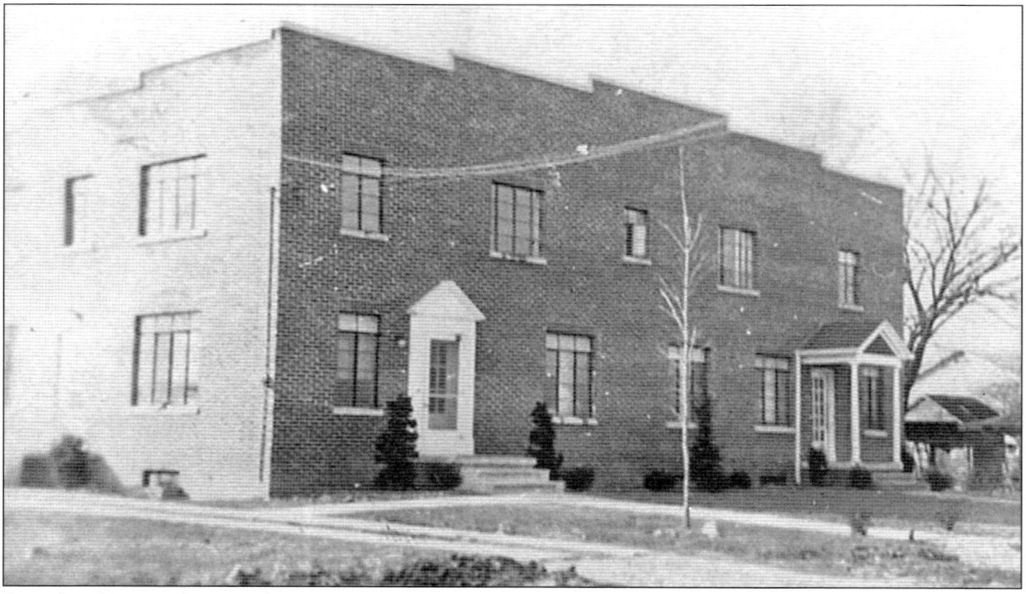

Broady's Hospital opened on East Bruce Street in 1940. For 10 years, the Broady family had living quarters inside the hospital. Dr. Robert A. Broady made frequent house calls as well as operating the busy clinic. When it was built, it was the only hospital between Knoxville, Tennessee, and Asheville, North Carolina. (Courtesy of Dr. Joseph Broady.)

Four

Serving the Community

A different world cannot be built by indifferent people.

—Peter Marshall

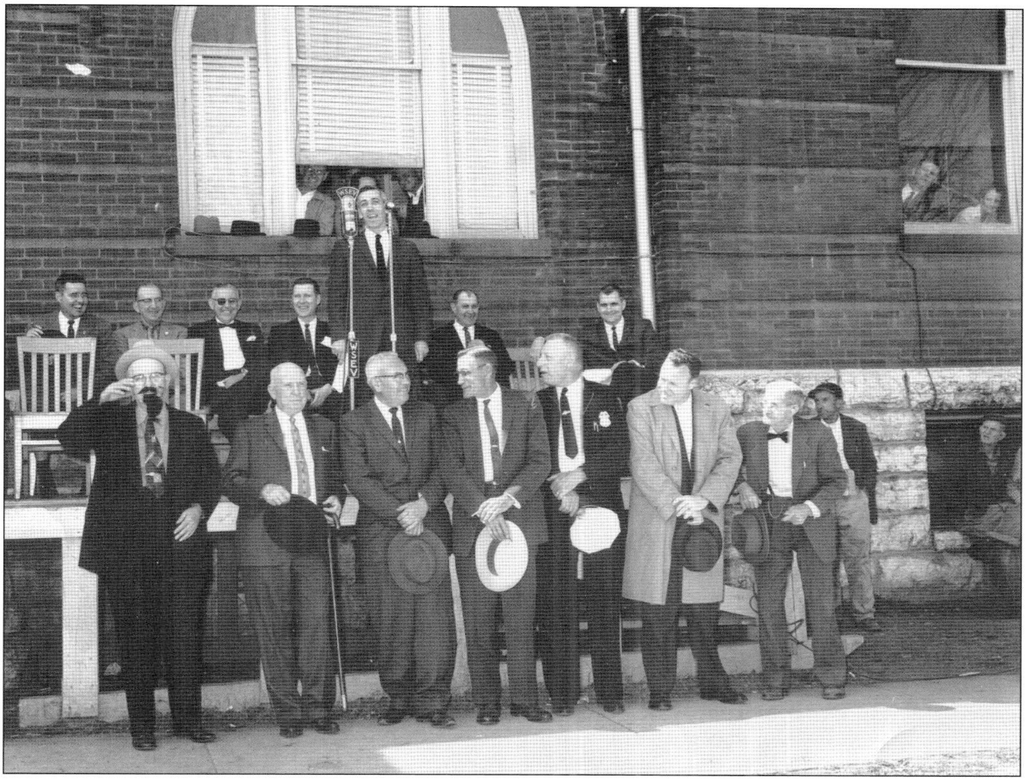

In 1961, local officials and former Sevierville mayors attend the 60th anniversary celebration of the town's incorporation. Shown here, standing before the microphone, Mayor Jimmie Temple addresses the crowd gathered on the courthouse lawn after the parade through town. (Courtesy of the *Mountain Press*.)

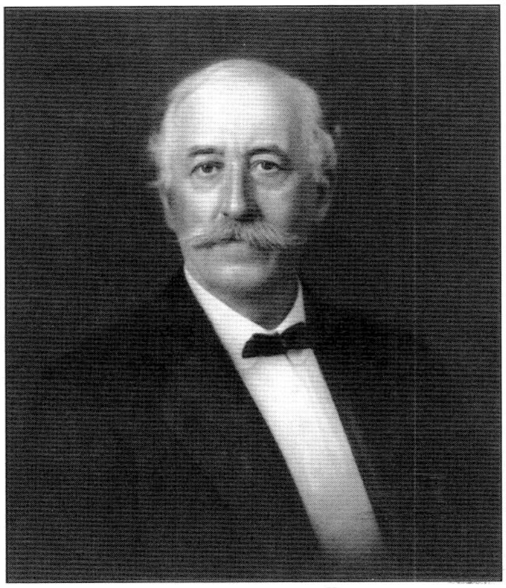

Judge Ambrose Paine was the mayor of Sevierville from 1901 until 1904. When Paine died in 1947, newspaper editor H.O. Eckel wrote the following tribute: "Judge Paine was a colorful figure in the history of Sevier County. He practiced law in all the courts of Sevier County and adjoining counties. Gov. Tom Rye appointed him circuit judge to fill out the term of Judge Henderson who had died. This is where Paine got the title of judge, and it stuck to him through all these years." (Courtesy of John B. Waters Jr.)

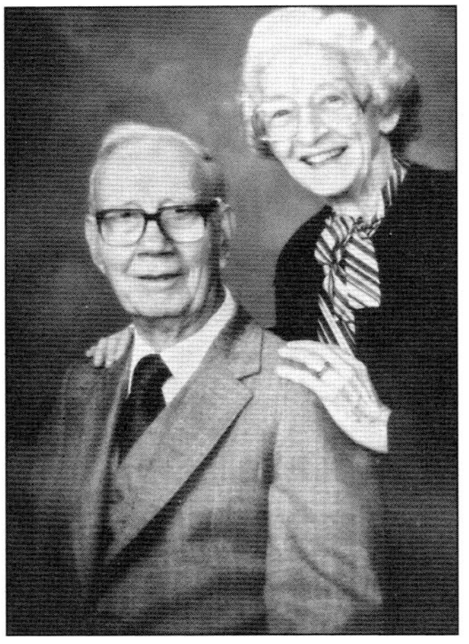

Physician Robert A. Broady and his wife, Ellen (Cox) Broady, moved to Sevierville in 1937 from China, where they had worked for five years as medical missionaries for the Presbyterian Church. Their first office was located on the floor above Wade's Department Store on Court Avenue. They delivered over 7,000 babies while practicing in Sevierville. (Courtesy of Dr. Joseph Broady.)

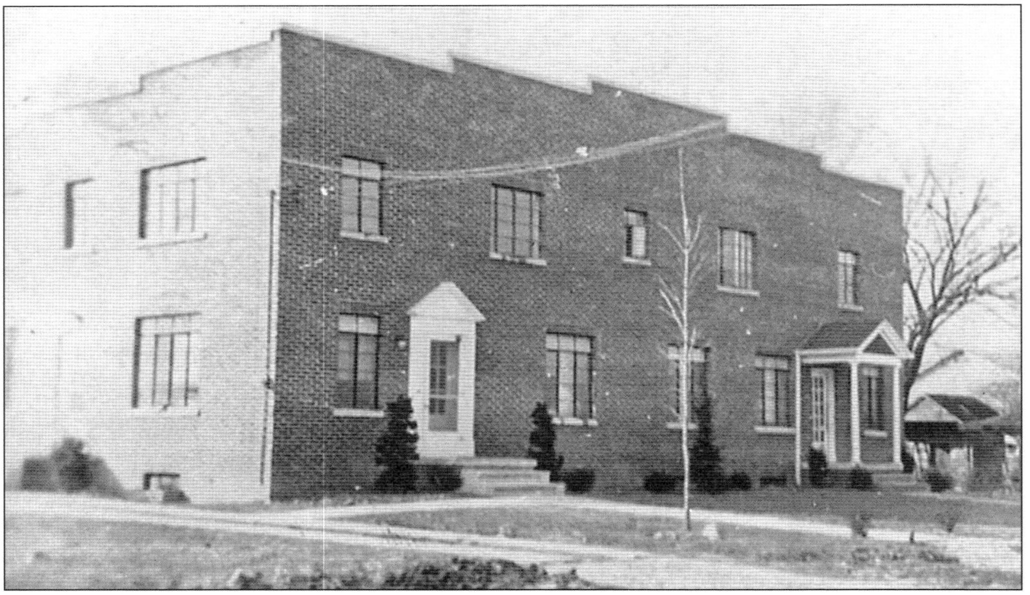

Broady's Hospital opened on East Bruce Street in 1940. For 10 years, the Broady family had living quarters inside the hospital. Dr. Robert A. Broady made frequent house calls as well as operating the busy clinic. When it was built, it was the only hospital between Knoxville, Tennessee, and Asheville, North Carolina. (Courtesy of Dr. Joseph Broady.)

Hugh Trotter was widely known by his nickname "Skip." He was an announcer for WSEV, the only radio station in Sevierville, and was active in various civic and church activities. When the Sevierville Chamber of Commerce formed in 1963, Trotter was elected the first chairman of the board of directors. (Courtesy of Sevierville Chamber of Commerce.)

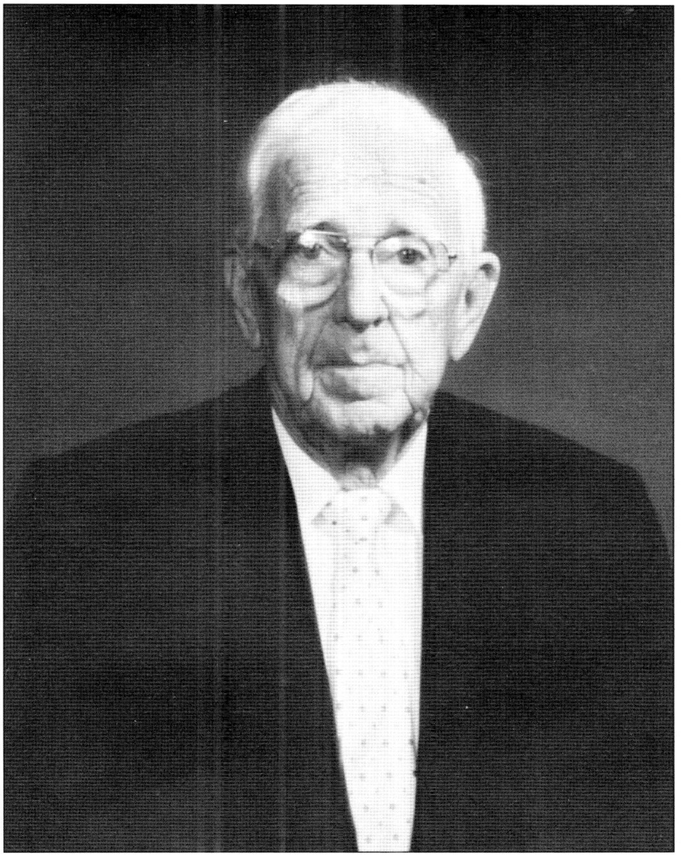

The first Sevierville Chamber of Commerce formed on June 16, 1963. Pictured from left to right are (seated): Lyle McNabb, Hugh Trotter, Ross Summitt; (standing) Jimmie Temple, Bo Roberts, E.W. Paine, John Hickey, Ray Reagan, and Charlie Bell who made up the first board of directors. (Courtesy of Sevierville Chamber of Commerce.)

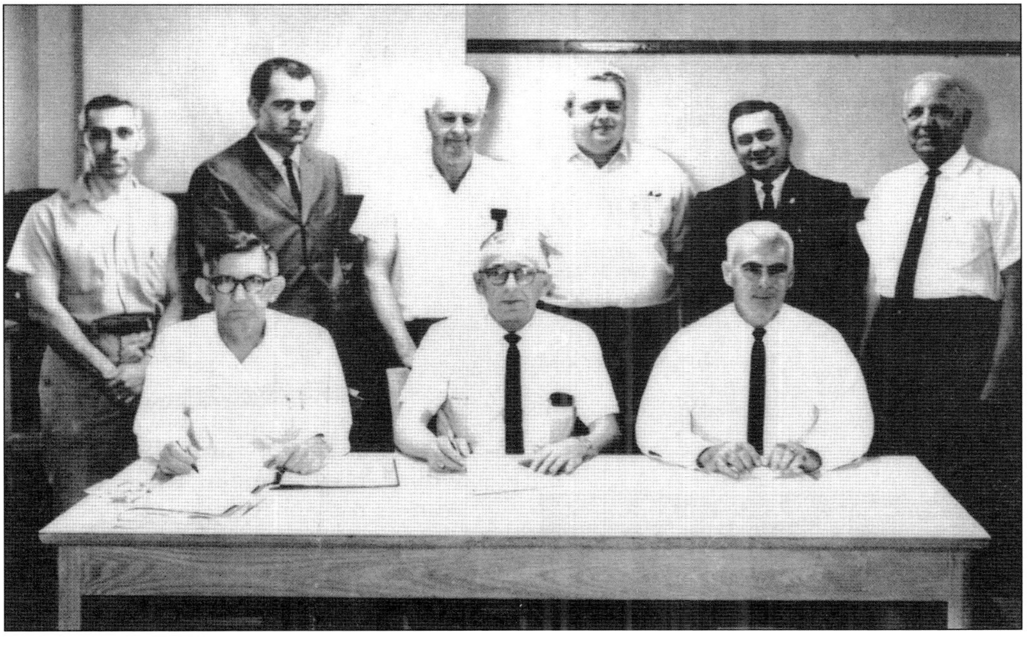

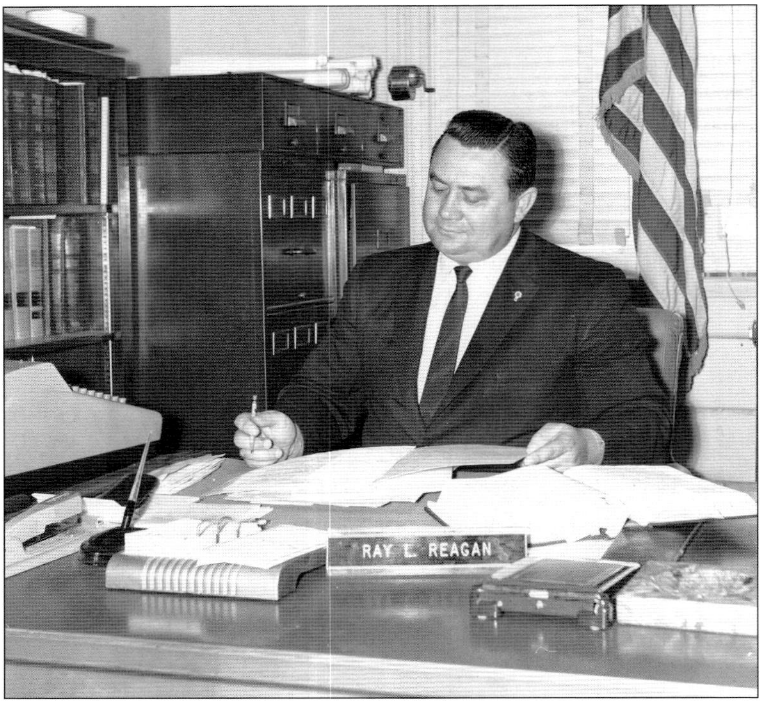

Judge Ray L. Reagan is photographed at his desk. He was a leader in an effort to bring a much-needed industrial park to Sevier County. The position of county judge changed to the current county mayor position. (Courtesy of Jimmie and Marie Temple.)

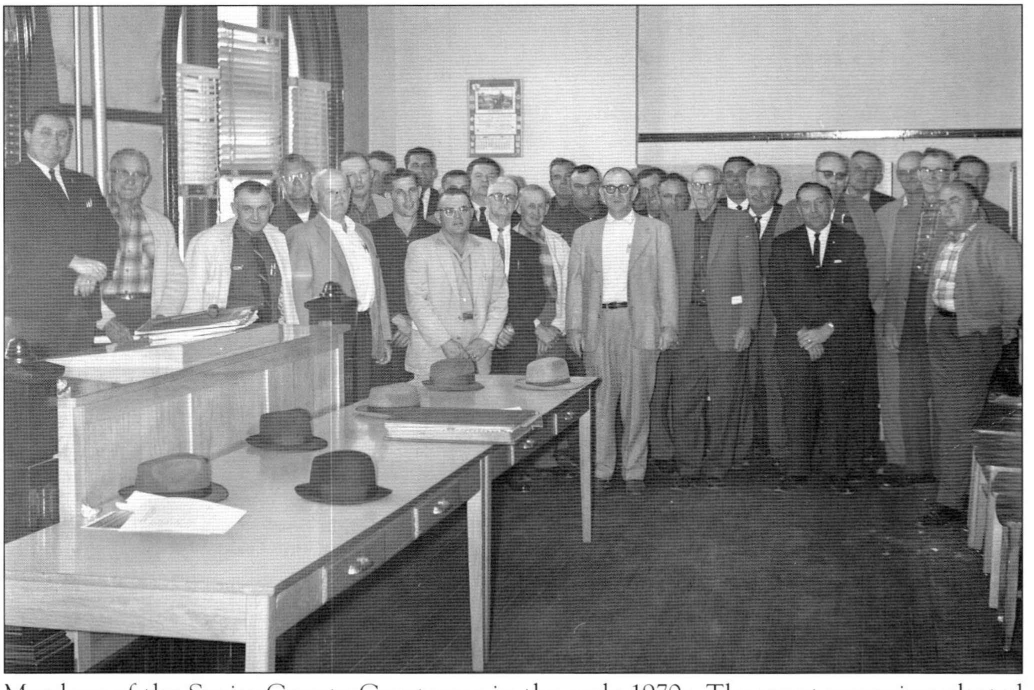

Members of the Sevier County Court pose in the early 1970s. The court comprises elected representatives from each civil district in the county. Formerly called justices of the peace, the title changed in recent years to county commissioner. In addition, the county court is now called the county commission. (Courtesy of Jimmie and Marie Temple.)

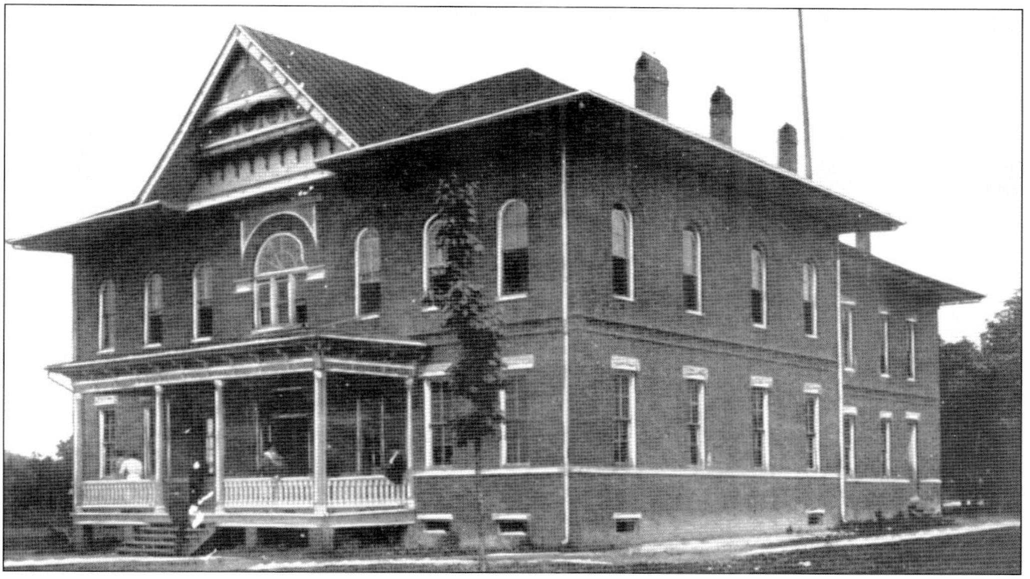

Murphy College was established on April 4, 1890. Shown here, the school was named in honor of J. Crawford Murphy, who helped establish the college. The brick used in the two-story building was made at a nearby kiln by Witt McMahan. Murphy College provided instruction for students from primary grades through college level. (Courtesy of King Family Library History Center, Herbert Lawson Collection.)

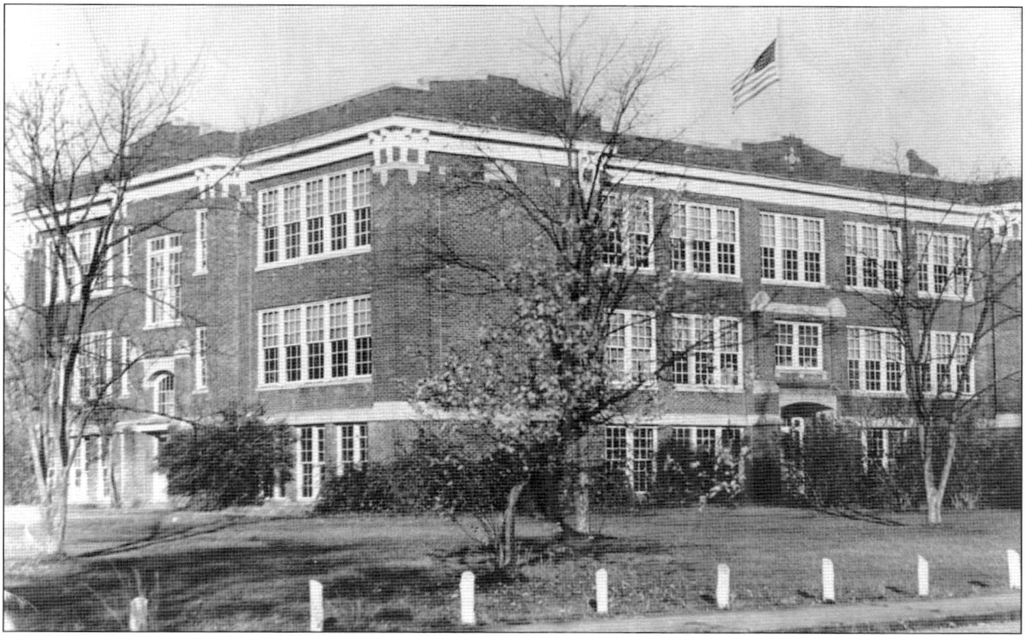

Classes in the new Sevier County High School began September 5, 1921. Located on High Street, the school served the public until 1968, when a new building was completed on Dolly Parton Parkway. At the time of construction, Sevier County High School was the largest brick structure ever built in Sevier County. (Courtesy of King Family Library History Center, Herbert Lawson Collection.)

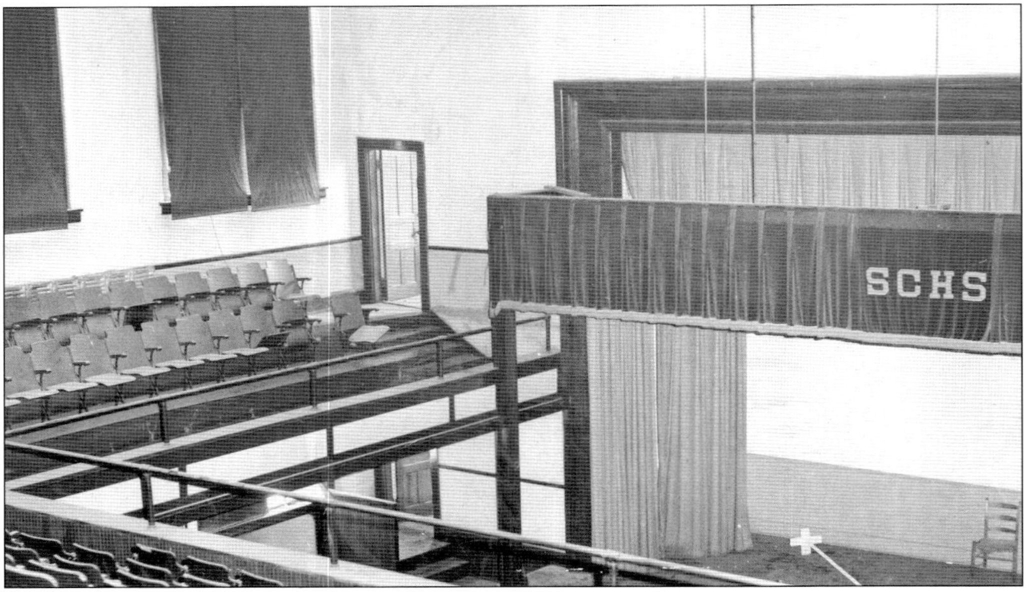

The auditorium of Sevier County High School is shown here, taken in the last years that the 1921 building was used. A weekly chapel program was held in the auditorium. By the time students were moved to the new location, this facility had become overcrowded. (Courtesy of the *Mountain Press*.)

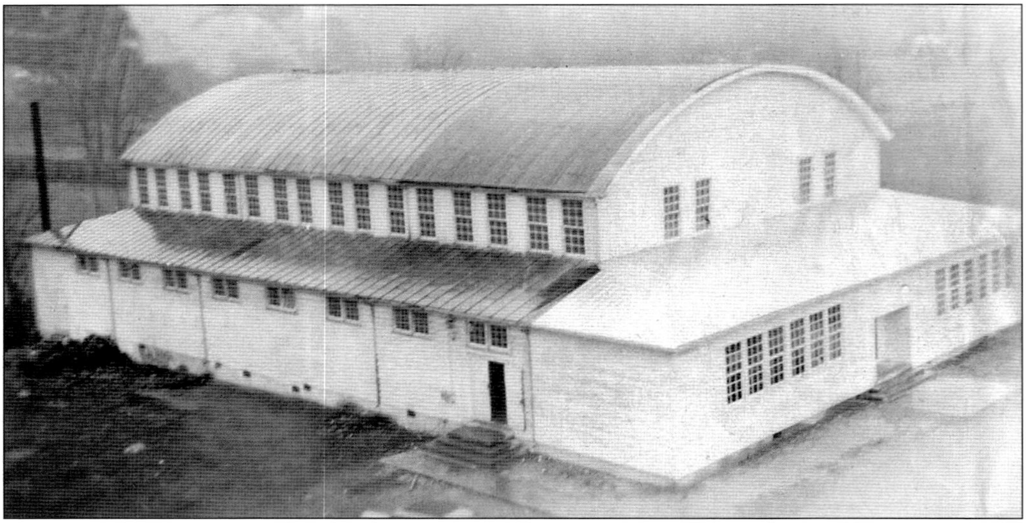

The Sevier County High School gymnasium was located directly behind the main 1921 building. Unable to accommodate the number of spectators who regularly attended the Smoky Bear's basketball events, games were held in Sevierville Elementary School gymnasium for several years before the new high school opened. (Courtesy of King Family Library History Center, Herbert Lawson Collection.)

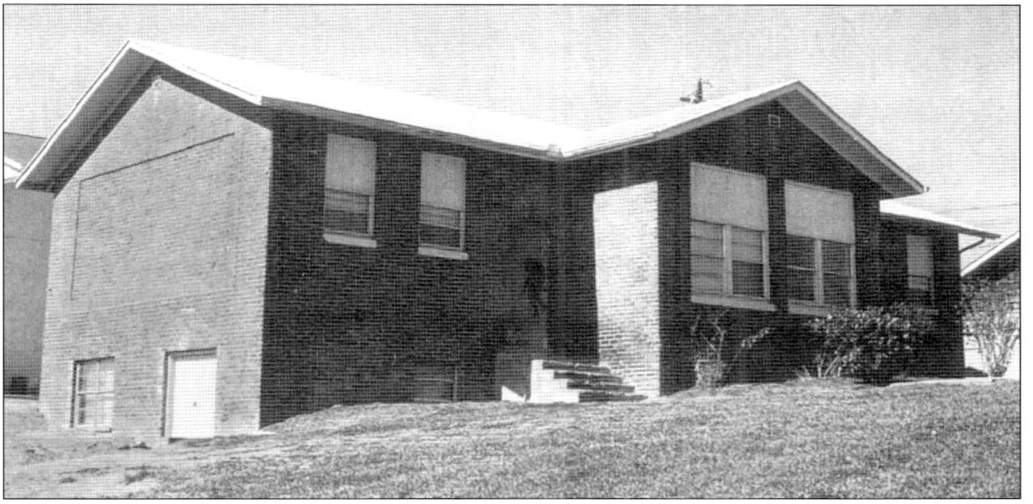

In 1923, the Pleasant View School was constructed in Sevierville for blacks. Built on property donated by Fred, James, and Newton McMahan, construction was funded by a grant from the Rosenwald Foundation. Mary McMahan, who was called Aunt Mary by her students, taught all eight grades. (Courtesy of the *Mountain Press*.)

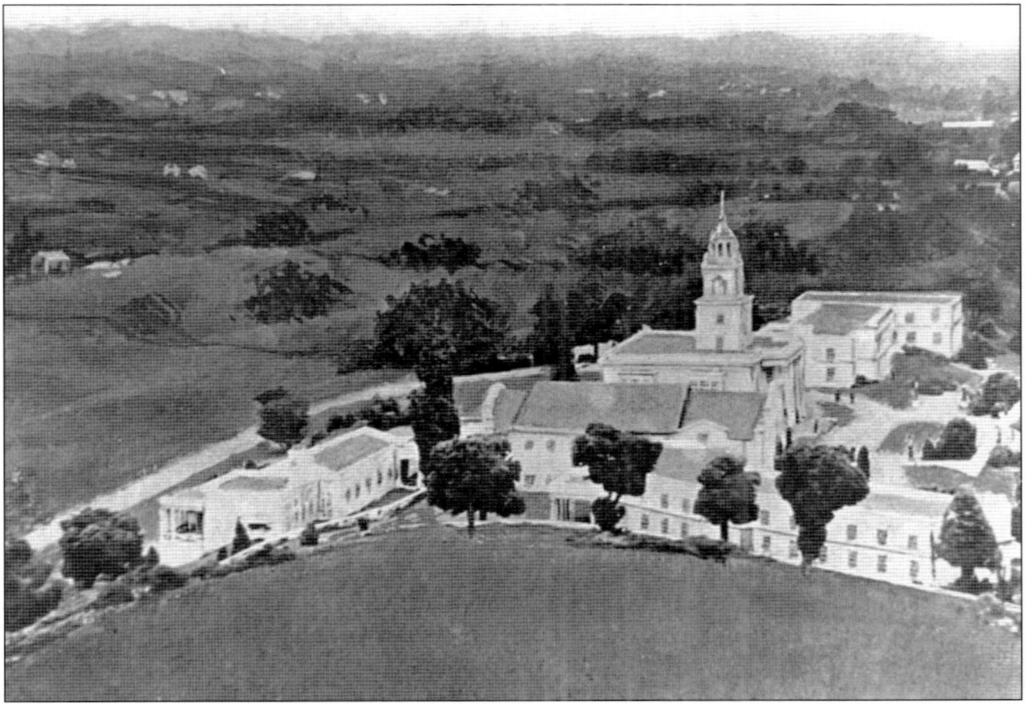

In 1923, when Murphy College moved to its new buildings on Thomas Hill, the name changed to Murphy Collegiate Institute. But, with the new public high school located only a few blocks away, the college did not survive. Doors closed in 1935 and the property was sold to the Church of God. The church operated a Bible training school on the site, until 1948, when they converted the buildings into an orphanage. (Courtesy of King Family Library History Center, Herbert Lawson Collection.)

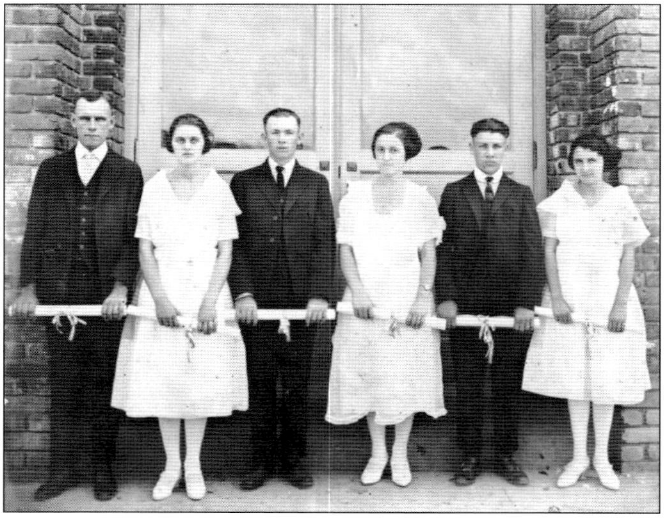

This photograph shows the Sevier County High School Class of 1922 posing in front of the new school. The students transferred from other schools in the county when the new school opened its doors in 1921. Pictured from left to right are Fred Lawson, Rushia Davis, Sam Huffaker, Kate Allen, George Ballard, and Edna Enloe.

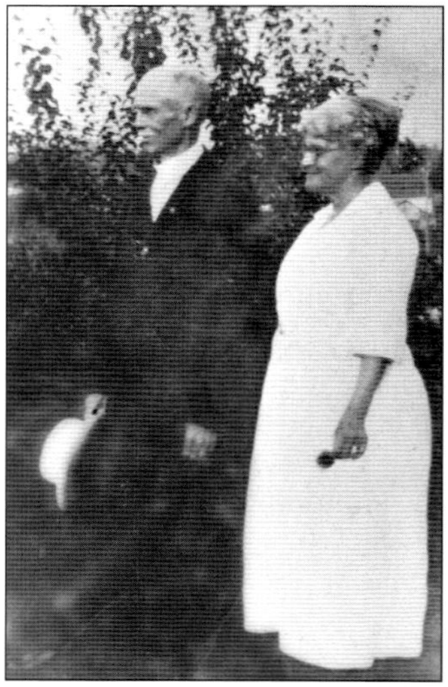

Dr. E.A. Bishop, pictured with his wife, became president of Murphy College in 1912. He led the school for over two decades, and the school never fully recovered from his death in 1925. Four presidents followed Dr. Bishop before the institution closed in 1936. (Courtesy of King Family Library History Center, Herbert Lawson Collection.)

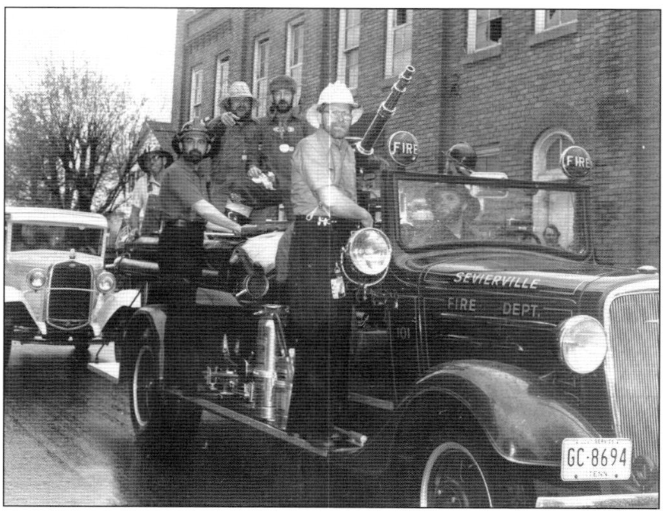

Volunteer firemen display holiday spirit aboard their vintage engine in this 1975 Sevierville Christmas parade. Standing on the running board are Jim Atchley (front) and Russell Hughes. (Courtesy of Jimmie and Marie Temple.)

Smoky the dalmatian displays unequivocal mastery over this fire hydrant. Smoky was one of many fearless dalmation mascots to assist the Sevierville's Finest over the years. In earlier days of all-volunteer fire-fighting teams, every caution light in town turned red to give them fast, unimpeded access. (Courtesy of the *Mountain Press*.)

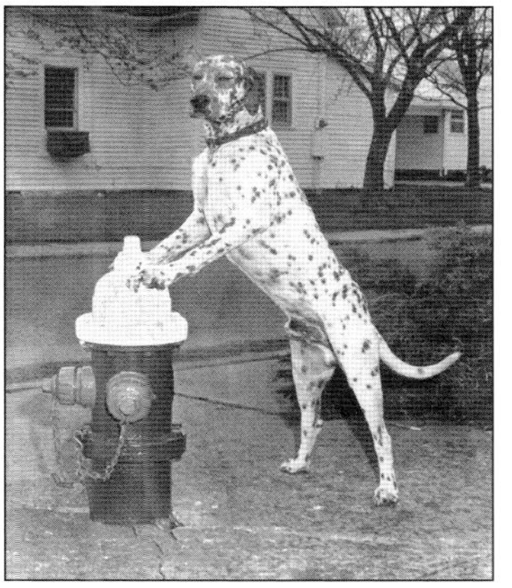

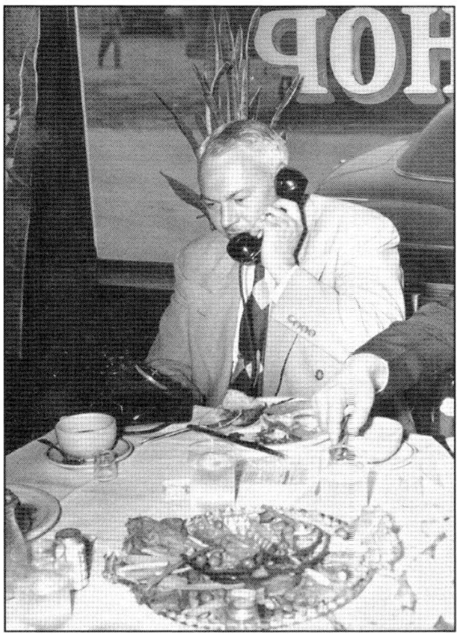

Mayor Robert Howard made the first direct-dial long-distance telephone call from Sevierville in 1951. The call was made from the coffee shop in the Central Hotel to Howard's sister-in-law in Orlando, Florida. The second call was made to his cousins in Ada, Oklahoma. (Courtesy of Mary Bob Rowe.)

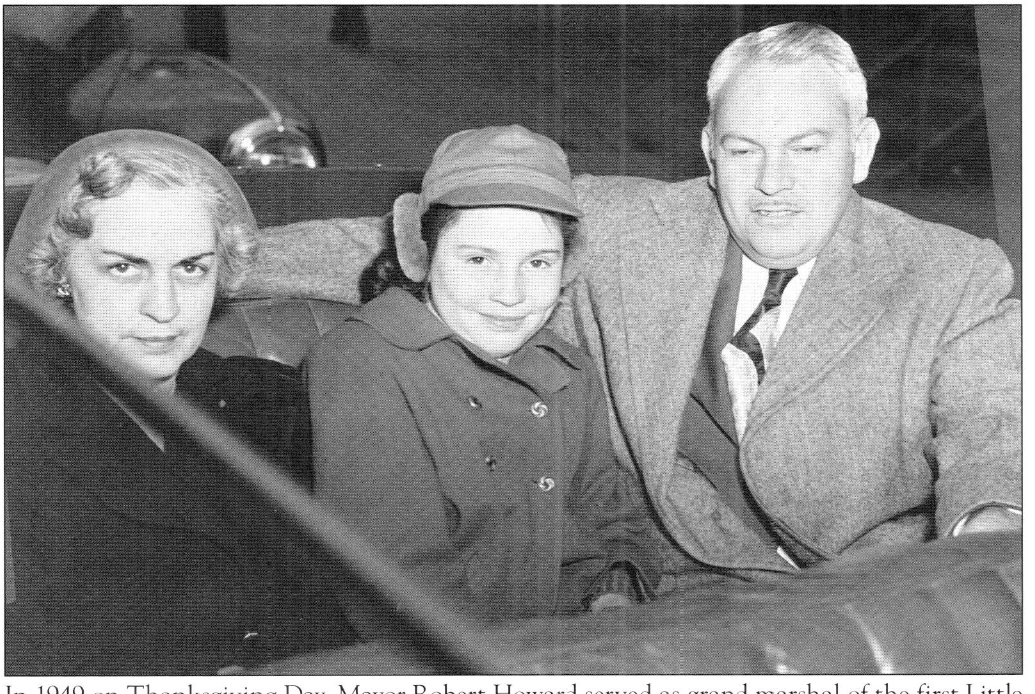

In 1949 on Thanksgiving Day, Mayor Robert Howard served as grand marshal of the first Little Smoky Bowl Parade. He is pictured with his wife, Mary (Temple) Howard, and daughter Mary. The parade was followed by a high school football game. The Little Smoky Bowl was sponsored by the Sevierville Lions Club. (Courtesy of Mary Bob Rowe.)

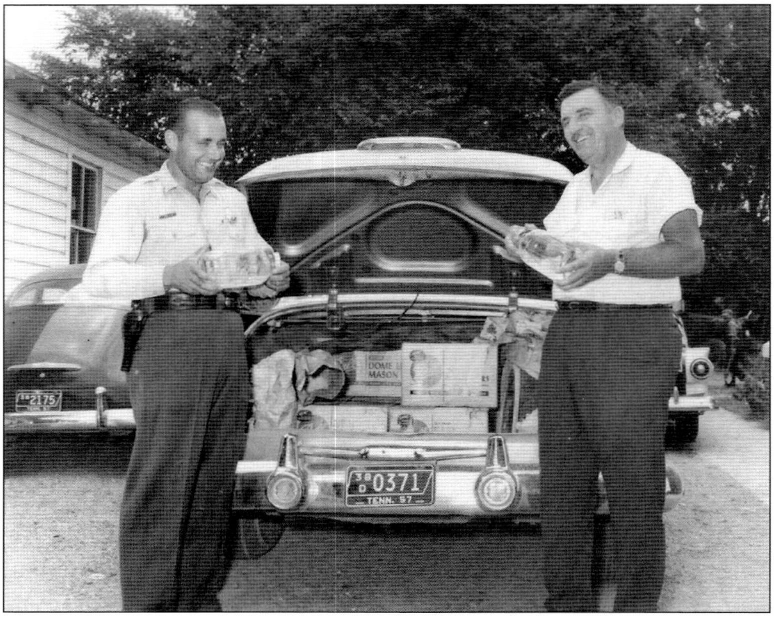

Tennessee state trooper T.J. Cantwell (left) and Sevier County sheriff Ray C. Noland are displaying moonshine they confiscated in this image taken in 1957. Noland served six terms as sheriff and was known to take a firm stand against any type of illegal activities. (Courtesy of Ersa Rhea Smith.)

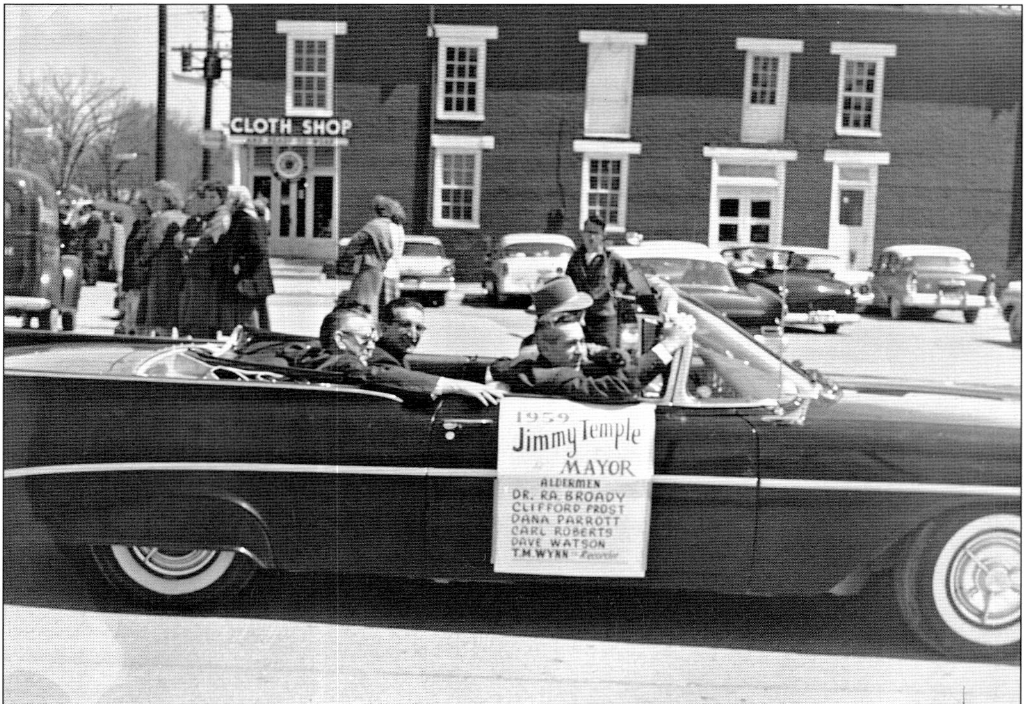

In this 1959 parade, the board rode through the streets of Sevierville in a convertible. While not all were on hand, the sign lists aldermen Robert Broady, Clifford Frost, Dana Parrott, Carl Roberts, Dave Watson, and recorder T.M. Wynn. Mayor Jimmie Temple rides in the front seat. Note that the sign says "Jimmy," though the mayor has always spelled it Jimmie. (Courtesy of the *Mountain Press*.)

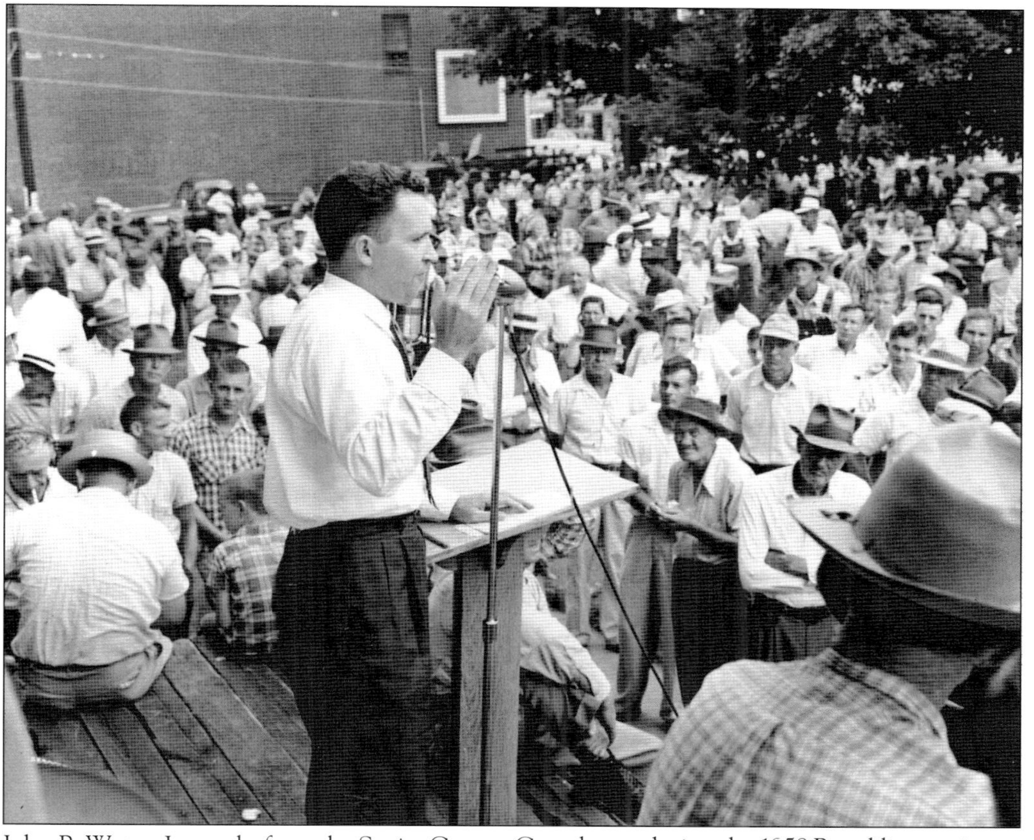

John B. Waters Jr. speaks from the Sevier County Courthouse during the 1958 Republican primary campaign for First District Congressman. (Courtesy of John B. Waters Jr.)

Gary Wade speaks at the local commemoration of America's bicentennial in 1976 as city officials and former mayors look on. City administrator Hulet Chaney, seated directly behind the speaker, organized the event. (Courtesy of city of Sevierville.)

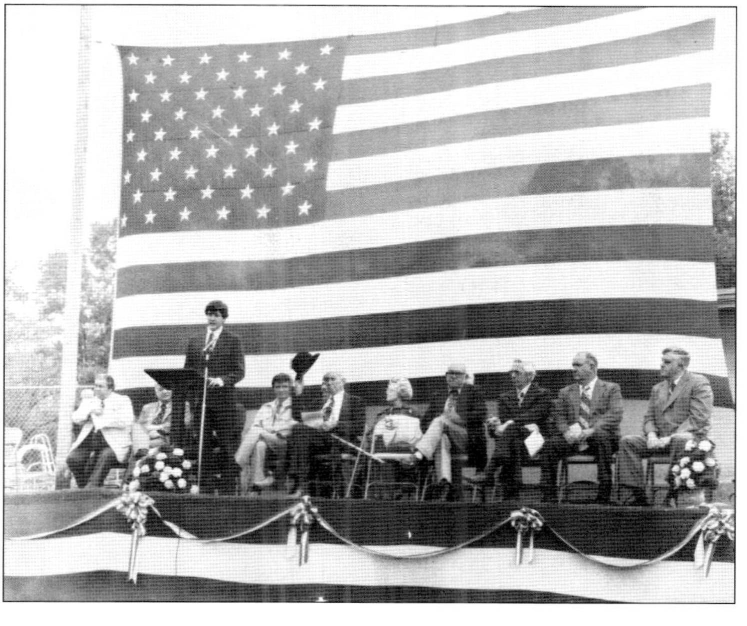

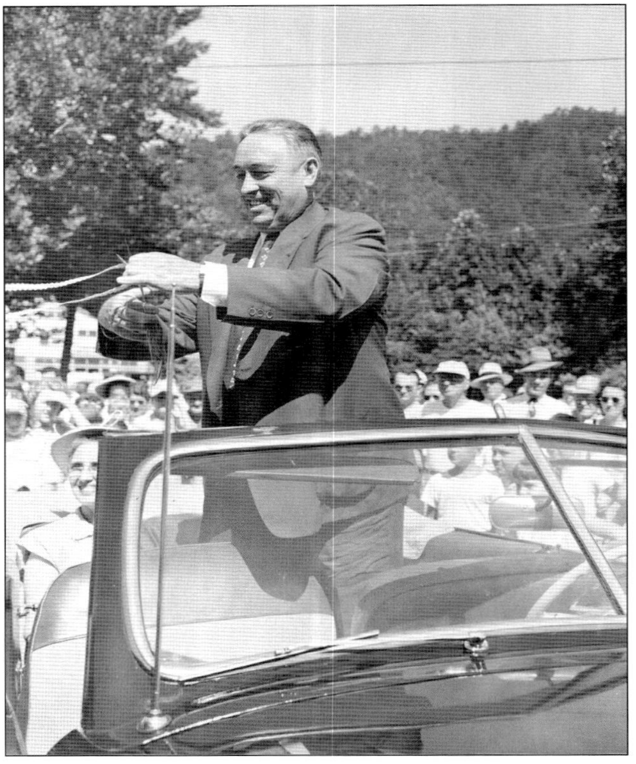

Tennessee governor Gordon Browning cuts the ribbon to open the 1951 Sevier County Fair. Browning was state governor from 1937 until 1939 and from 1947 until 1953. He was enroute to Gatlinburg when local officials persuaded him to stop in Sevierville for the ribbon-cutting honor. (Courtesy of Jimmie and Marie Temple.)

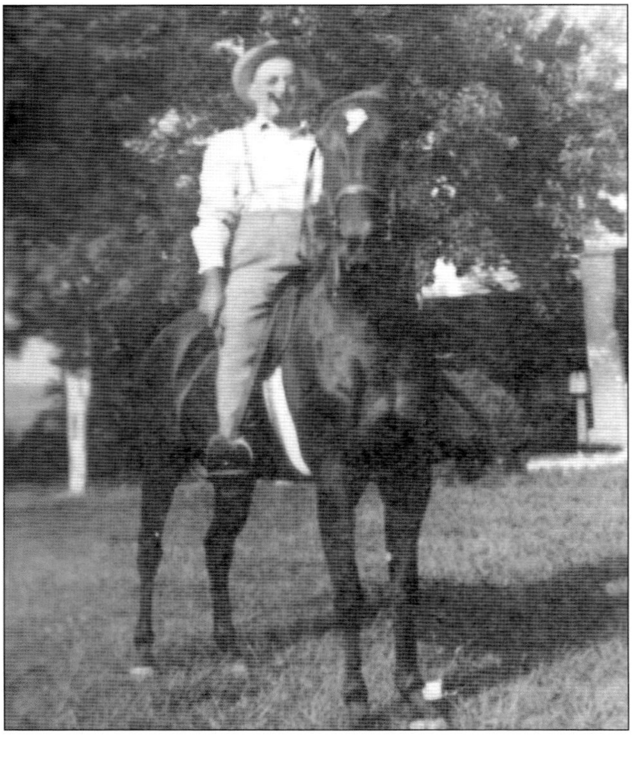

Well-known physician John Ogle is pictured riding his horse at Five Oaks Farm. Dr. Ogle began his practice at age 21 in Harrisburg, where he met and married Blanche Wayland in 1908. He made house calls day and night, traveling by horse. In 1924, Ogle bought Five Oaks Farm and moved his office to downtown Sevierville (Courtesy of King Family Library History Center, Tim Fisher Collection.)

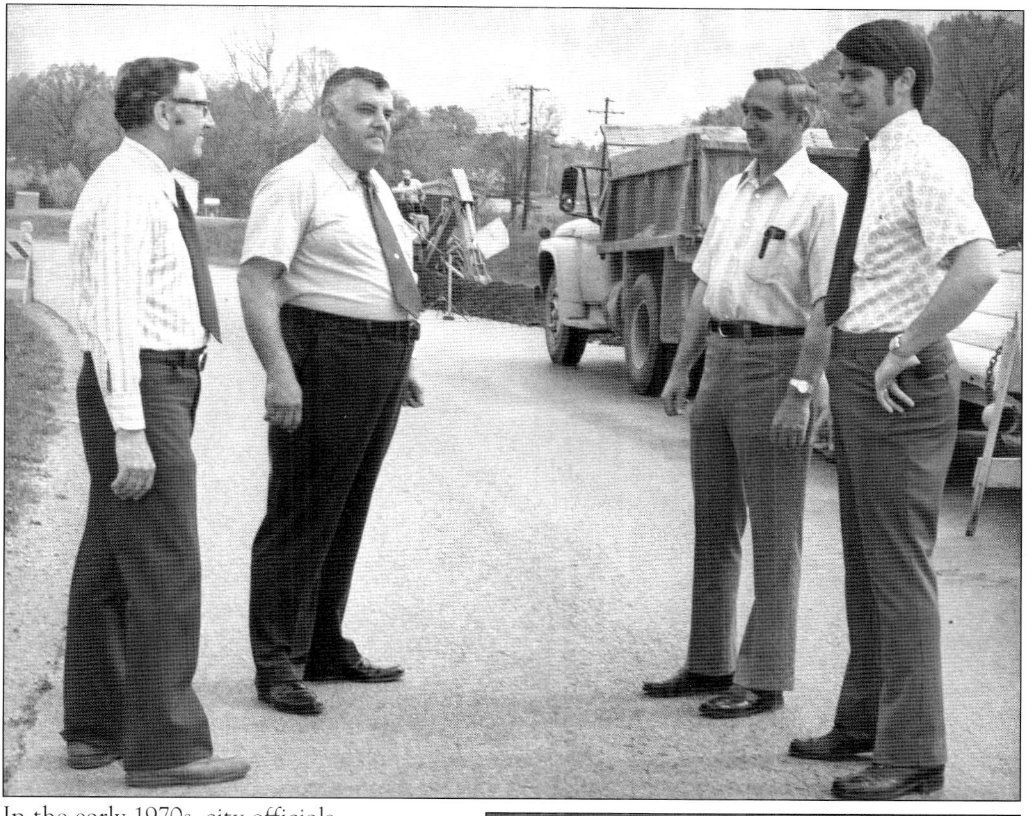

In the early 1970s, city officials were photographed discussing city infrastructure. From the left are Lou Lightner, Mayor Herbert Lawson, Jack Delozier, and C.L. Overman. Lawson was elected in 1971. Meetings of the board were held at the Sevierville Fire Department at that time. (Courtesy of King Family Library History Center, Herbert Lawson Collection.)

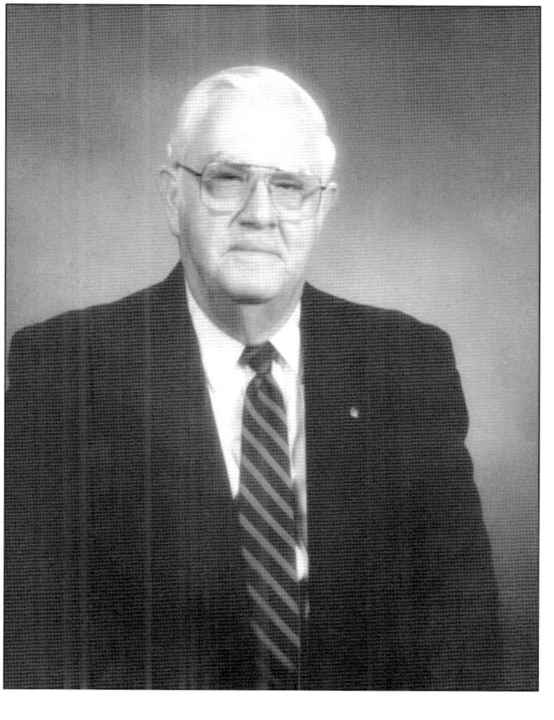

Before Herbert Lawson was elected mayor in 1971, he succeeded Hugh Trotter as the second chair of the Sevierville Chamber of Commerce board. Lawson operated the Corner Store in Sevierville, volunteered with the Sevierville Volunteer Fire Department, and sang in the First Baptist Church choir. (Courtesy of Sevierville Chamber of Commerce.)

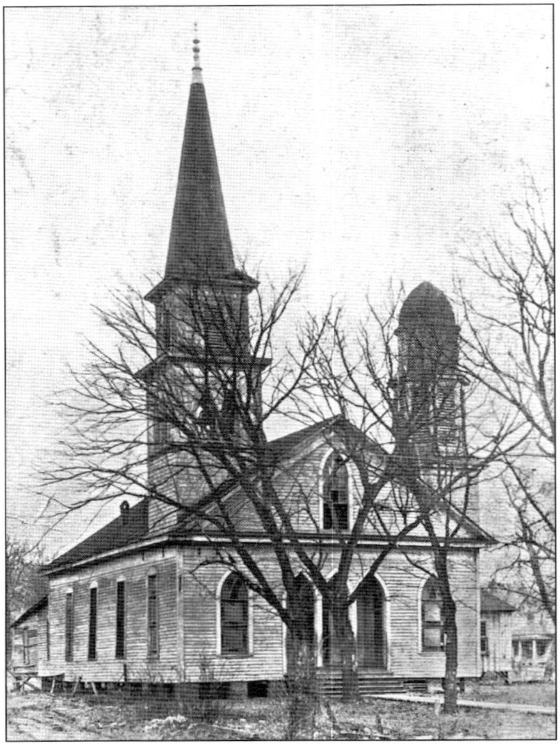

Originally called Forks-of-the-River Baptist Church, the First Baptist Church constructed their third building in 1876, shown here. The building was in the vicinity of the old Forks-of-the-River Cemetery. The new church cost $1,443, and the fund-raising process was led by P.H. Stafford. The congregation moved to its new location in 1924. (Courtesy of King Family Library History Center, Herbert Lawson Collection.)

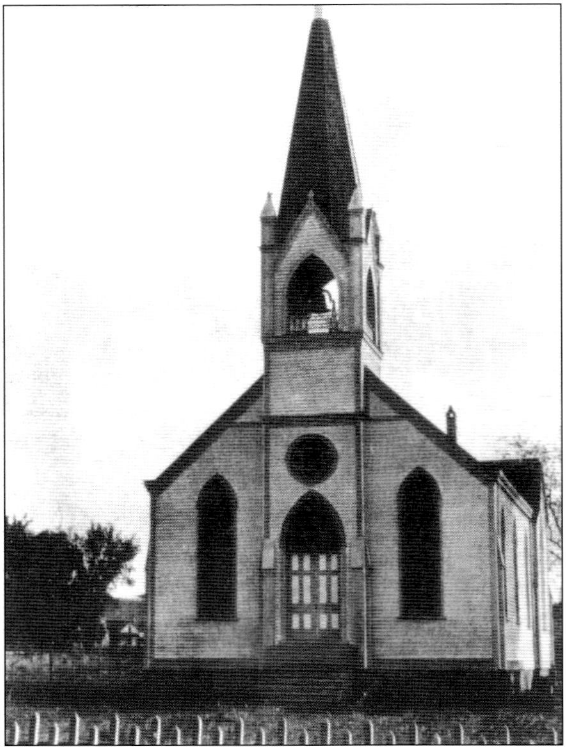

Located on the south side of East Main Street, the Methodist-Episcopal Church (south) was constructed in 1893. A white frame building with a tall steeple and a bell, the structure was graced with tall stained-glass windows donated by members in memory of loved ones. (Courtesy of King Family Library History Center, Herbert Lawson Collection.)

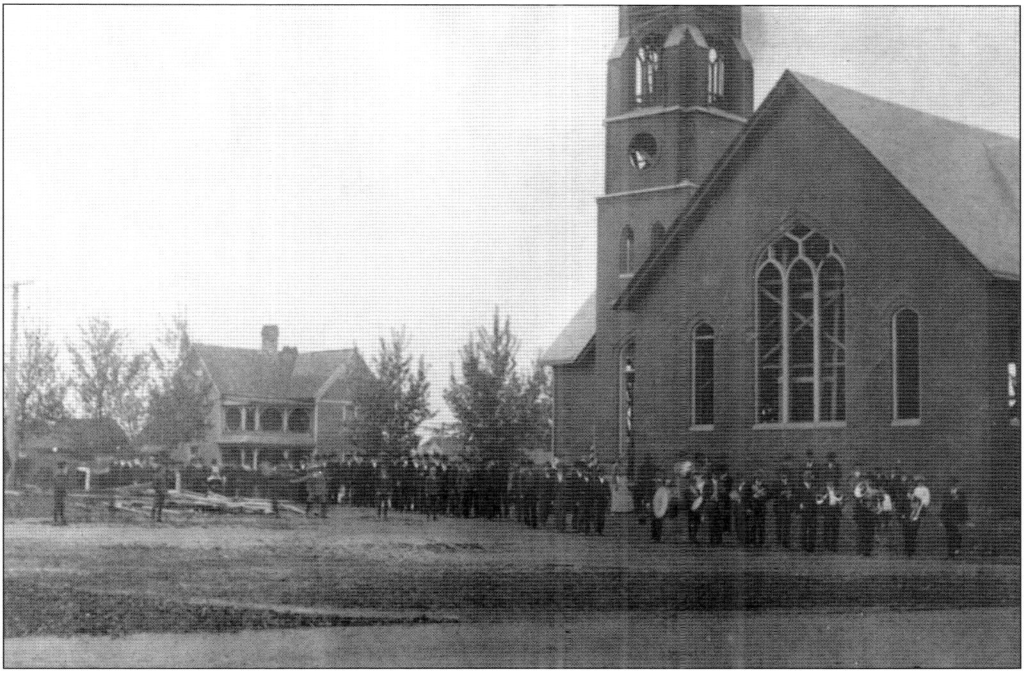

In 1908, a new Methodist-Episcopal Church (north) was dedicated. A photograph commemorating the event shows the east side of the new brick building, facing Cedar Street. Not completely finished, scaffolding inside the church can be seen through the windows. On this summer day, a brass band and the congregation were on hand; building debris is still visible on the left. The residence in the background is the W.G. Caton house. (Courtesy of King Family Library History Center, Herbert Lawson Collection.)

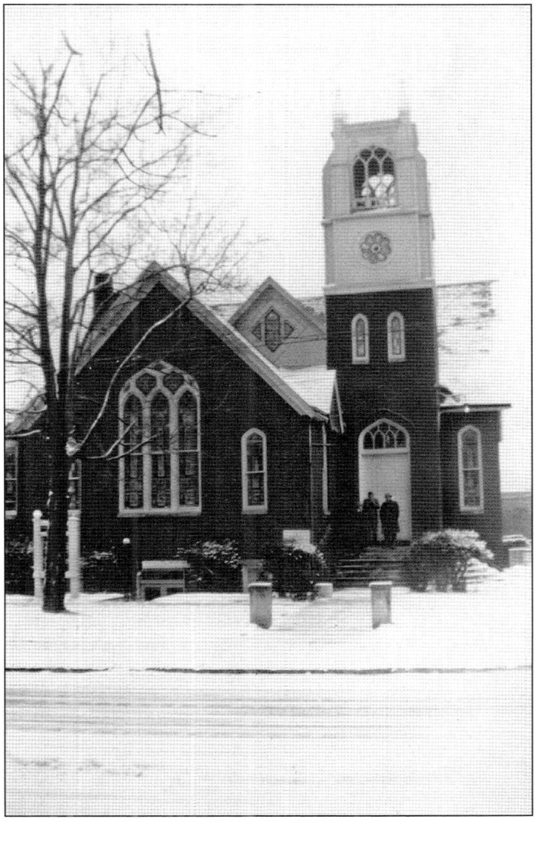

In 1940, the two Methodist-Episcopal Churches (north and south) merged and worshiped together at the Cedar Street site. In 1968, the church merged with the Evangelical United Brethren Church and became known as the United Methodist. Ground breaking for a new building took place in 1969. (Courtesy of the *Mountain Press*.)

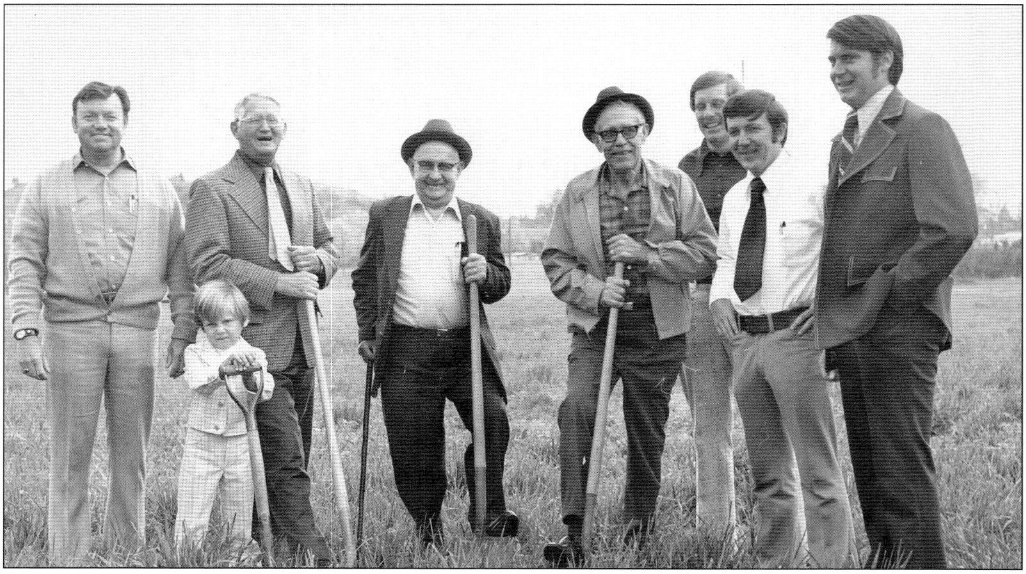

In 1973, the ground breaking for a new swimming pool in Sevierville City Park was captured. Pictured left to right are an unidentified contractor, Mayor Cliff Davis, Mayor Davis's grandson John Rader, Alderman Tip Snapp, Alderman Charles Franklin, city park representative Bob Atchley, City Recorder Hulet Chaney, and city administrator C.L. Overman. (Courtesy of King Family Library History Center, Herbert Lawson Collection.)

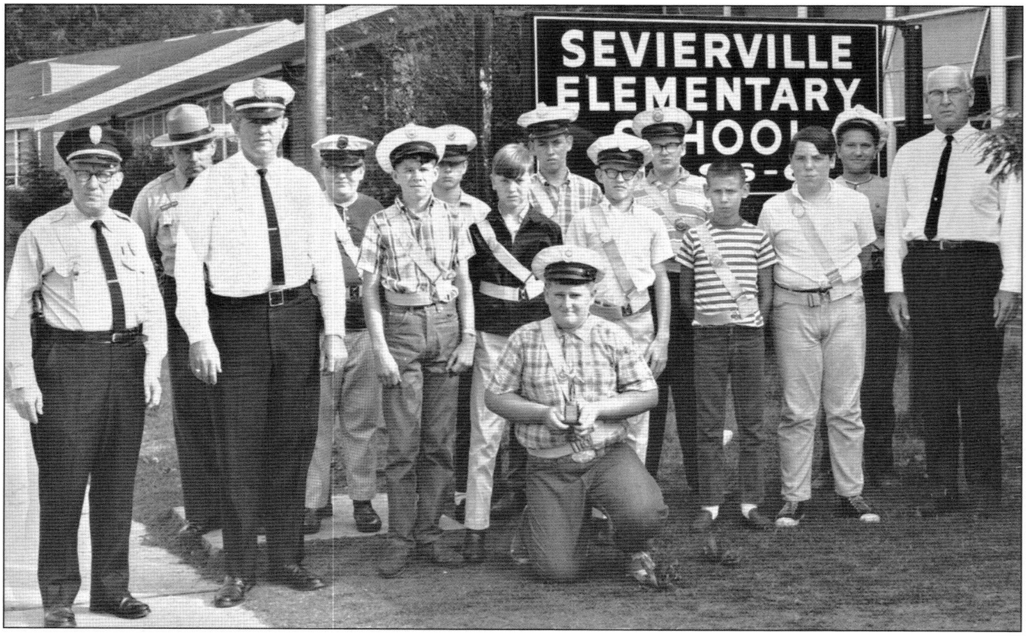

Shown here is the Sevierville Elementary School Safety Team from the 1960s. From left to right are (first row, kneeling) Tony Shults; (second row) police officer Carmen Townsend, chief of police M.T. Helton Jr., Leroy Maples, David Kerr, David Jordon, James Flynn, Barry Kelly, and principal Raymond Russell; (third row) GSMNPS ranger Howard Corpus, Craig Noland, Mike Lynch, Billy Carr, Keith Beason, and Carroll Huskey. (Courtesy of the *Mountain Press*.)

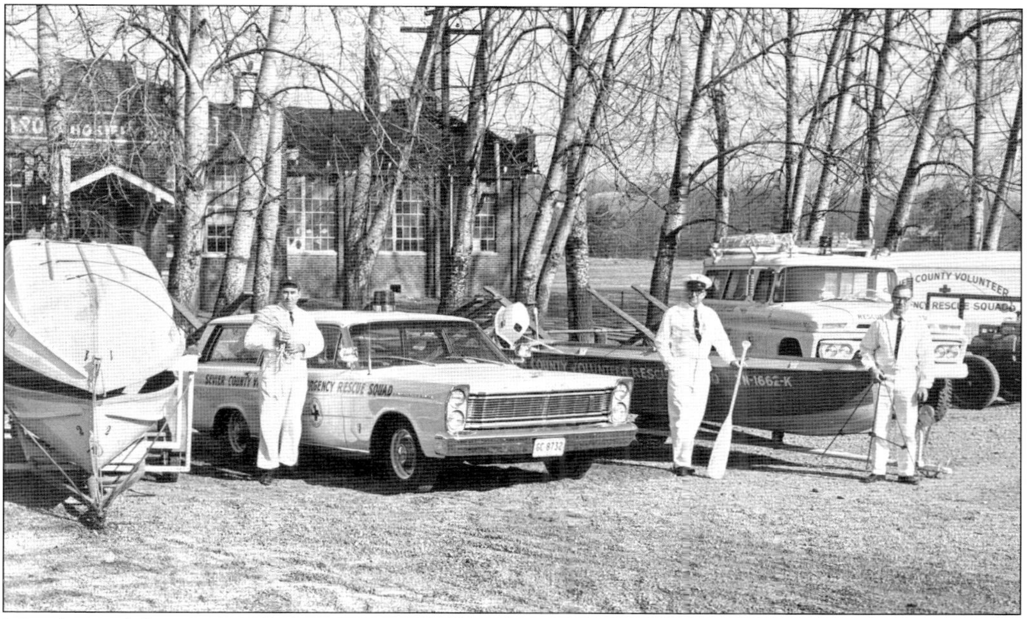

Members of the Sevier County Rescue Squad display the range of their emergency vehicles from their headquarters on East Bruce Street. The loyal team of volunteers has served Sevier County citizens in times of need for half a century. (Courtesy of the *Mountain Press*.)

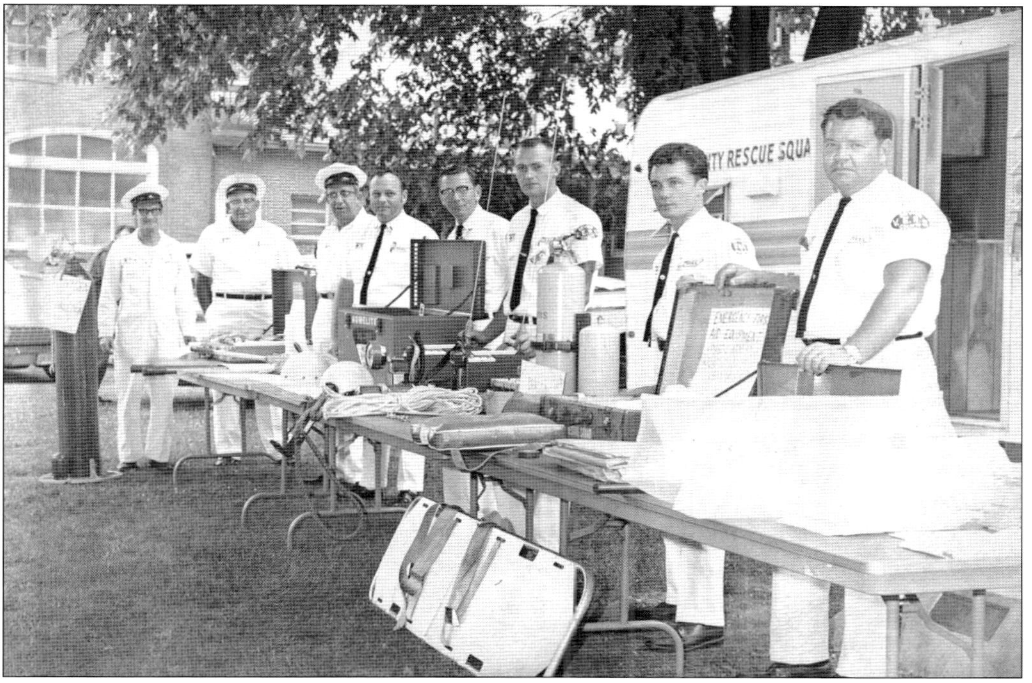

The Sevierville Rescue Squad poses with rescue and medical equipment on the courthouse lawn to educate taxpaying residents and to solicit operating funds. From left to right are: Ralph Fortenberry, Pleas Proffitt, Johnny Allison, Kenneth Moon, Glen Turner, Ed White, C.A. Ownby, and Carlton White. (Courtesy of the *Mountain Press*.)

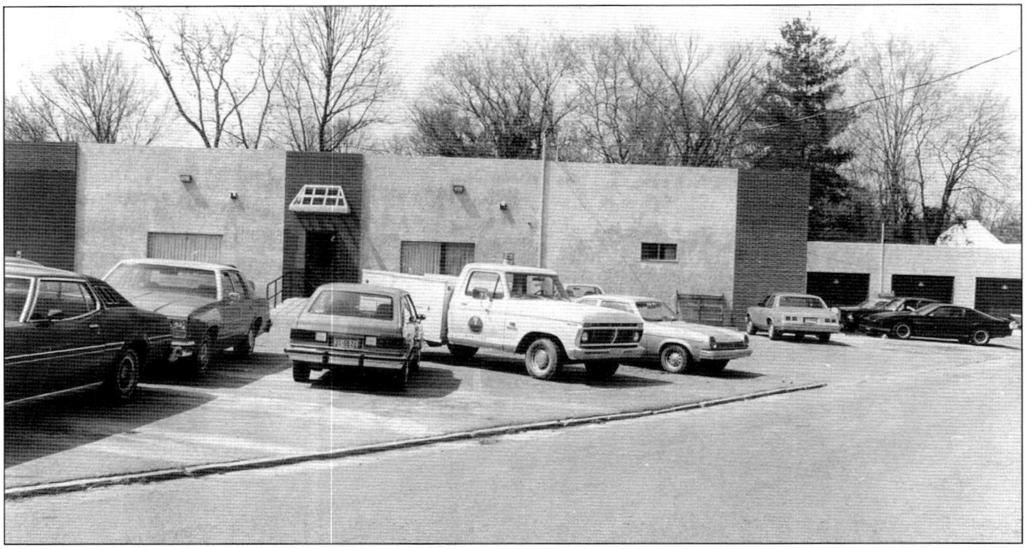

The Sevierville Police Department did not have formal headquarters until 1972, when the city obtained the old McNelly-Whaley Ford Building at the intersection of Grace Avenue and Park Road. The building was shared with city hall. (Courtesy of the *Mountain Press*.)

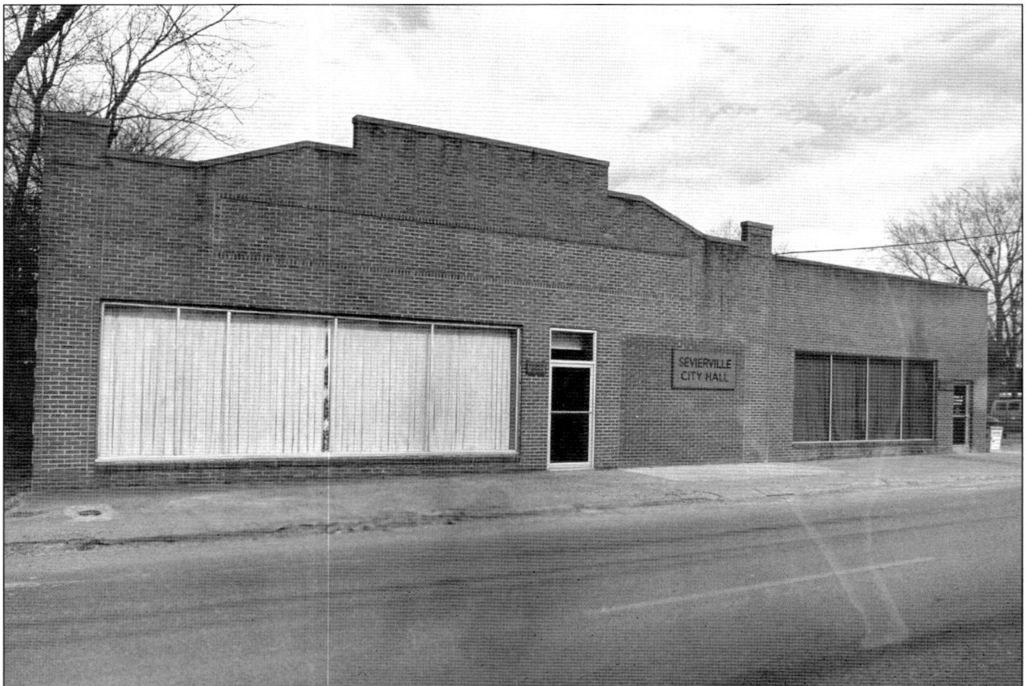

Sevierville's first city hall was the front section of the old McNelly-Whaley Ford Dealership on Park Road. The city board meetings were held in the Sevier County Courthouse for many years and in the fire hall before moving to this location in 1972. (Courtesy of the *Mountain Press*.)

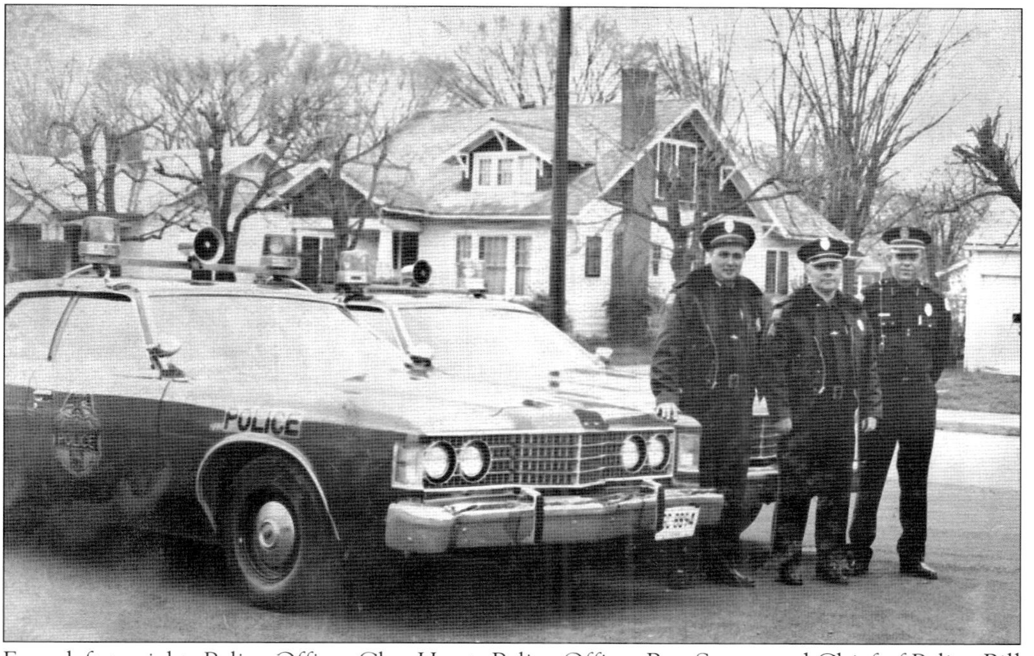

From left to right, Police Officer Cleo Hurst, Police Officer Ray Suggs, and Chief-of-Police Bill Tyson pose in front of Sevierville's first official police headquarters on Grace Avenue. (Courtesy of the *Mountain Press.*)

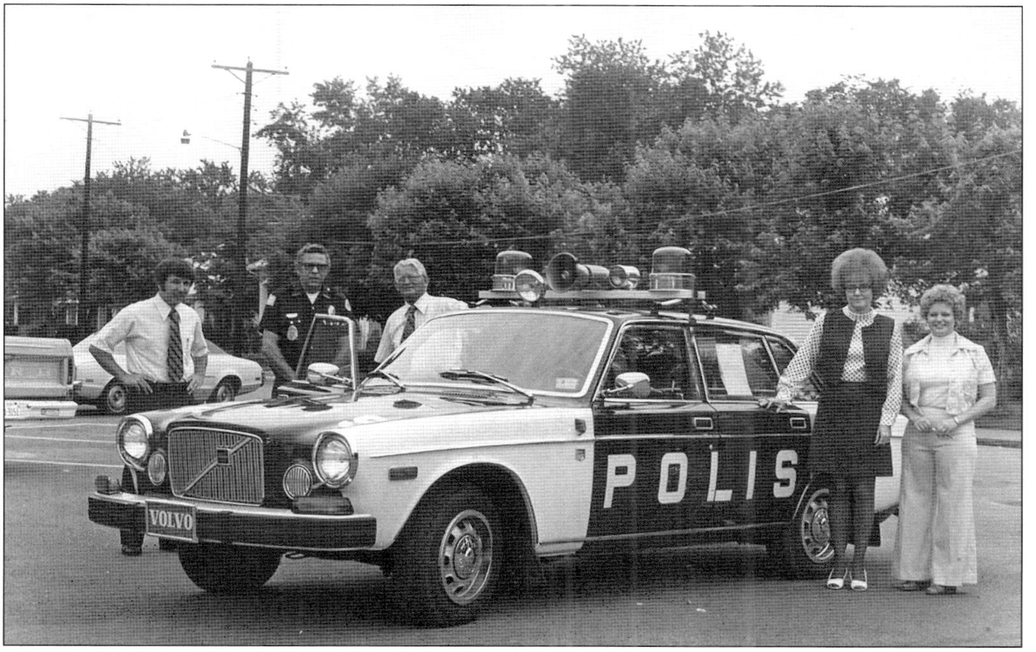

Posing by a Swedish-made police car are (left to right) Hulet Chaney, Chief-of-Police Chief Bill Tyson, Mayor Cliff Davis, Pat Valentine, and Pat Schettini. The foreign car was spotted commuting through the city, and local officials saw an opportunity for a great photograph. (Courtesy of the *Mountain Press.*)

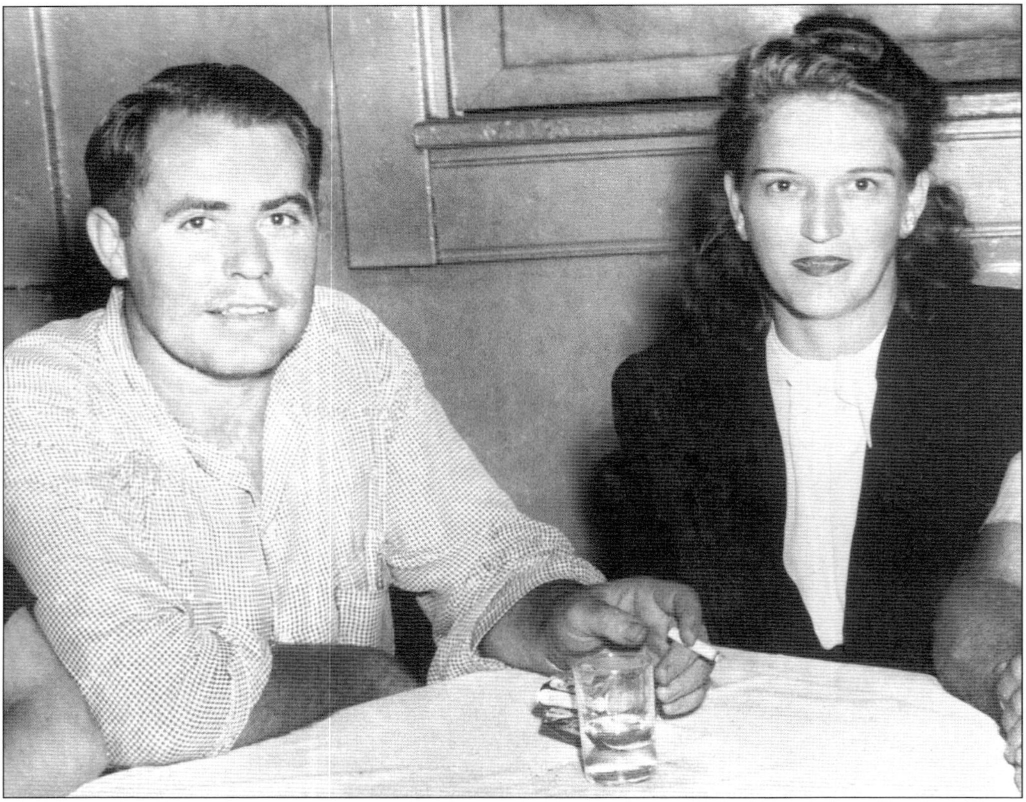

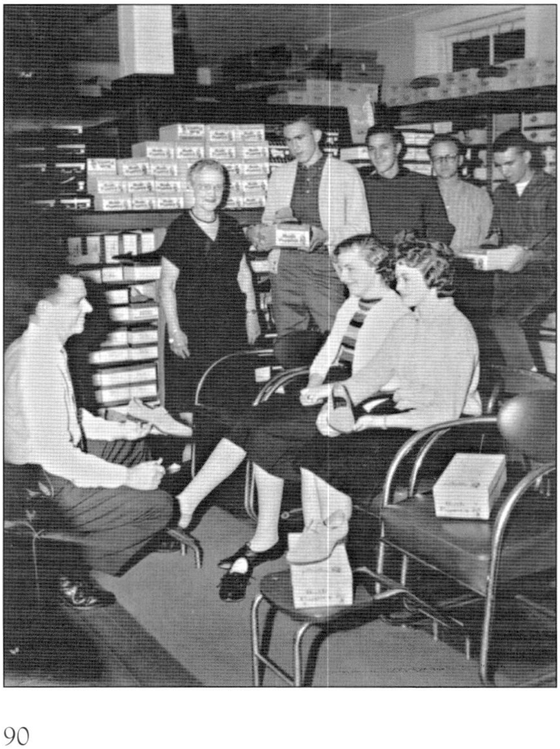

Carl Smith and his wife, Ollie (Lowe) Smith, operated several businesses in Sevierville. The couple started with a small grocery store and boardinghouse on Newport Highway. Later they operated the Sandwich Shop on Bruce Street and another restaurant on Court Avenue. Mr. Smith became a very successful real estate developer and constructed several motels, including the Smoky Bear Motor Inn on the new highway to Gatlinburg. (Courtesy of Dr. Steve Madison.)

Wade's Department Store on Court Avenue was in operation for three decades by owner Victoria Atchley Wade and her son Dwight. Shown here, Salesman James Turner shows wares to two unidentified customers, seated. Mrs. Wade (standing) assists. The four men standing are unidentified. (Courtesy of Sevierville Chamber of Commerce.)

Five

Sevierville Living

Time is but a stream I go fishing in.

—Henry David Thoreau

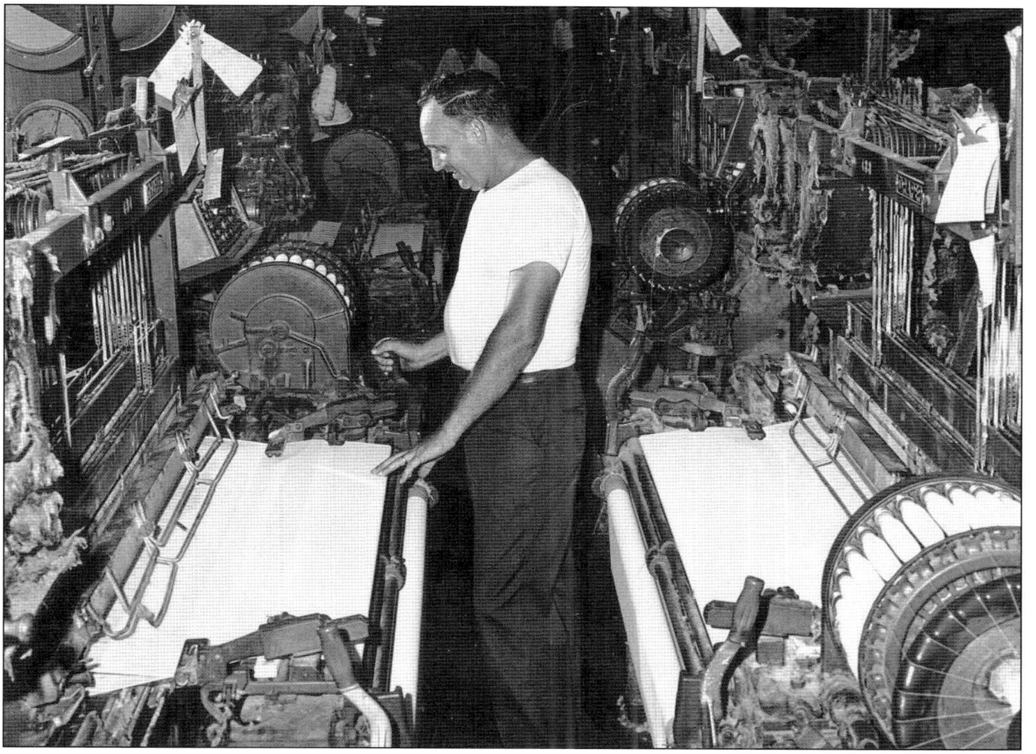

In 1955, Cherokee Textile Mills relocated from Knoxville to Sevierville, bringing with it several hundred local jobs. Some Knoxville employees chose to make the 50-mile-round-trip daily commute to and from Sevierville to retain jobs, but the mill's presence was still a big boost to the local economy. Shown here, Mayford H. Kerr operates a loom in the weaving department. (Courtesy of King Family Library History Center.)

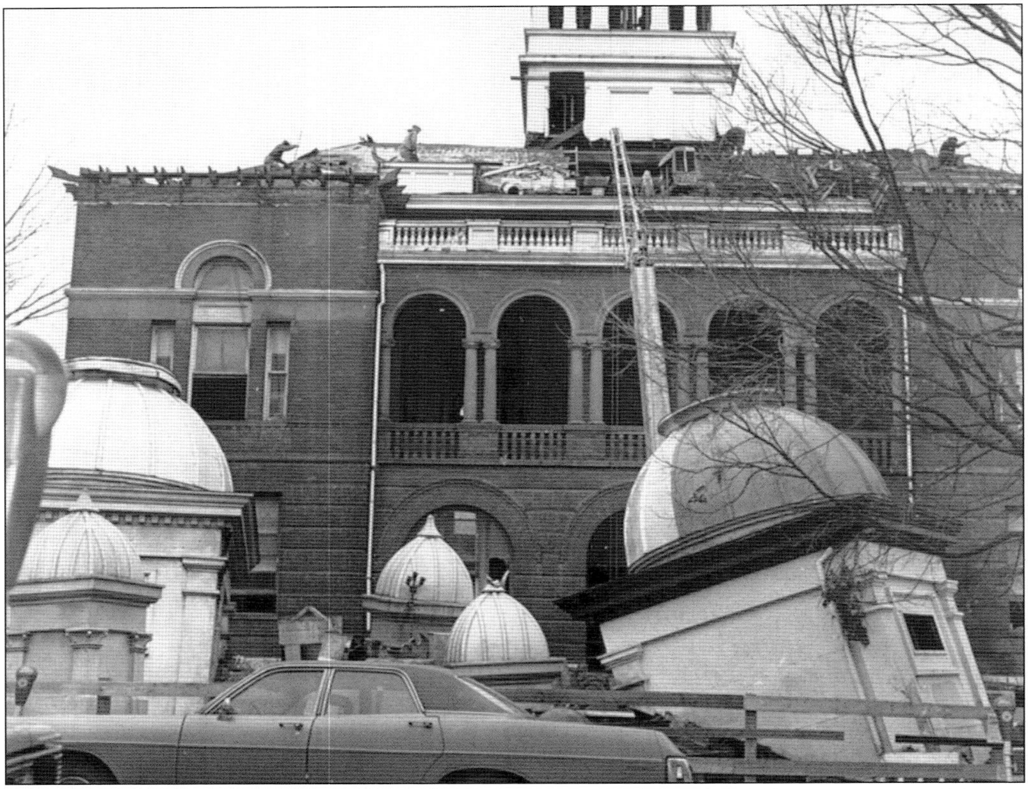

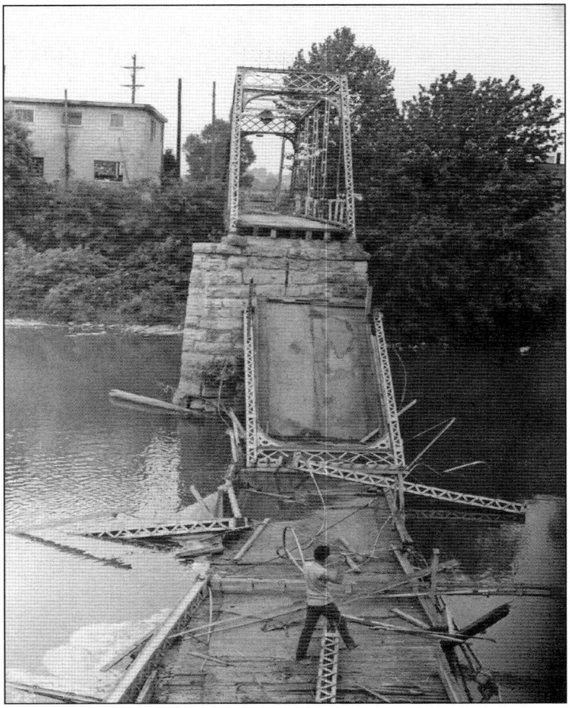

In the early 1970s, renovation of the courthouse began. The interior had to be demolished without damaging the building's exterior. The roof of the old building was removed, and the decorative cupolas were stored in the yard, shown here. The interior walls were also removed, except those supporting the tower. (Courtesy of the *Mountain Press*.)

In the fall of 1961, the old five-span steel bridge that crossed the east fork of the Little Pigeon River collapsed moments after a truck had crossed the bridge. Built in 1893, the old bridge was the only crossing between Sevierville and all points north in Sevier County. (Courtesy of the *Mountain Press*.)

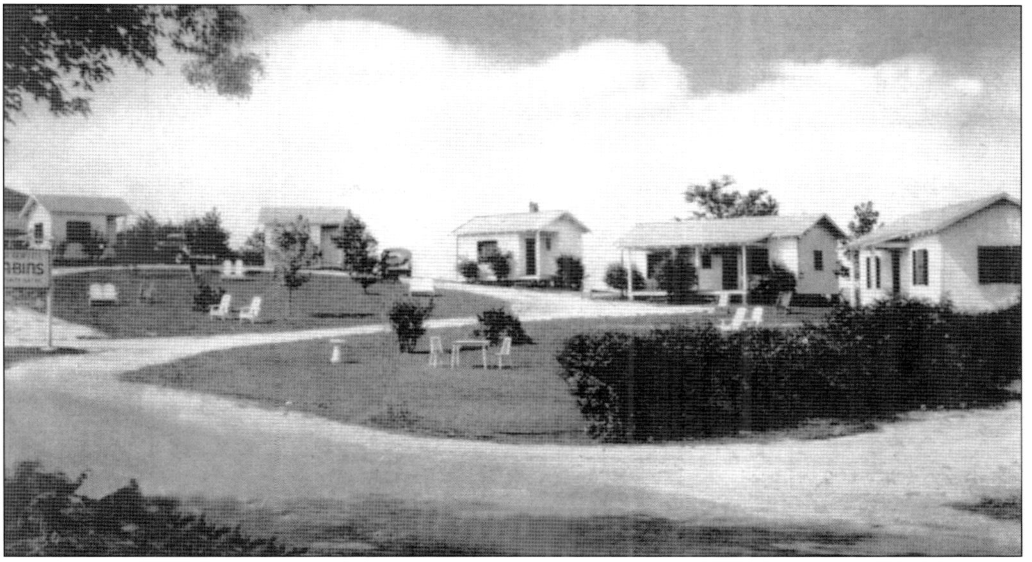

Shortly after the Great Smoky Mountains National Park was established, Mack Marshall and his wife, Minnie Belle, developed a group of tourist cottages on Park Road, naming them the Round Top Cottages. The Marshalls were among the first of many families offering economical lodging for tourists. (Courtesy of King Family Library History Center, Herbert Lawson Collection.)

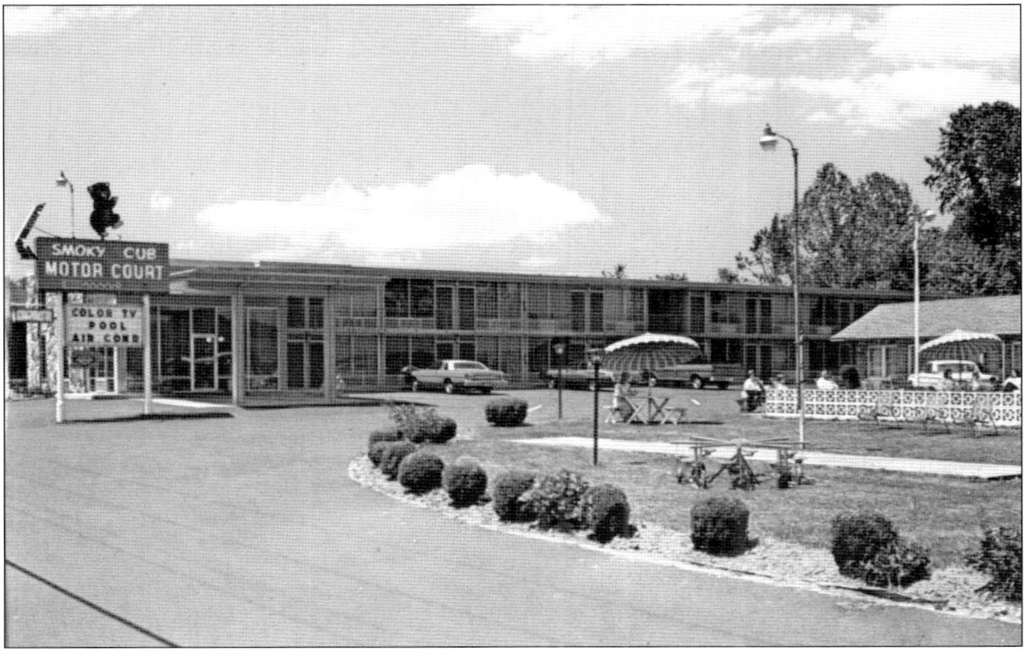

Carl and Ollie Smith constructed the Smoky Bear Motor Inn in the 1940s. After the business changed hands several times, Arvine and Betty May purchased the building at a 1963 public auction. They changed the name to Smoky Cub Motel and operated the business for 22 years. (Courtesy of Betty May.)

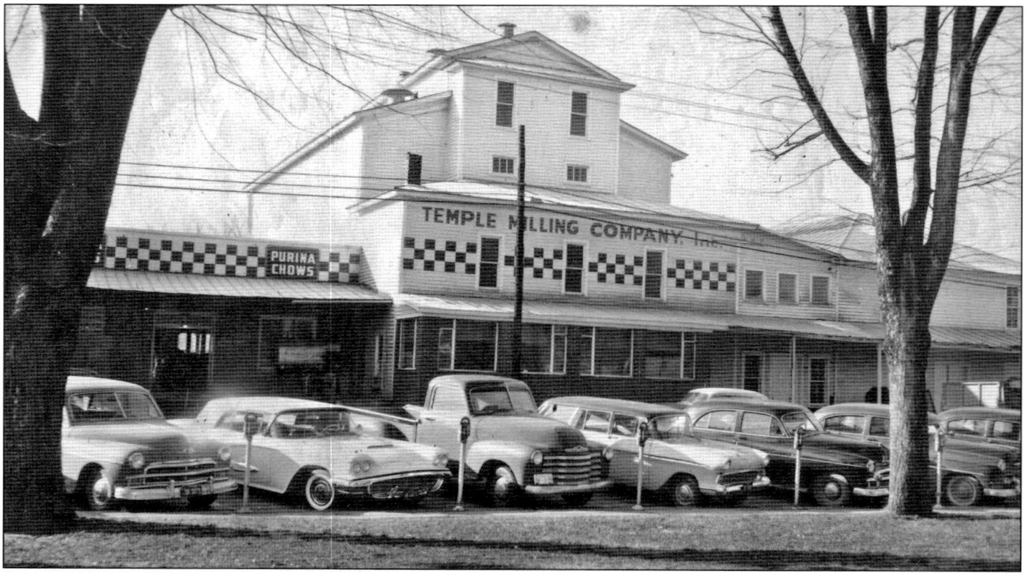

In 1934, John and Effie (Benson) Temple took over management of the Stanley McMahan Milling Company. Originally called Walker Milling Company, the Temple family operated the business for over half a century. Jimmie Temple became manager after his father stepped down in 1952. (Courtesy of Jimmie and Marie Temple.)

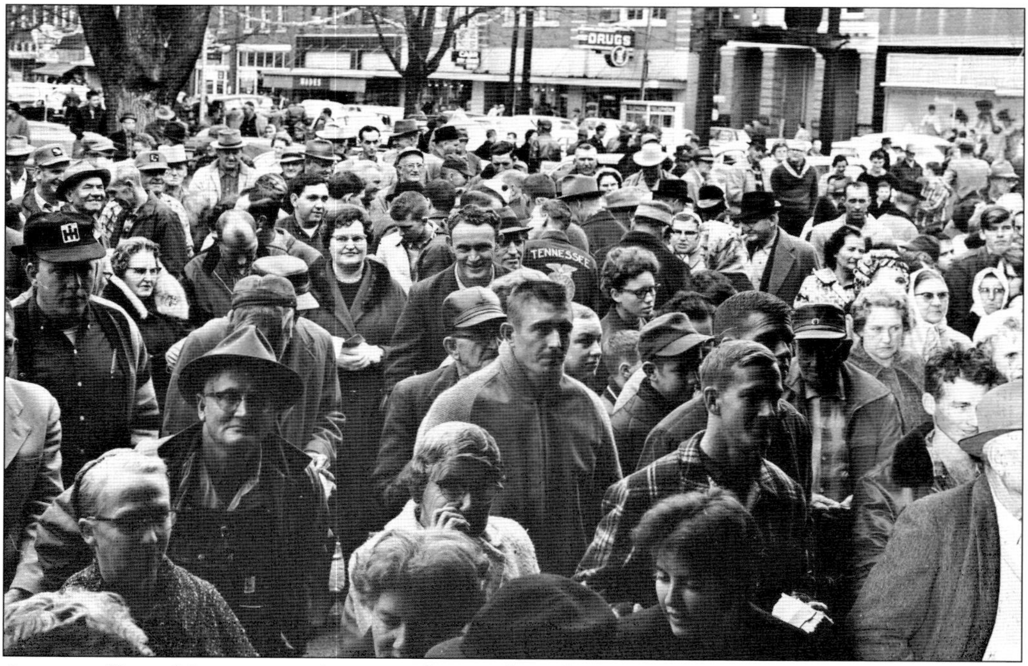

A group of hopeful winners gathers outside Temple Milling Company for the Mike and Ike drawing. Sponsored by Purina, the event was held each December for several decades, and it culminated in drawings for various food-related prizes. Photographed in the 1950s, this particular crowd awaits the drawing for two Purina-fed pigs, Mike and Ike, one representing sales and one representing money paid on accounts. (Courtesy of Jimmie and Marie Temple.)

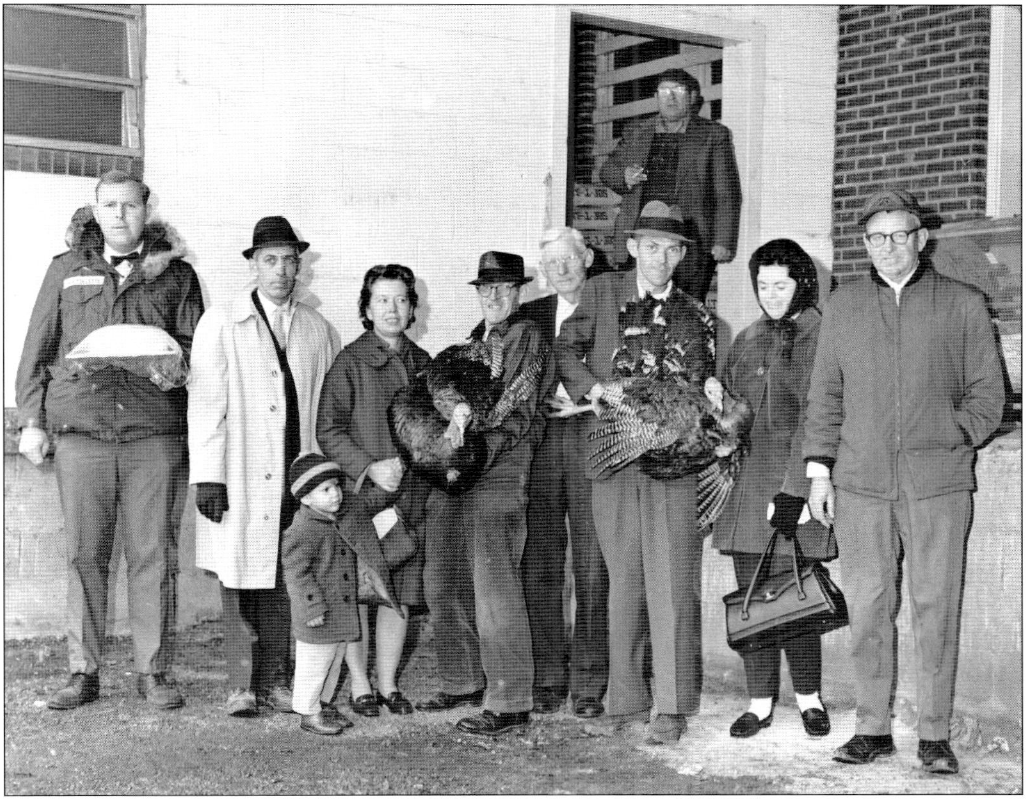

Prizes at the Temple Milling Company Mike and Ike Program might include turkeys, mill, flour, and (shown here) Mrs. Temple's homemade coconut cake. Carl LaFollette was the lucky cake winner. (Courtesy of Jimmie and Marie Temple.)

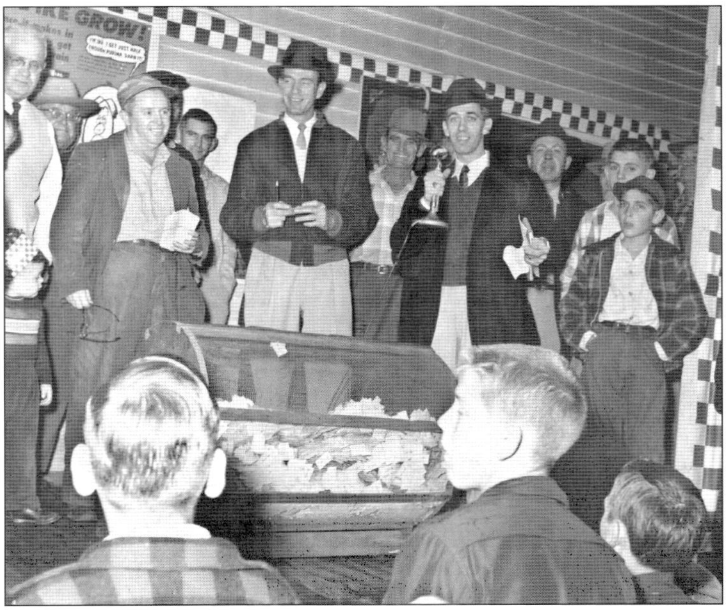

Broadcast live on the local radio station, WSEV, the Purina Mike and Ike Program drew hundreds of people to downtown Sevierville. Special recognition was given to the oldest man, oldest woman, and the person with the most children, in attendance. (Courtesy of Jimmie and Marie Temple.)

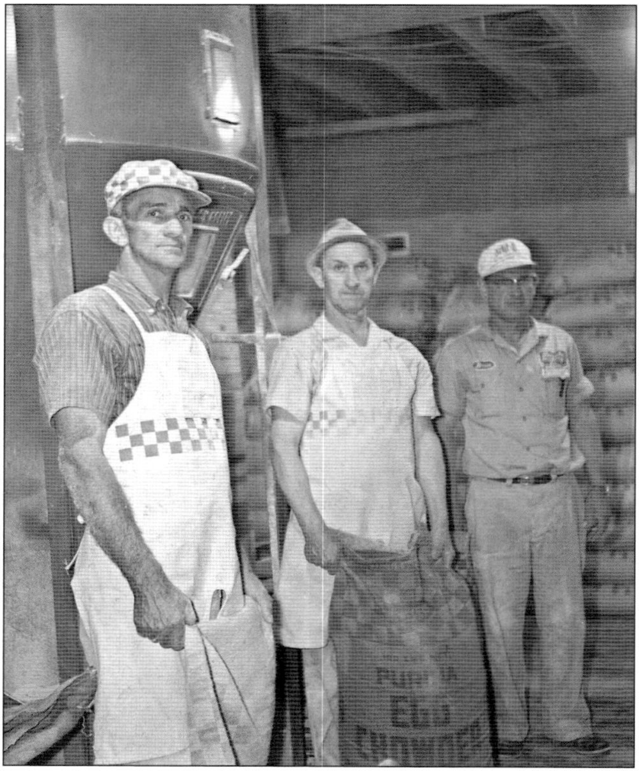

Temple Milling Company employees (left to right) Lihugh Whaley, Bates Ward, and Bruce Ward pose by their workstations. The Ward brothers worked together at the mill for several years. (Courtesy of Jimmie and Marie Temple.)

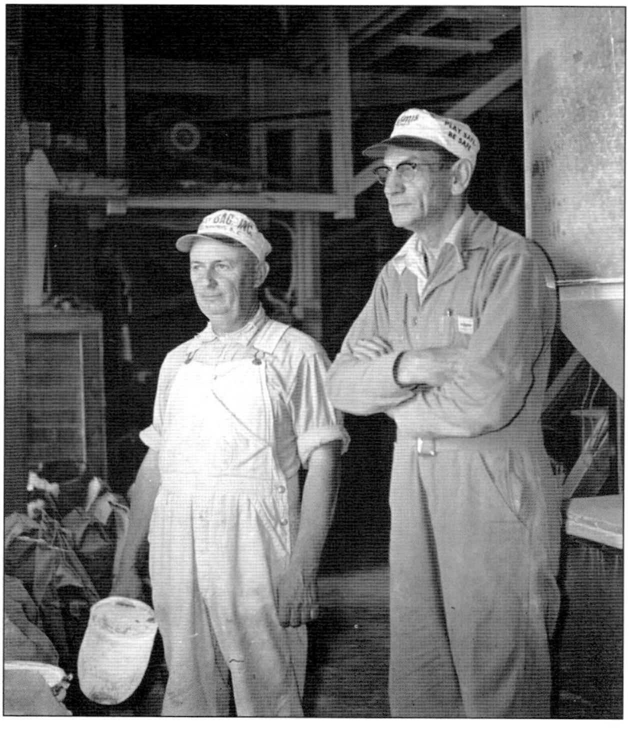

The Thomas brothers, (left) Lee and millwright Ed, pose at a work break at Temple Milling Company. Lee Thomas worked for John E. Temple his entire life, beginning at a chair factory in Oak City. Temple brought Lee to Sevierville to be his miller, and he worked for the family for 44 years. (Courtesy of Jimmie and Marie Temple.)

Effie (Benson) Temple, John E. Temple's wife, works at her desk at Temple Milling Company. In addition to her duties as a homemaker and mother, Temple worked by her husband's side all of her life. She lived to age 98. (Courtesy of Jimmie and Marie Temple.)

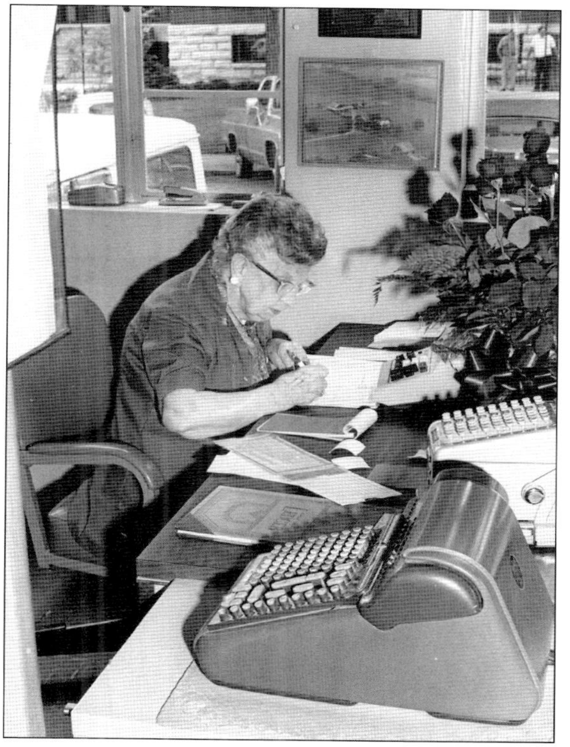

A Temple Milling Company delivery truck makes its way down a narrow county road. The deliveryman hauled Log Cabin Meal, Snow Top Flour, and Temple Eggs throughout Sevier County primarily to country stores. (Courtesy of Jimmie and Marie Temple.)

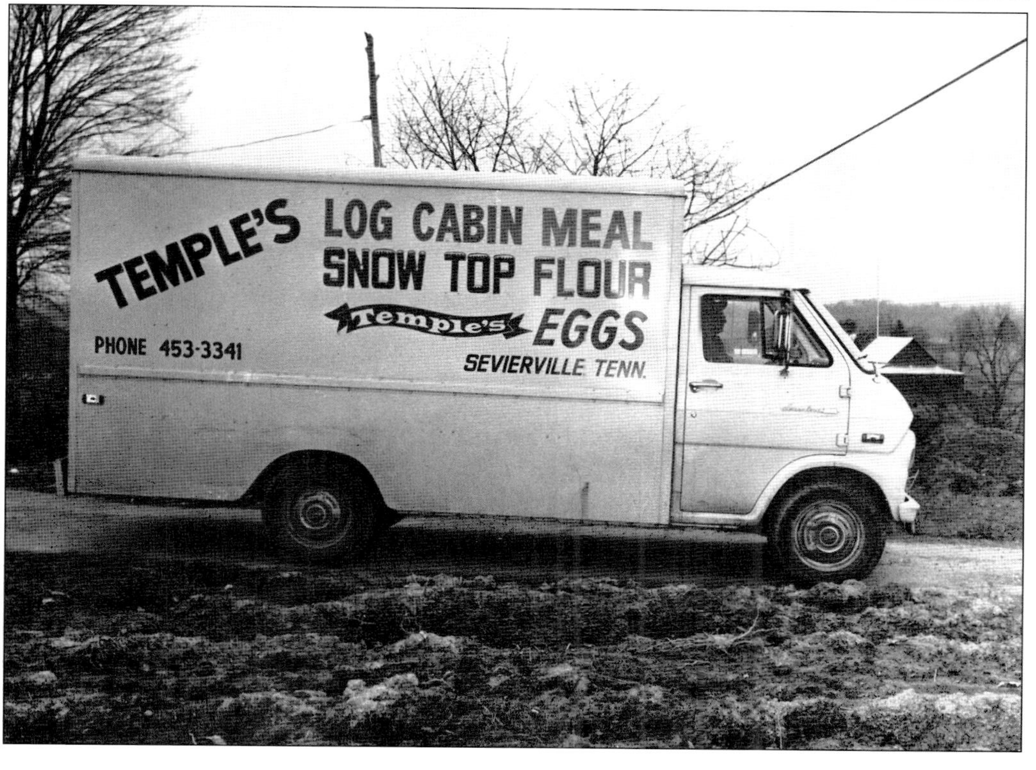

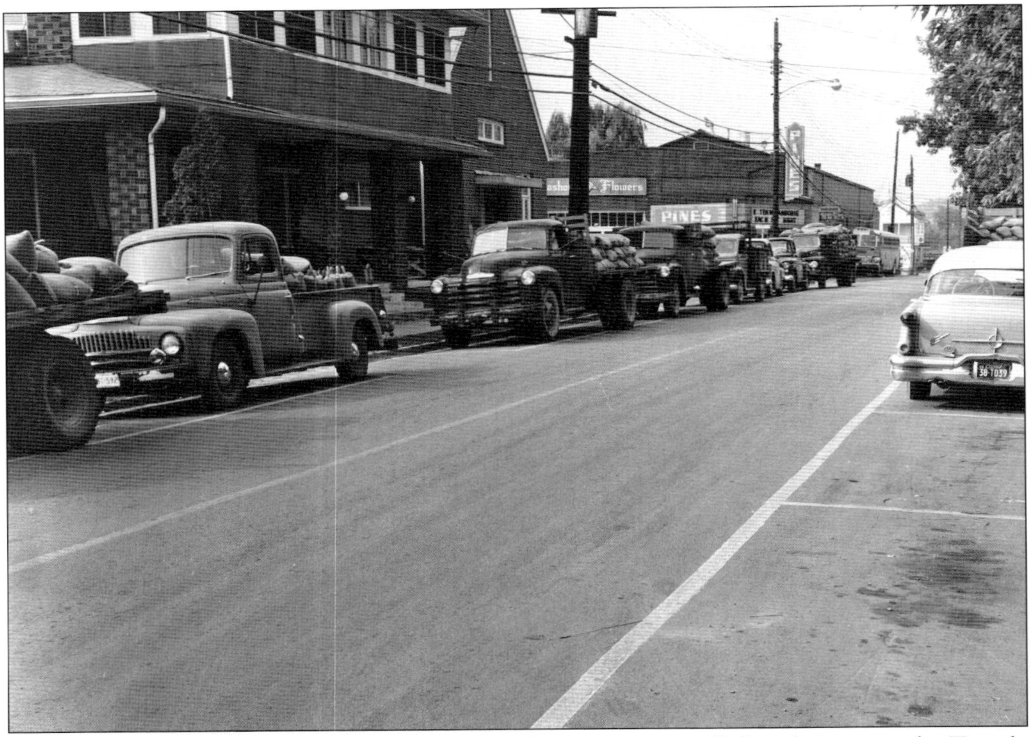

Wheat-filled trucks line up on Court Avenue as farmers wait to sell their harvest to the Temple Milling Company. This photograph also shows Rawlings Funeral Home, the Pines Theatre, and Bashor's Florist on the left. (Courtesy of Jimmie and Marie Temple.)

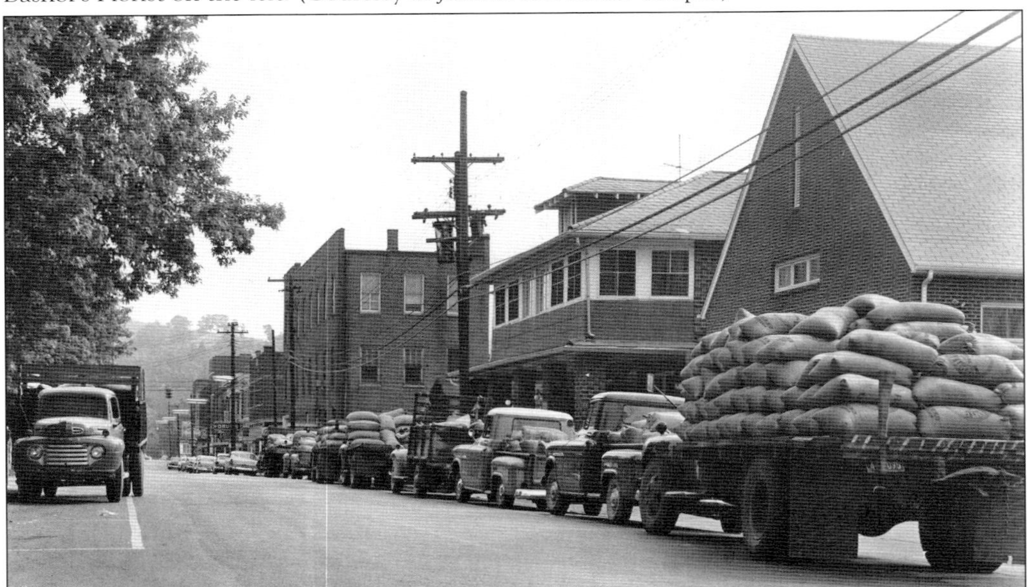

This photograph, facing north on Court Avenue, shows Sevier County farmers lined up by Temple Milling Company to sell wheat. Local merchants welcomed the day wheat was sold because many farmers visited their businesses after they were paid. (Courtesy of Jimmie and Marie Temple.)

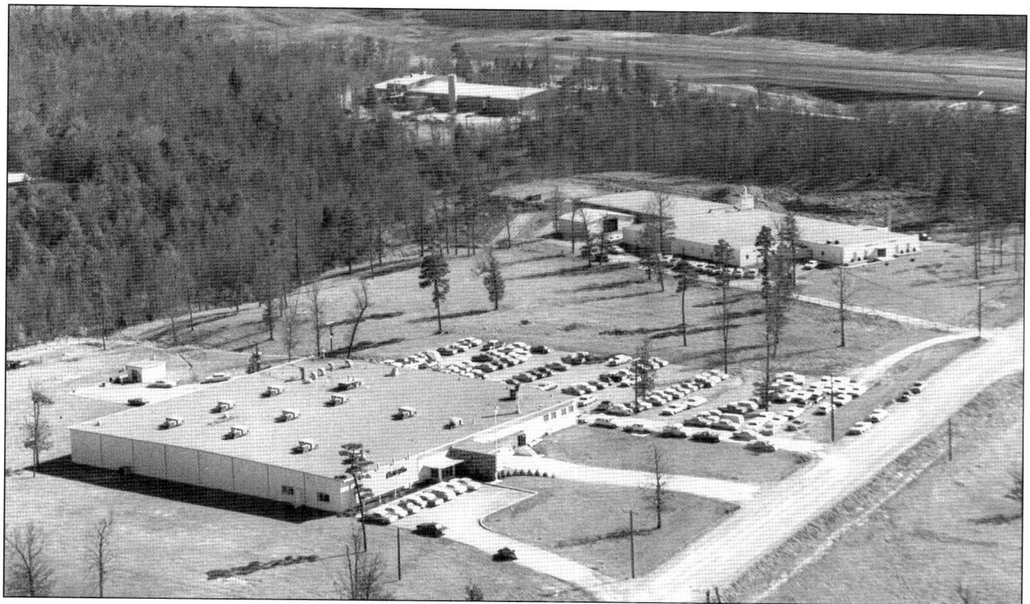

Electro-Voice, a manufacturer of audio equipment, opened a plant in the new Ray L. Reagan Industrial Park in 1965, shown here. The new Sevier County High School was constructed across the street a few years later. Electro-Voice headquarters was in Buchanan, Michigan. (Courtesy of the *Mountain Press*.)

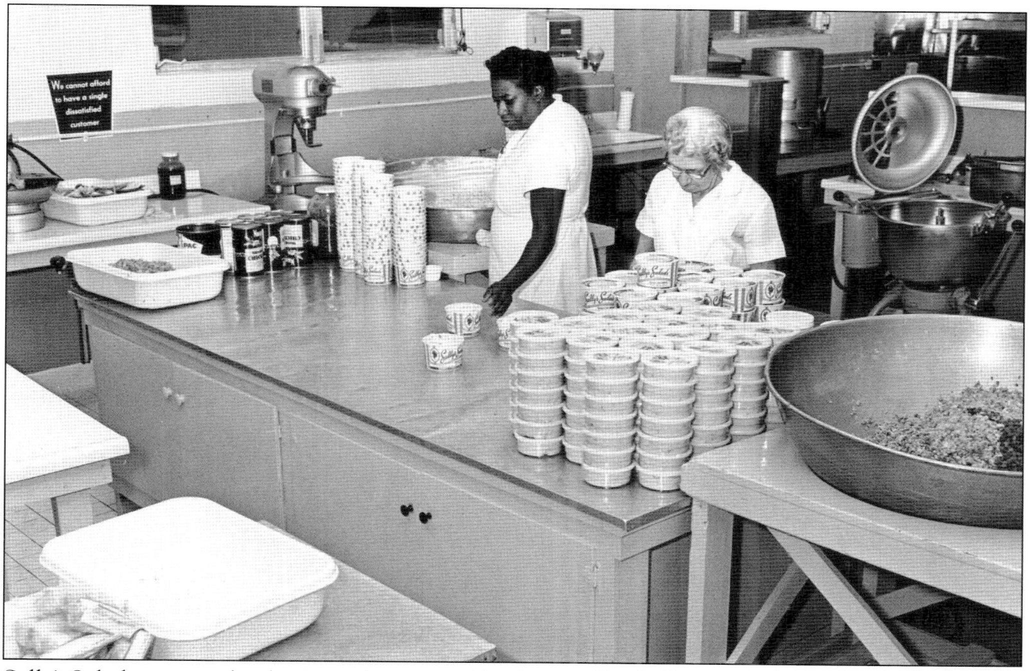

Sally's Salads was another business that opened in the new Ray L. Reagan Industrial Park. Established in 1959 by Grant and Sara Beth Cantwell, the company grew to become Smoky Mountain Vending Company. The Cantwells were among the most philanthropic individuals in Sevier County, giving generously to many worthwhile organizations. (Courtesy of the *Mountain Press*.)

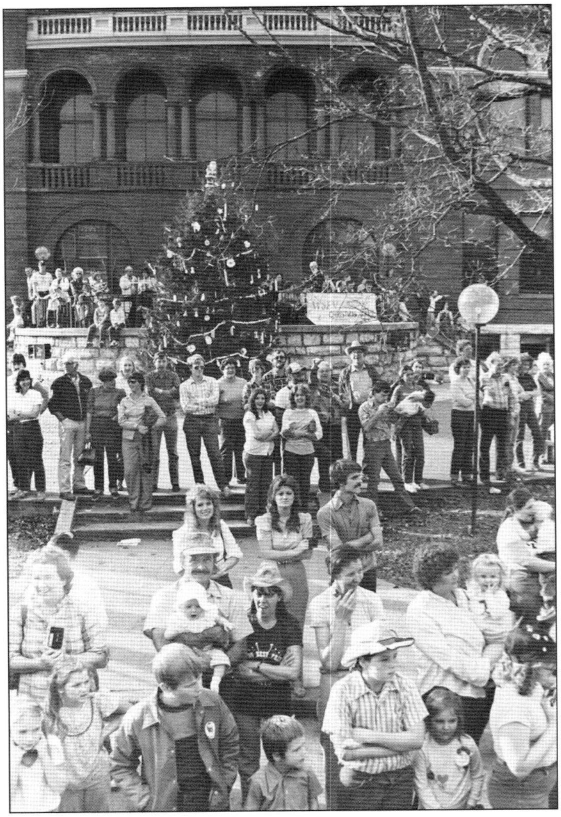

A crowd gathers in front of the Sevier County Courthouse to watch the annual Sevierville Christmas Parade. The parade has been staged every December since 1963, sponsored by the Sevierville Chamber of Commerce. (Courtesy of the *Mountain Press.*)

The Sevierville Christmas Parade travels east down Bruce Street in 1979, while hundreds of spectators line the sidewalks. The annual parade has always been billed as a hometown event. The Sevier County High School Marching Band has participated in every parade. (Courtesy of the *Mountain Press.*)

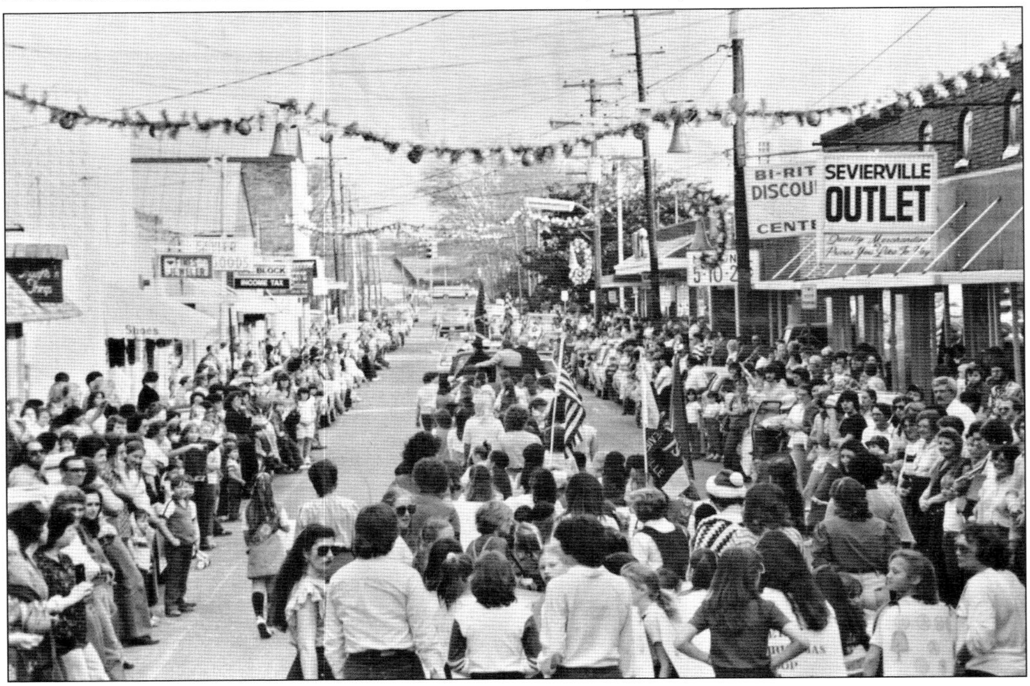

Alfred Newman and his brother John operated Newman's Cafe on Bruce Street from 1956 until 1988. The brothers also ran a Taxi Company in Sevierville before purchasing the building at public auction and opening the cafe, shown here. Alfred Newman is standing behind the counter. (Courtesy of Johnnie Faye Newman.)

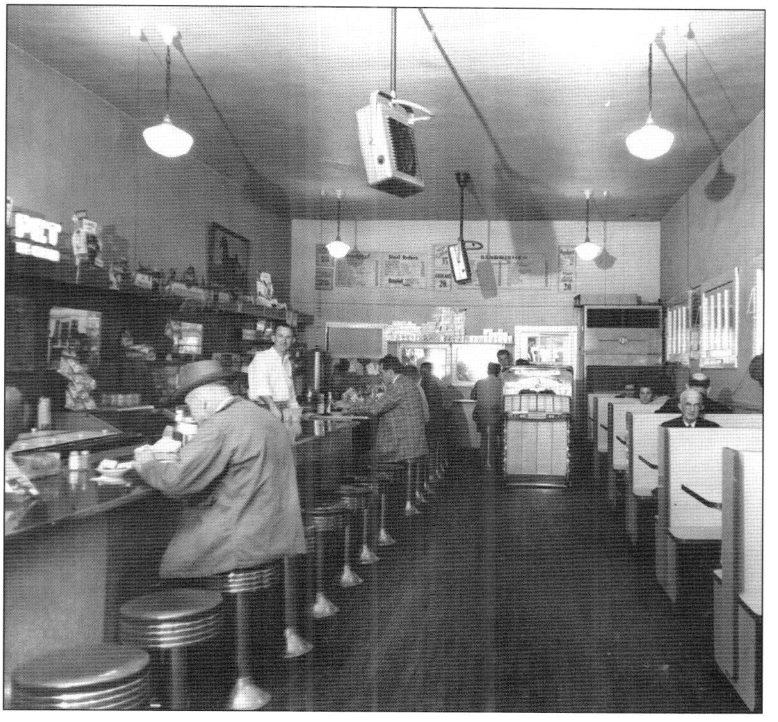

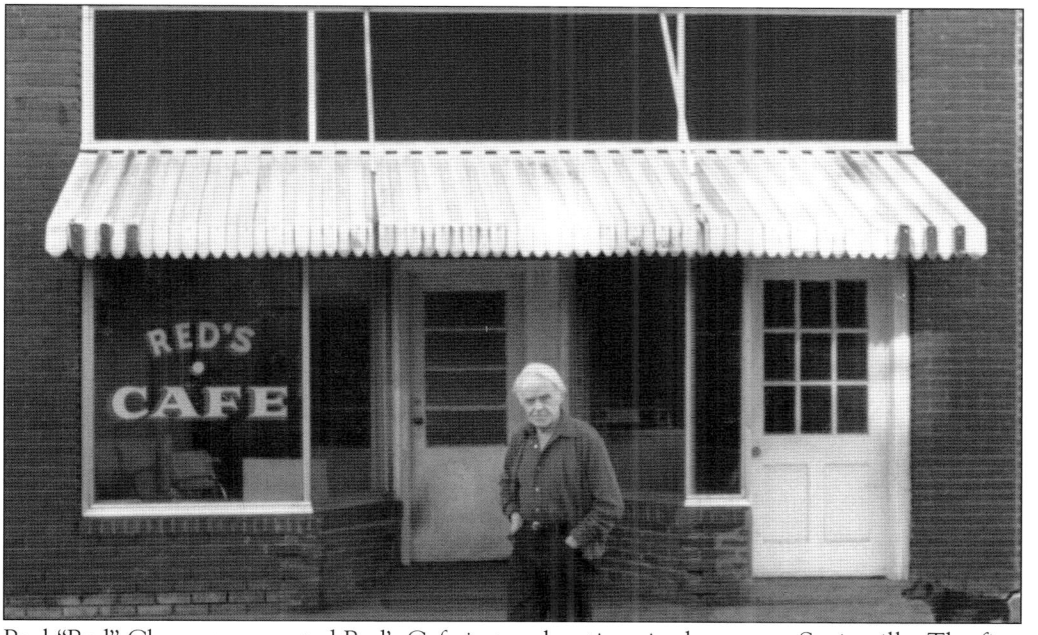

Paul "Red" Clevenger operated Red's Cafe in two locations in downtown Sevierville. The first was on Bruce Street across from the post office. Clevenger is photographed here in front of the second location on Court Avenue. Clevenger was esteemed for his mouth-watering hamburgers; he never served French fries. (Courtesy of Marie Clevenger Cameron.)

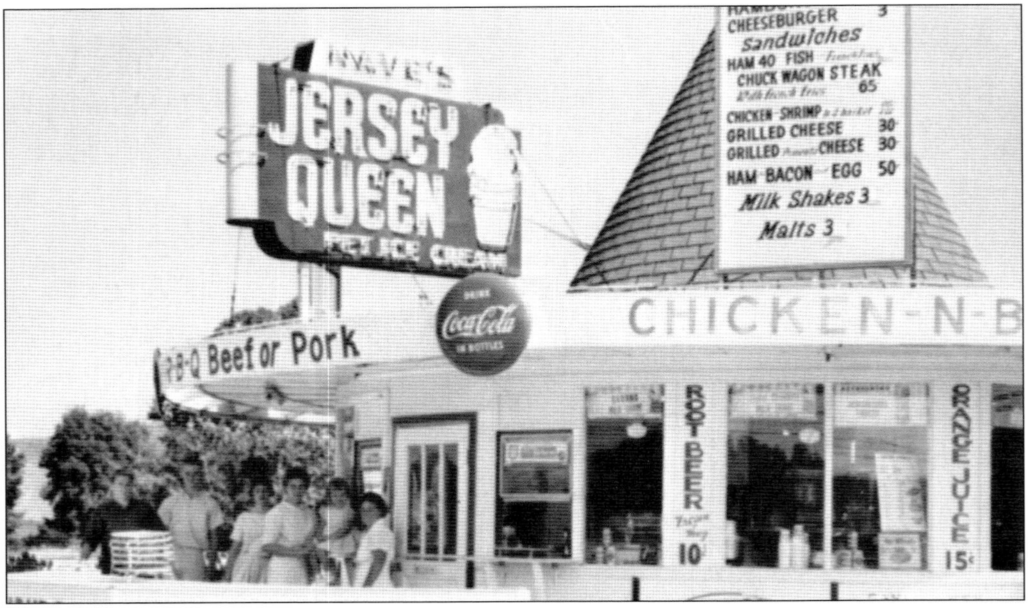

Jersey Queen, located on Gatlinburg Highway (Parkway), was a popular purlieu for teenagers. Located next door to the Tastee-Freeze, both drive-in restaurants served short orders, such as hamburgers, hotdogs, soft drinks, and milk shakes. (Courtesy of Sevierville Chamber of Commerce.)

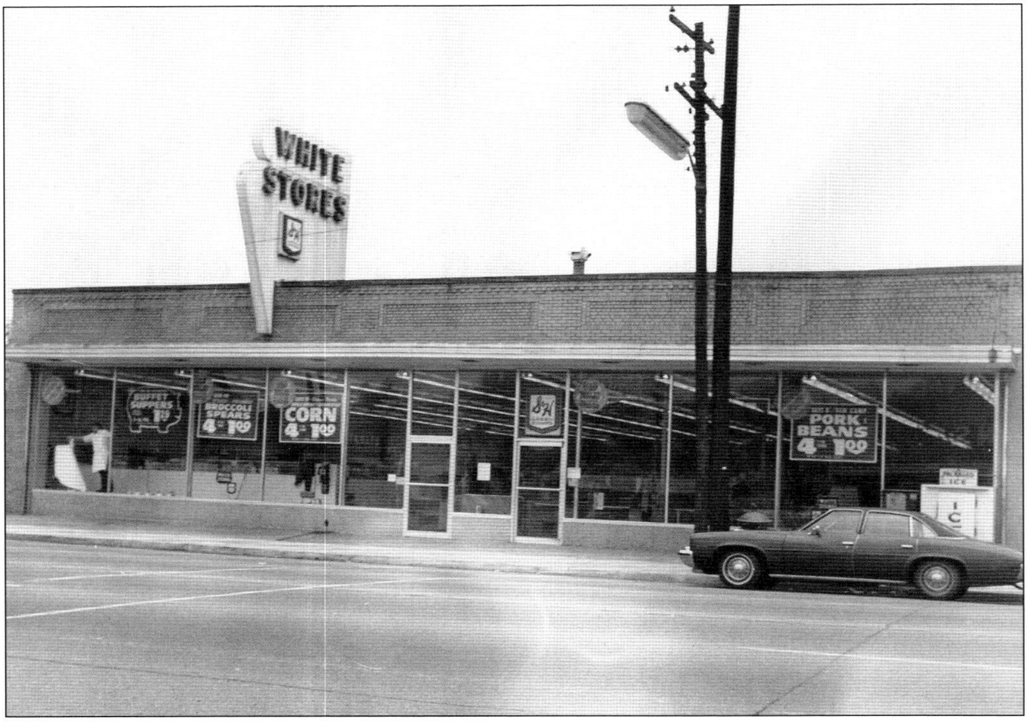

The White Store, a supermarket on East Main, was part of a Knoxville-based chain owned by Dwight McDonald. Earnest Lawson was store manager of the Sevierville store for many years. (Courtesy of the *Mountain Press*.)

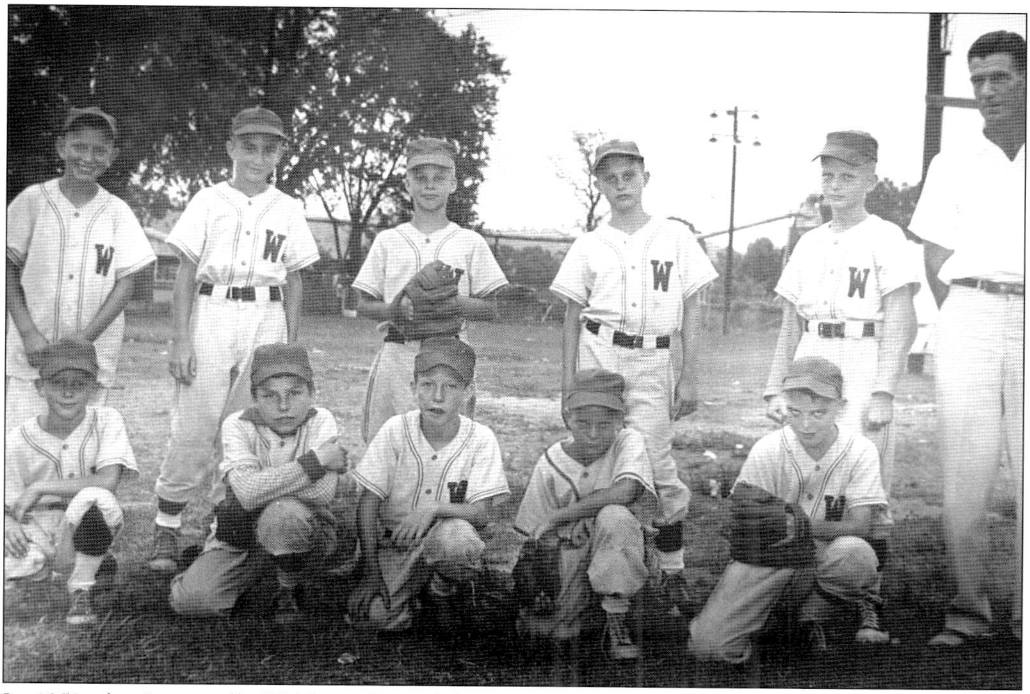

In 1953, the Sevierville Wildcats formed, becoming the city's first Little League baseball team. Pictured left to right are (first row) Jack Stoffle, Jerry Gorenflo, Larry Mize, Larry Helton, and Maurice Moore; (second row) Jimmy Valentine, Harold Loy, Al Schmutzer Jr., John Sims, Bob Allen, and coach Archie Moore. (Courtesy of Robert Allen.)

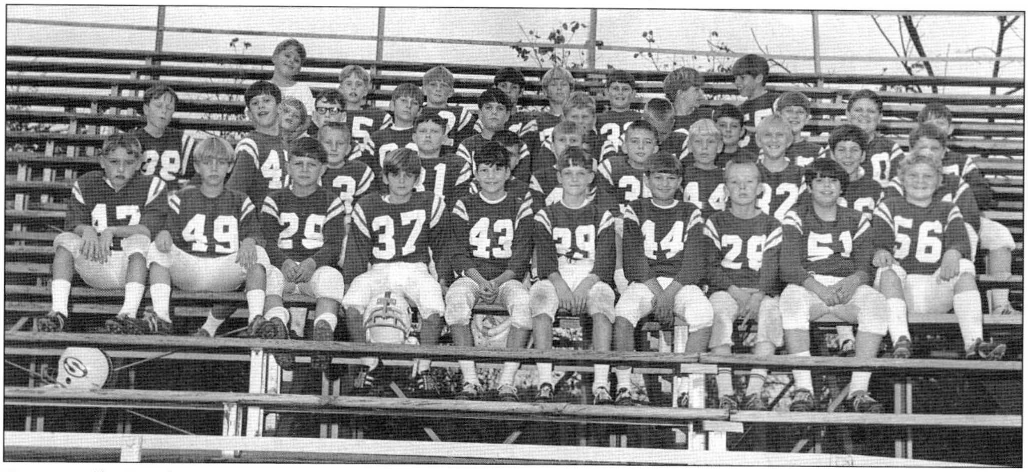

Sevierville Little League football players are pictured in 1971. From left to right are (first row) Randy Jenkins, Terry Carr, Joel Sutton, Jimmy Burchfiel, Danny King, Bryan Stubblefield, Dennis McCarter, Duane Whaley, Robbie Murphy, and Tony Davis; (second row) Kenny Jenkins, Toby Ward, Tony Tarwater, Steve Ward, Jeff Dodgen, Jeff Russell, Mike Catlett, Ricky Blair, Jeff Whaley, Roger McMahan, and Joe Kenner; (third row) Johnny Justus, Mike Leatherwood, Jeff Ramsey, David Grim, Ricky Randles, Ray Hodges, Thomas Rice, Robin Smith, Randy Parton, and R.L. Henderson; (fourth row) Howard Clinton, Kirk McGaha, Rodney Tarwater, Tim Holt, Gary McMahan, Mark Rutledge, Mitch Webb, and Buster England. (Courtesy of the *Mountain Press*.)

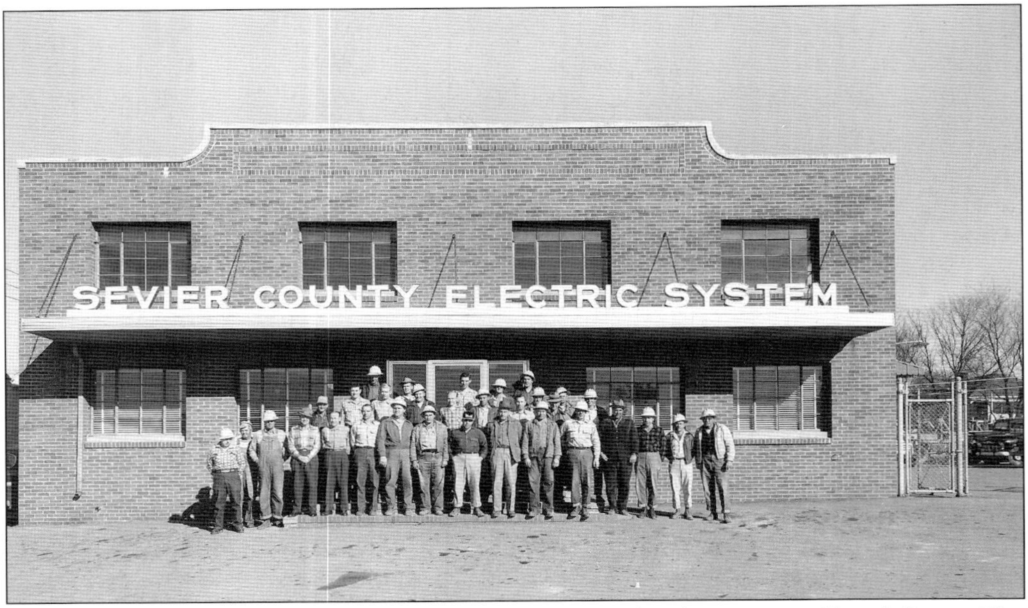

Sevier County Electric System employees pose at company headquarters on Church Street. The business is now located on Dolly Parton Parkway, next to the municipal complex. (Courtesy of Allen Robbins.)

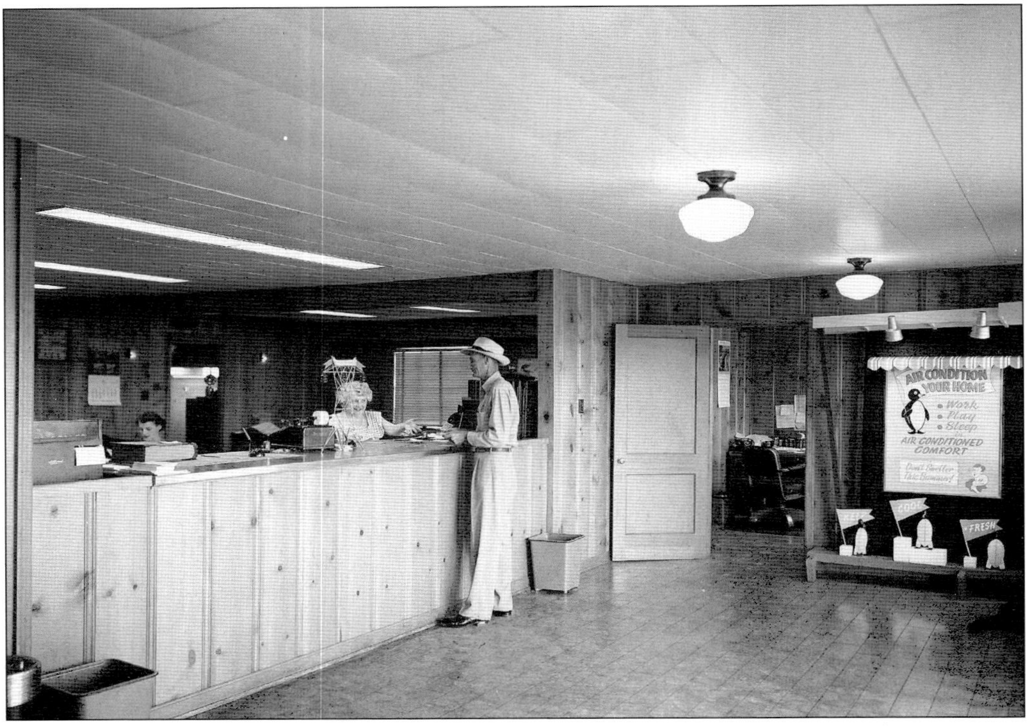

A lobby receptionist waits on a customer at the Sevier County Electric System. The company's first board was elected in 1939 and the city of Sevierville purchased the company in 1940; Hugh Blair was the first superintendent. (Courtesy of Allen Robbins.)

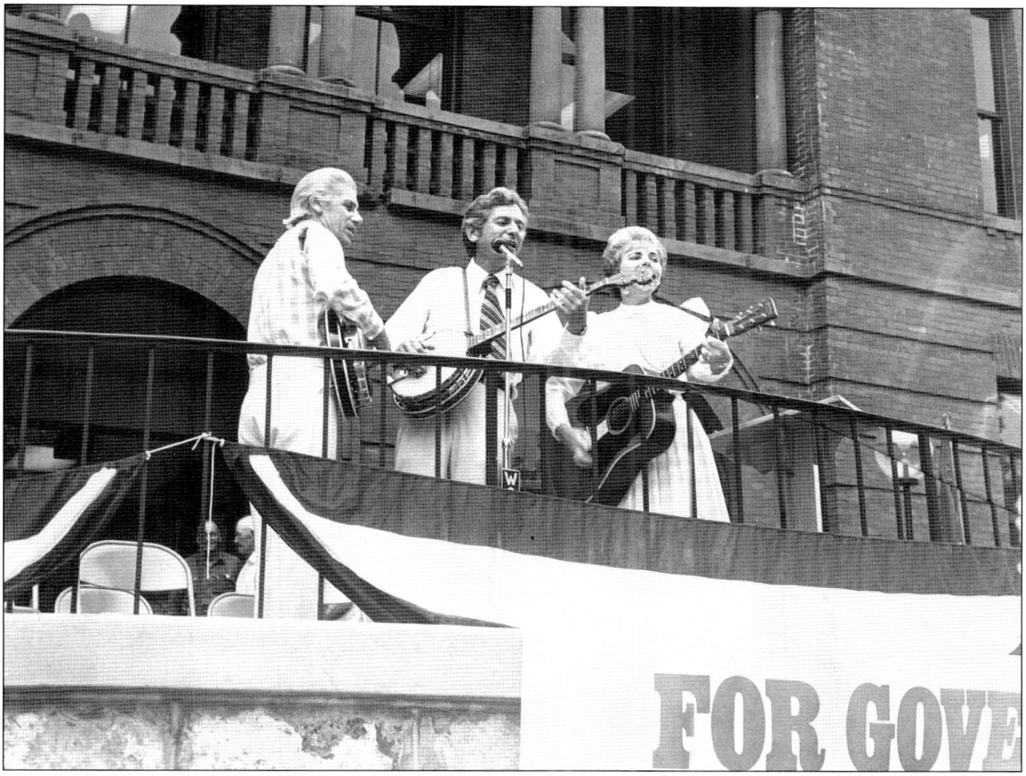

Country-music entertainers Bonnie Lou (right) and Buster Moore (left) entertain a political gathering for Lamar Alexander during his 1978 campaign for governor. Politicians often featured live entertainment as a prelude to their speeches. Most political events took place on the courthouse lawn. (Courtesy of the *Mountain Press*.)

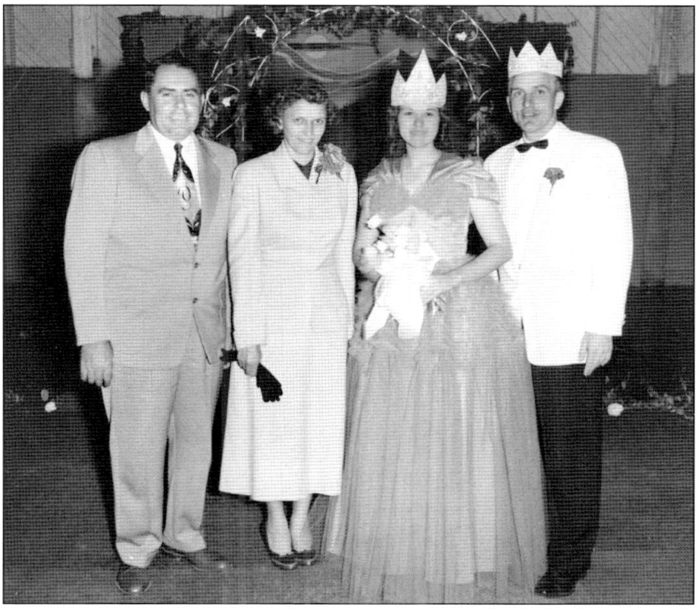

In 1953, Betty Jo Smith was crowned Miss Lee College. Her parents traveled to Cleveland, Tennessee, to attend the ceremony. Photographed left to right are Carl Smith, Ollie Smith, Betty Jo, and John Daniels–crowned Mr. Lee College. (Courtesy of Dr. Steve Madison.)

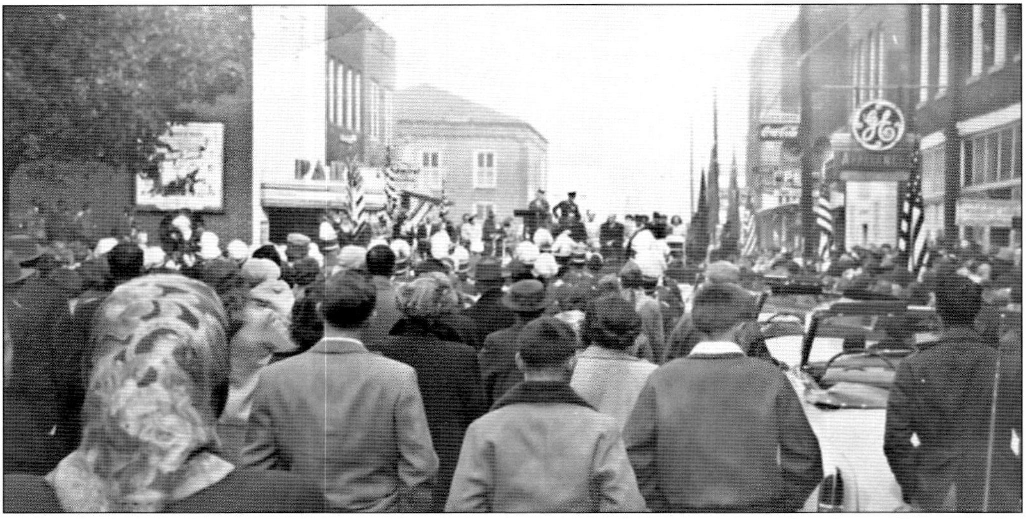

In 1953, a large crowd turned out on the streets of Sevierville to support and welcome home Otha Emert, who was prisoner-of-war during the Korean Conflict. (Courtesy of King Family Library History Center, Herbert Lawson Collection.)

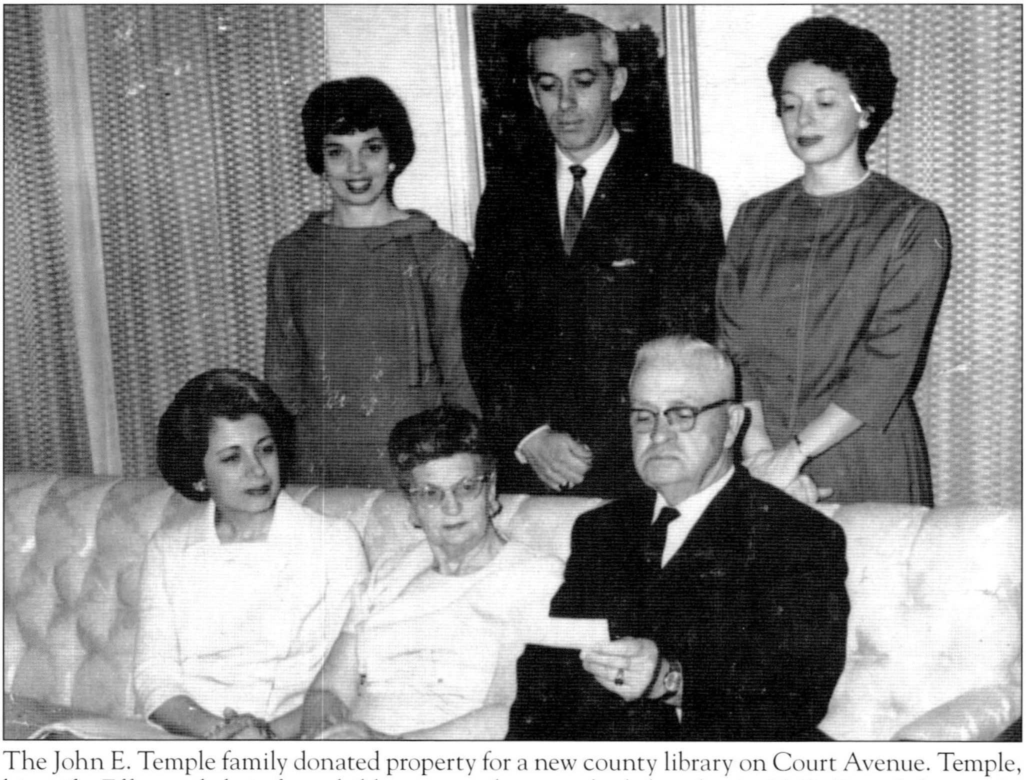

The John E. Temple family donated property for a new county library on Court Avenue. Temple, his wife, Effie, and their four children were photographed that day in 1966. From left to right are (first row) Frankie Temple Cutshaw, Effie Benson Temple, John E. Temple; (second row) Mary Joyce Temple Hughes, Jimmie Temple, and Patsy Temple Waters. (Courtesy of Jimmie and Marie Temple.)

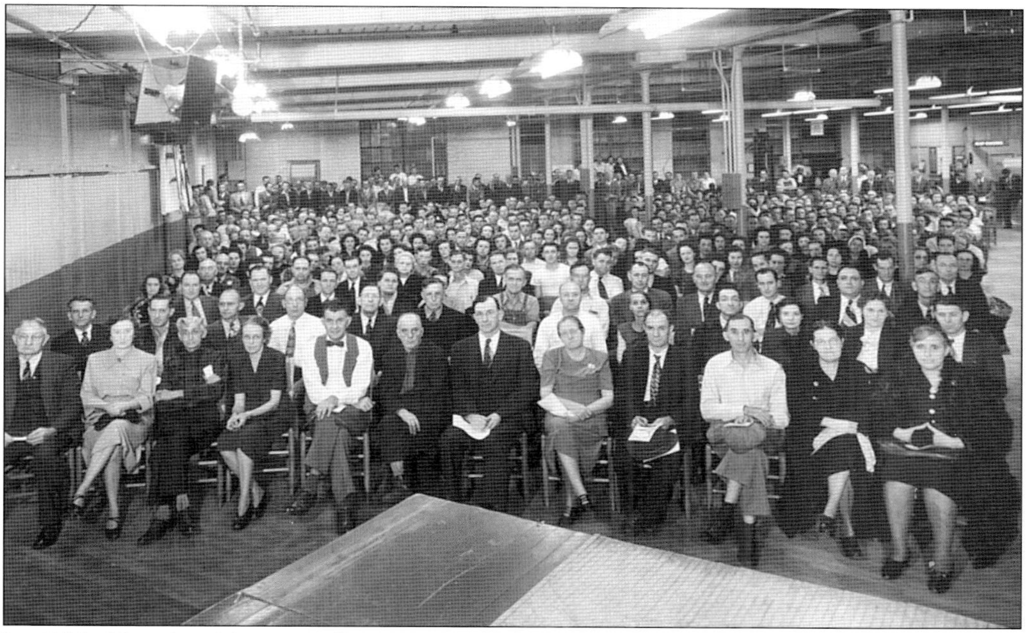

In 1954, Cherokee Textile Mills announced plans to relocate from Knoxville to Sevierville. Employees were gathered for the announcement, shown here, at the Sutherland Avenue facility. Reaction to the news was mixed in Knoxville; many employees were willing to commute. In Sevierville, the economic benefits and opportunities brought about were greeted with wholesale delight. (Courtesy of King Family Library History Center.)

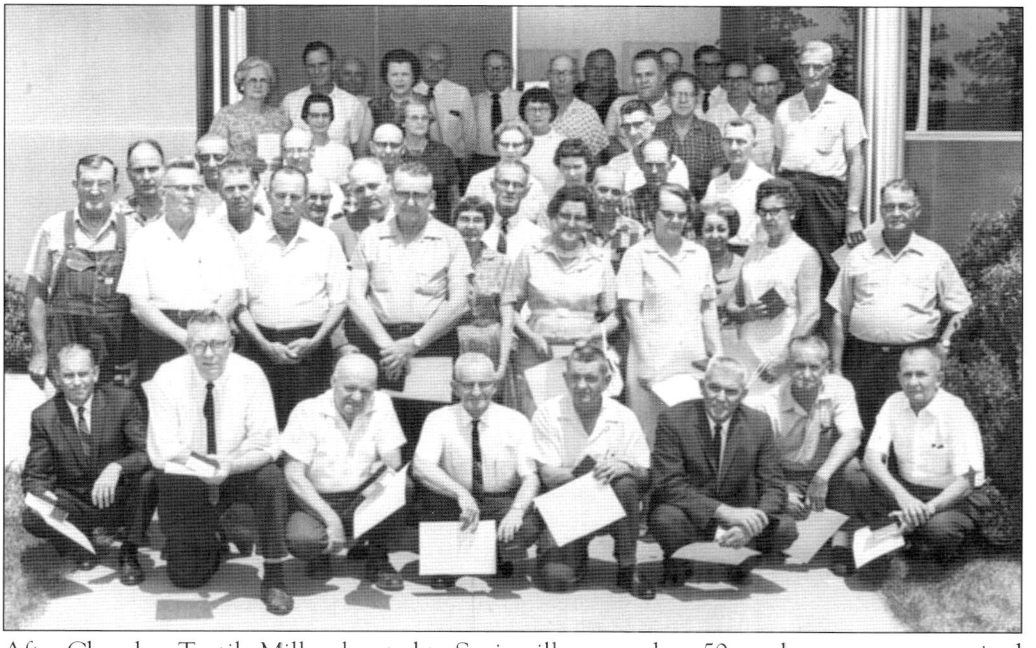

After Cherokee Textile Mills relocated to Sevierville, more than 50 employees were recognized each year for their years of service. Many residents worked for the mill for more than 50 years. (Courtesy of King Family Library History Center.)

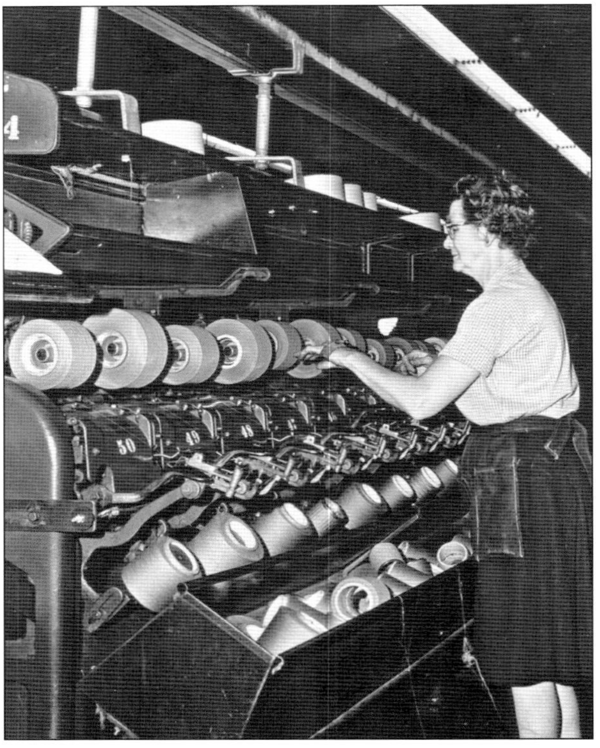

Cherokee Textile Mills usually operated six days a week for the half-century the mill was in operation in Sevierville. Shown here is a lady hard at work doing her daily routine. In the best of times, the mill ran six days a week. (Courtesy of King Family Library History Center.)

Large bales of cotton shown here are unloaded at Cherokee Textile Mills. The first step in the milling process was "carding" the cotton; from there, it was dispatched to the spinning department. (Courtesy of King Family Library History Center.)

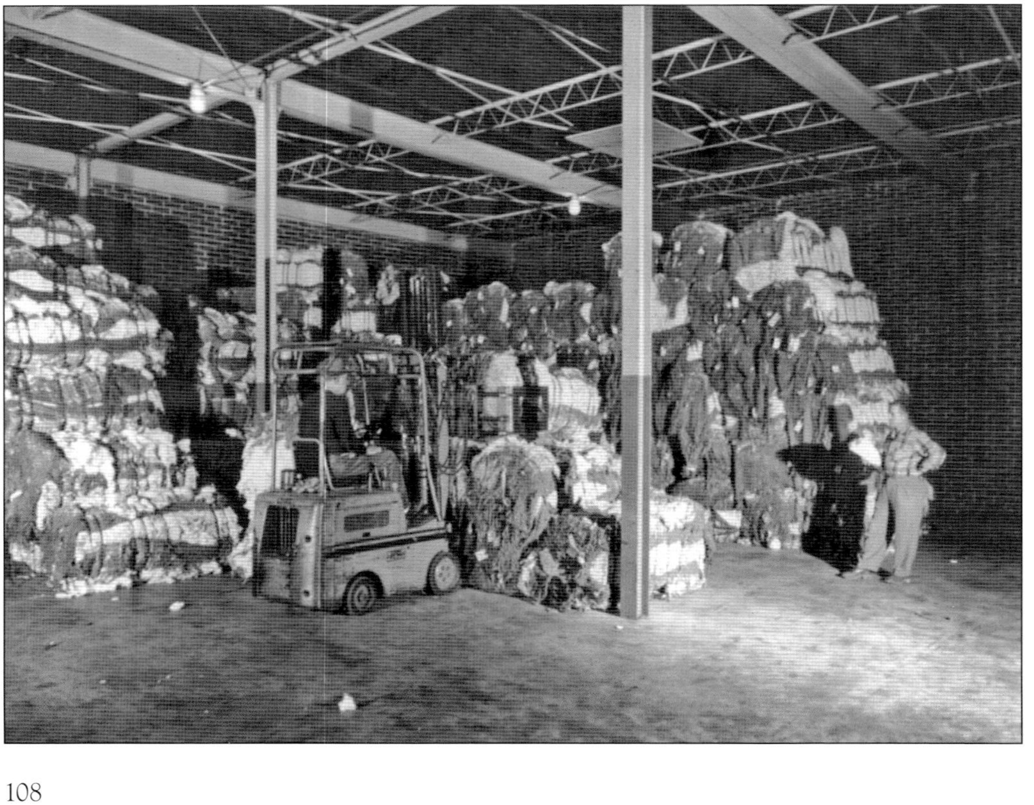

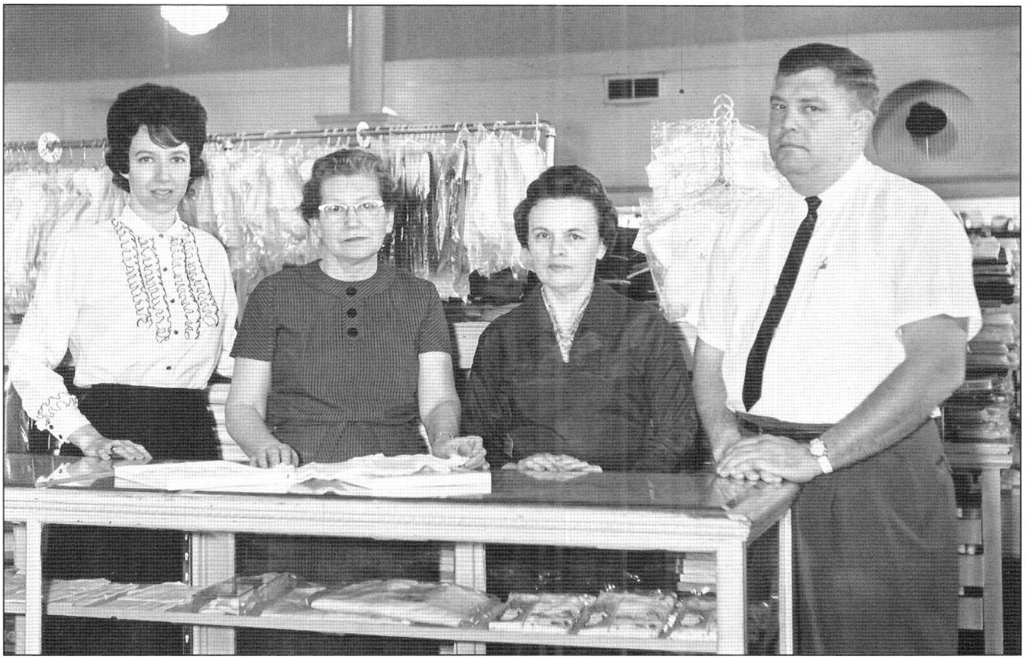

Photographed here are employees of the Corner Store, a dry-goods emporium that was located on the northeast corner of Bruce Street and Court Avenue. Herbert Lawson managed the store for many years. Lawson served a term as mayor from 1971 until 1973, often conducting day-to-day city business in the store. Posing left to right, sales clerks Charlotte Stott Blalock, Ruth Conner Douglass, and Pauline Hill Lindsey are joined by Lawson. (Courtesy of King Family Library History Center, Herbert Lawson Collection.)

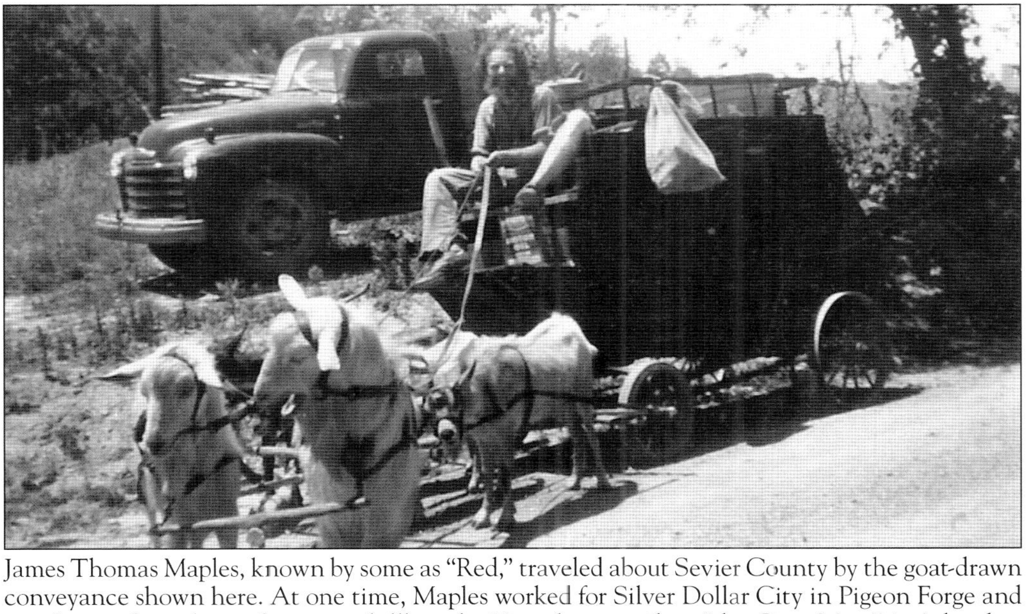

James Thomas Maples, known by some as "Red," traveled about Sevier County by the goat-drawn conveyance shown here. At one time, Maples worked for Silver Dollar City in Pigeon Forge and was featured on their advertising billboards. His other moniker, "the Goat Man," isn't hard to peg. (Courtesy of King Family Library History Center, Herbert Lawson Collection.)

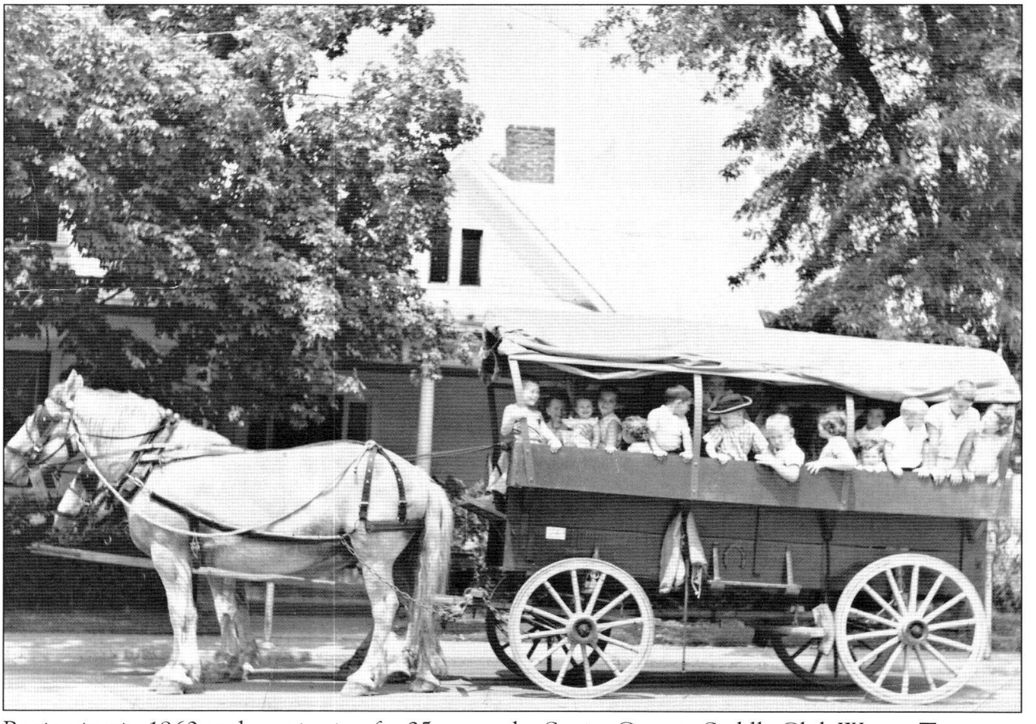

Beginning in 1960 and continuing for 25 years, the Sevier County Saddle Club Wagon Train was an eagerly anticipated tradition that entertained hundreds who enjoyed equestrian activities and old-time fun. Here, a wagon of Temple kinfolk proceeds down the Court Avenue venue. (Courtesy of Jimmie and Marie Temple.)

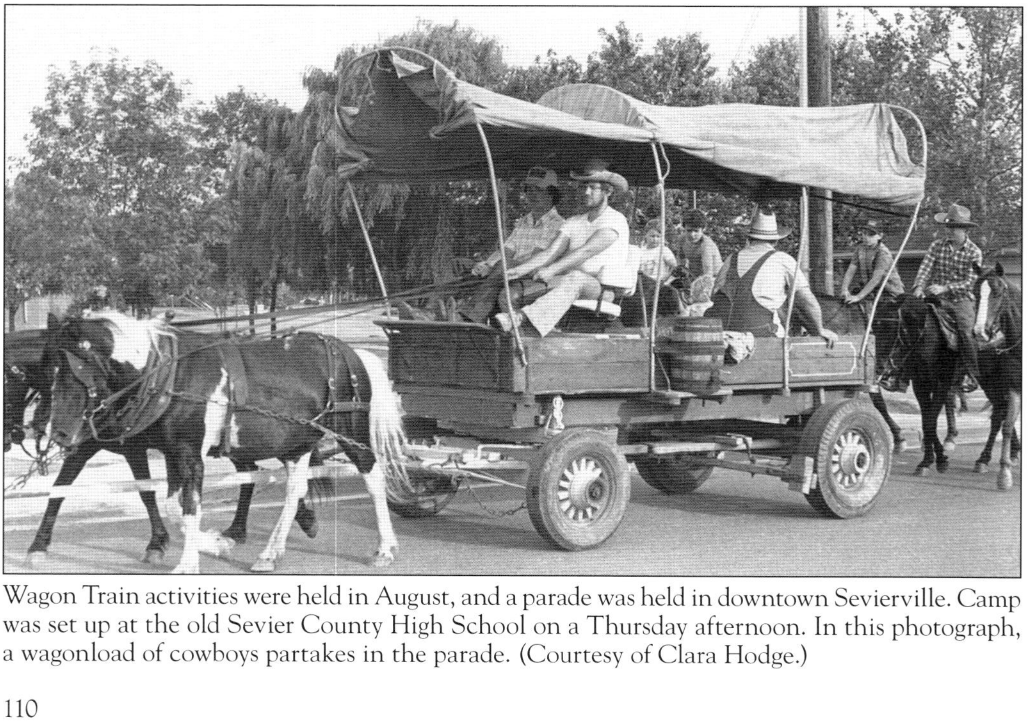

Wagon Train activities were held in August, and a parade was held in downtown Sevierville. Camp was set up at the old Sevier County High School on a Thursday afternoon. In this photograph, a wagonload of cowboys partakes in the parade. (Courtesy of Clara Hodge.)

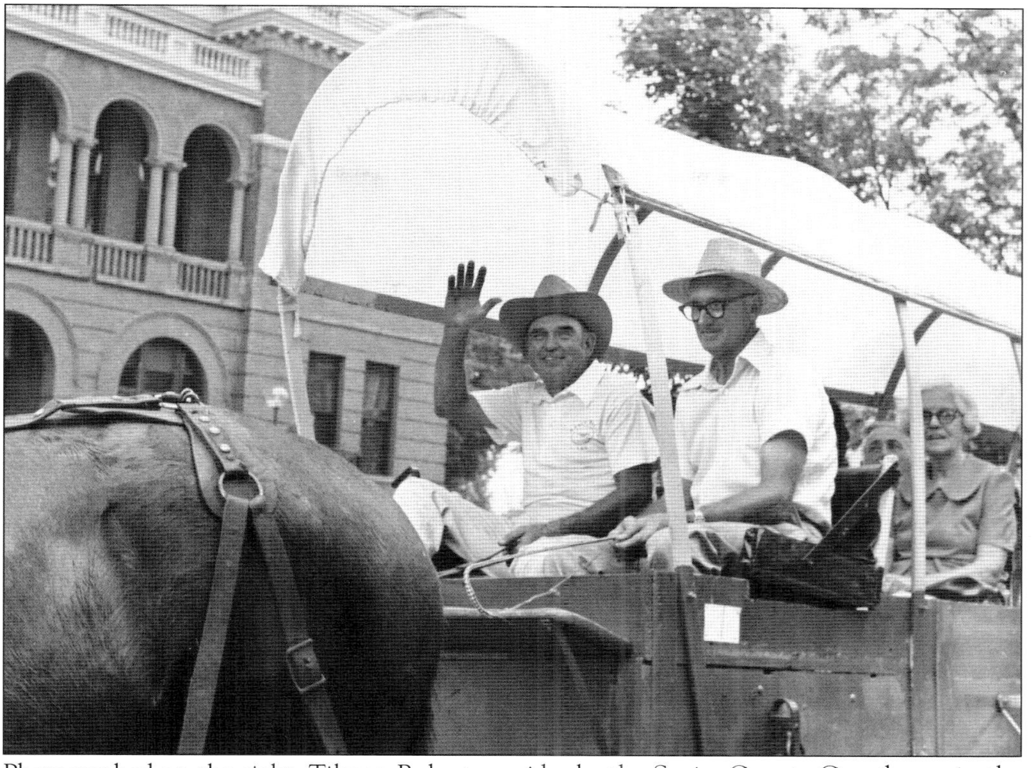

Photographed on the right, Tilman Robertson rides by the Sevier County Courthouse in the Wagon Train parade. Robertson served as wagonmaster for nearly all of the 25 Wagon Train parades held in Sevierville. He also facilitated a Sunday morning worship service each year during the event. (Courtesy of Clara Hodge.)

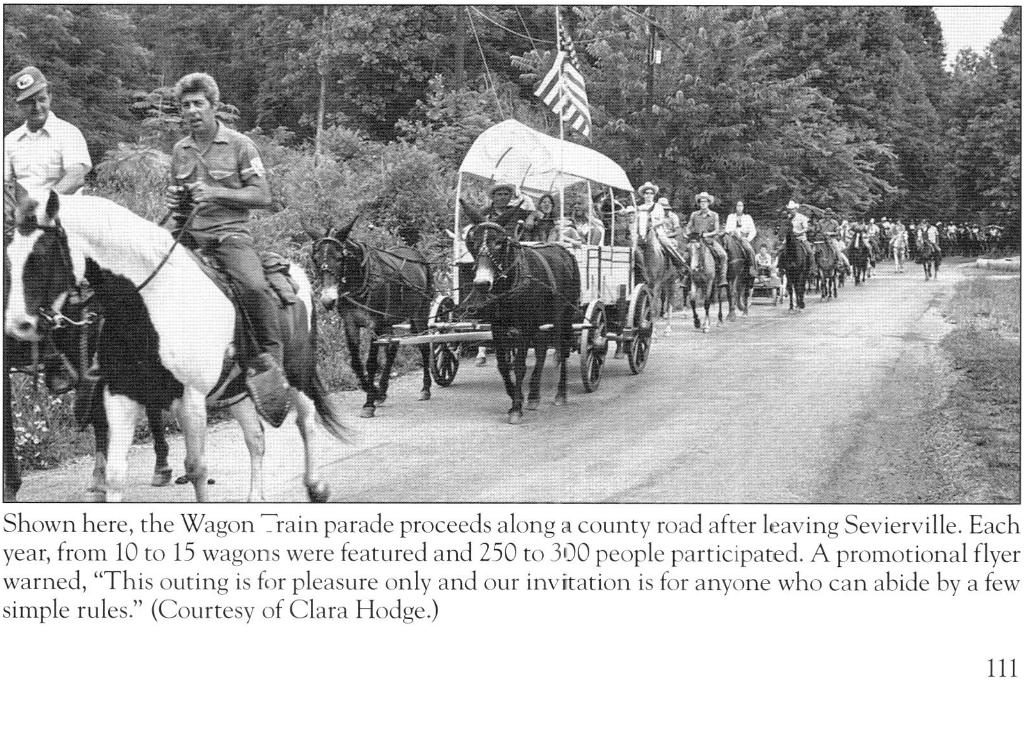

Shown here, the Wagon Train parade proceeds along a county road after leaving Sevierville. Each year, from 10 to 15 wagons were featured and 250 to 300 people participated. A promotional flyer warned, "This outing is for pleasure only and our invitation is for anyone who can abide by a few simple rules." (Courtesy of Clara Hodge.)

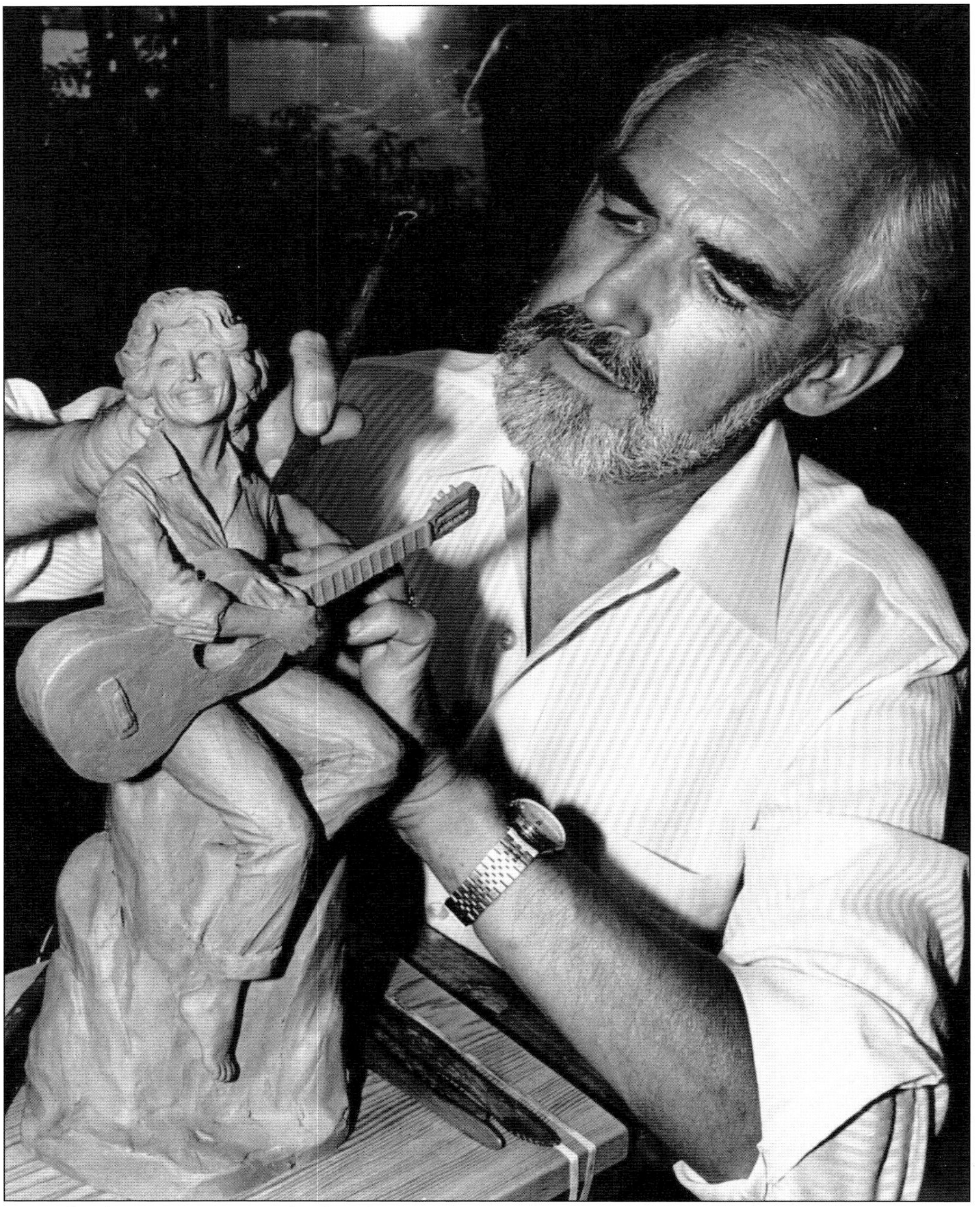

Artist/sculptor Jim Gray worked with a Sevier County committee on plans to locate a six-and-a-half-foot bronze statue of Dolly outside the Sevierville County Courthouse. In 1985, Gray began with the 10-inch proposed model shown here. Gray's bust of Gov. John Sevier is displayed in the courthouse's interior hall. (Courtesy of Sevierville Chamber of Commerce.)

In 1986, Jim Gray prepared the five-foot mountain boulder for the six-and-a-half-foot statue of Dolly Parton. The mountain stone, on which Dolly is seated, was chosen to represent Dolly's Smoky Mountain roots. (Courtesy of Sevierville Chamber of Commerce.)

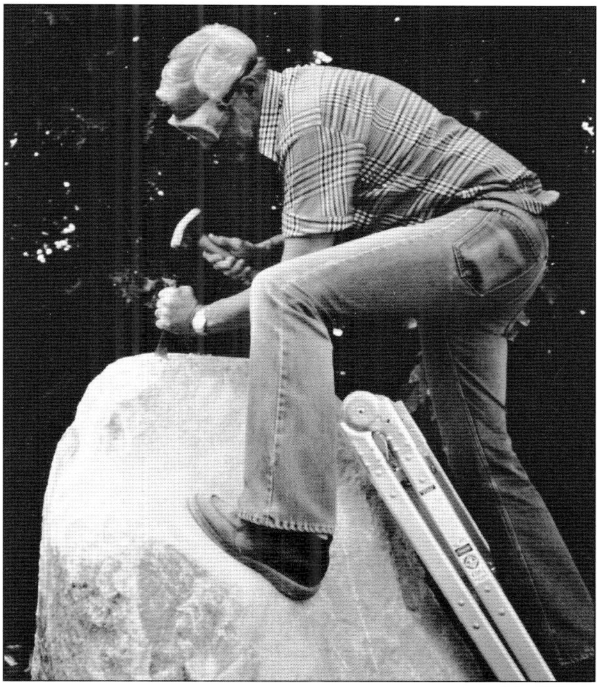

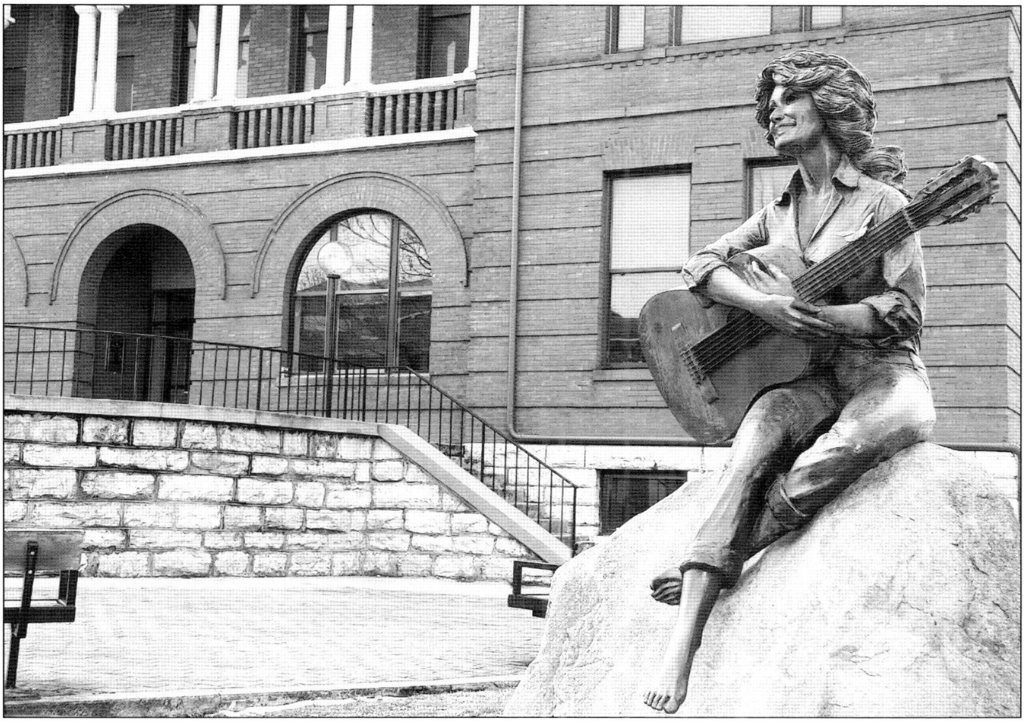

One of the most frequently asked questions at the Sevierville Visitor Center is, "How can I find the Dolly statue?" Over the years, thousands of visitors worldwide have stood on the Sevier County Courthouse lawn to view the famous statue. (Courtesy of Sevierville Chamber of Commerce.)

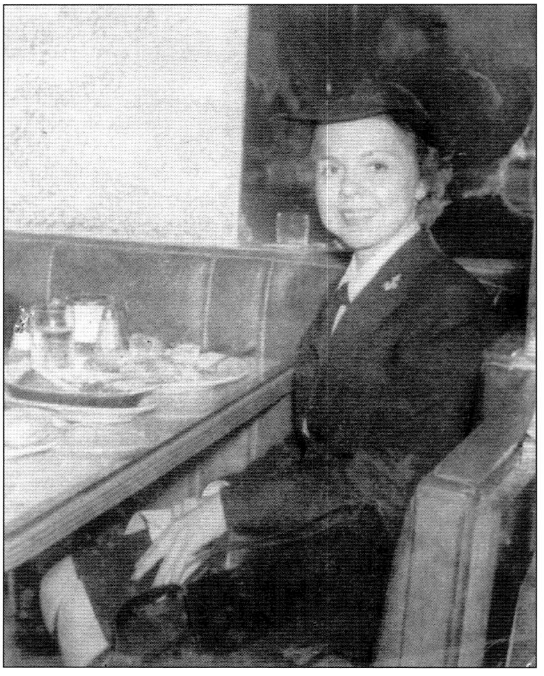

Artist Frances (Wade) Ostergren poses in 1944 dressed in her US Navy WAVE uniform. She returned to Sevierville, her hometown, in 1960. She began traveling throughout Sevier County sketching churches and schools along with the Sevier County courthouse and its tower, swinging bridges, landscapes, and homes. Her watercolor paintings hang in homes and public buildings throughout Sevier County and beyond. (Courtesy of King Family Library, Frances Wade Ostergren Collection.)

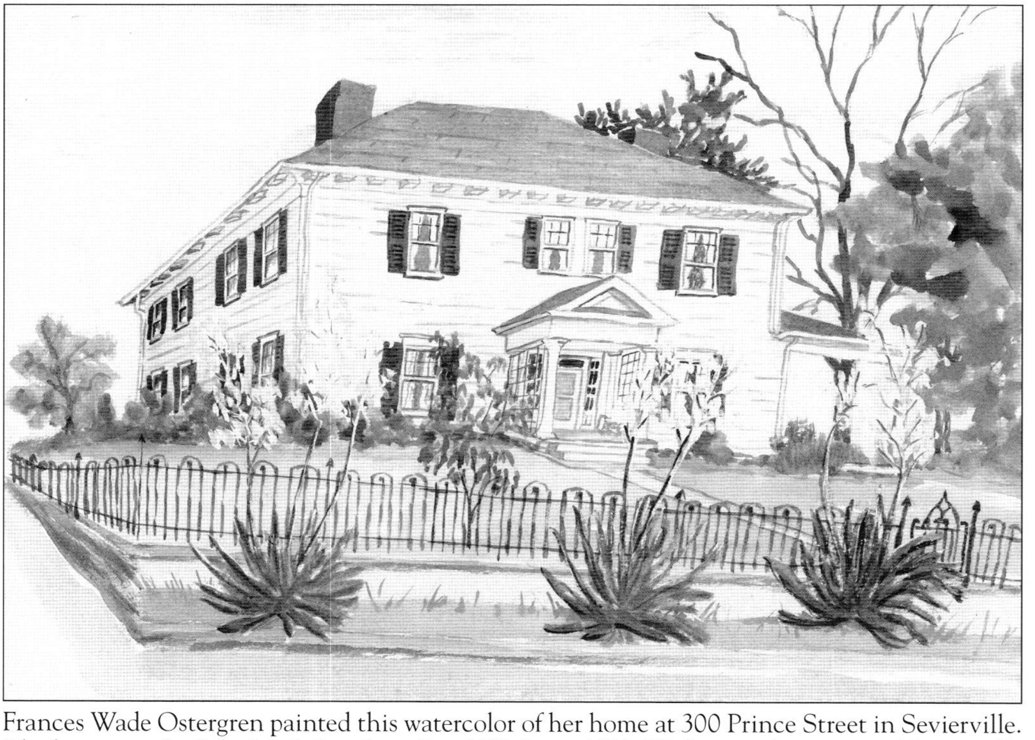

Frances Wade Ostergren painted this watercolor of her home at 300 Prince Street in Sevierville. The house was built by her father, Jerry Reed Wade, in 1920. Wade served as mayor of Sevierville for one term in the mid-1940s. The artist resided in the house while practicing her art. (Courtesy of King Family Library, Frances Wade Ostergren Collection.)

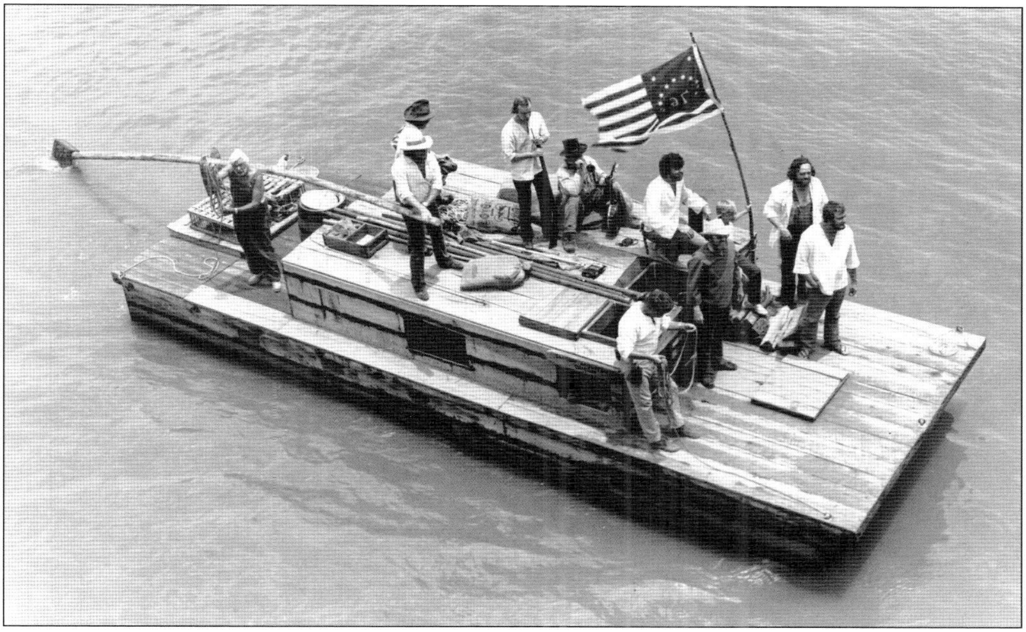

During America's 1976 bicentennial celebration, local men, photographed here, crafted a replica of the old flatboats that once transported goods from Appalachian communities to the Gulf of Mexico. They christened the vessel *The Smoky Mountain Queen* and journeyed from Douglas Lake to New Orleans. (Courtesy of the *Mountain Press*.)

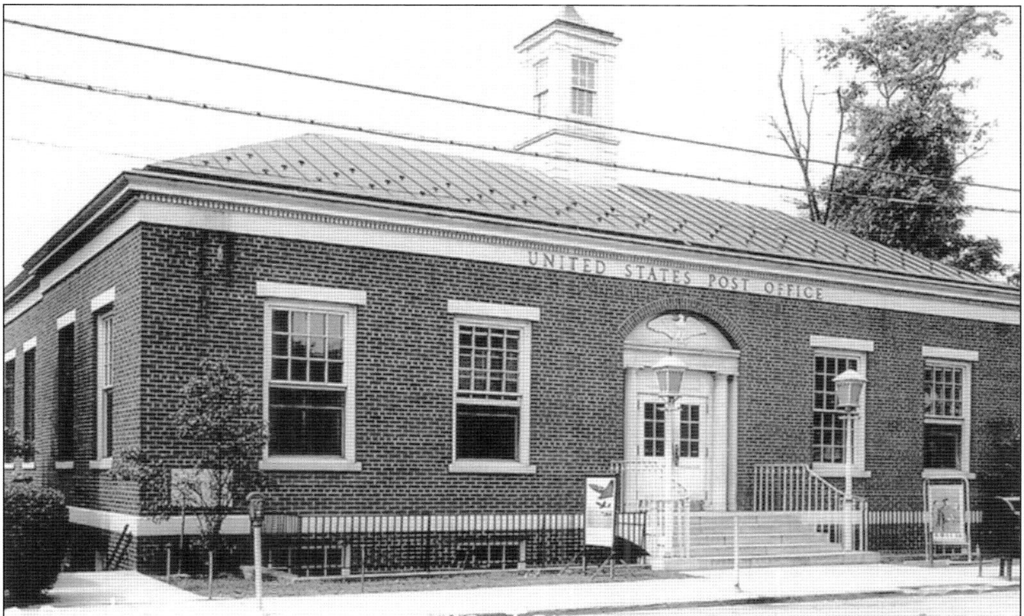

The Sevierville Post Office was located in various buildings before the Works Progress Administration constructed this attractive building in 1940. It is located on the southwest corner of Bruce Street and Park Road. When Dixie Bowers resided on the property, she planted the magnolia tree on the corner, which survives today, a century later. (Courtesy of Sevierville Chamber of Commerce.)

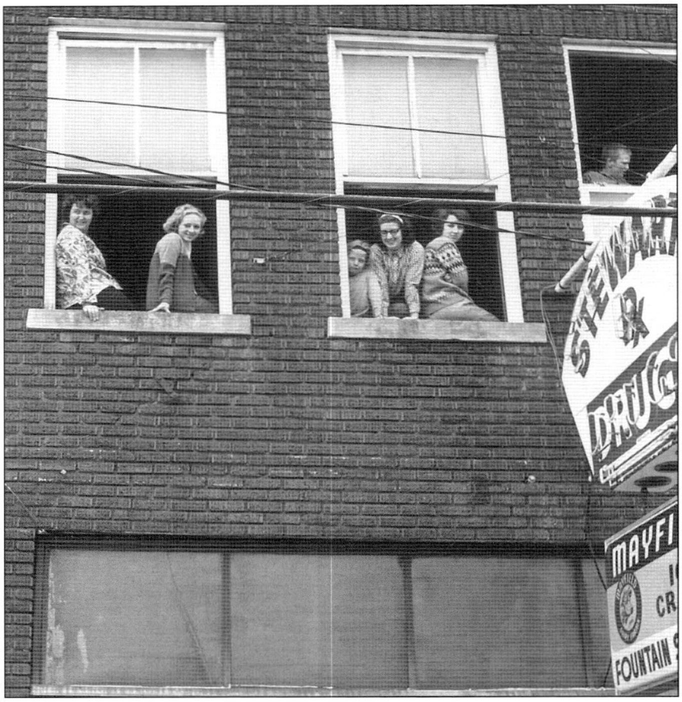

Spectators photographed here watch the Sevierville Christmas Parade from the second-story window over Stewart's Drug Store on Court Avenue. Stewart's Drug Store is now located on the Forks-of-the-River Parkway. (Courtesy of King Family Library History Center, Herbert Lawson Collection.)

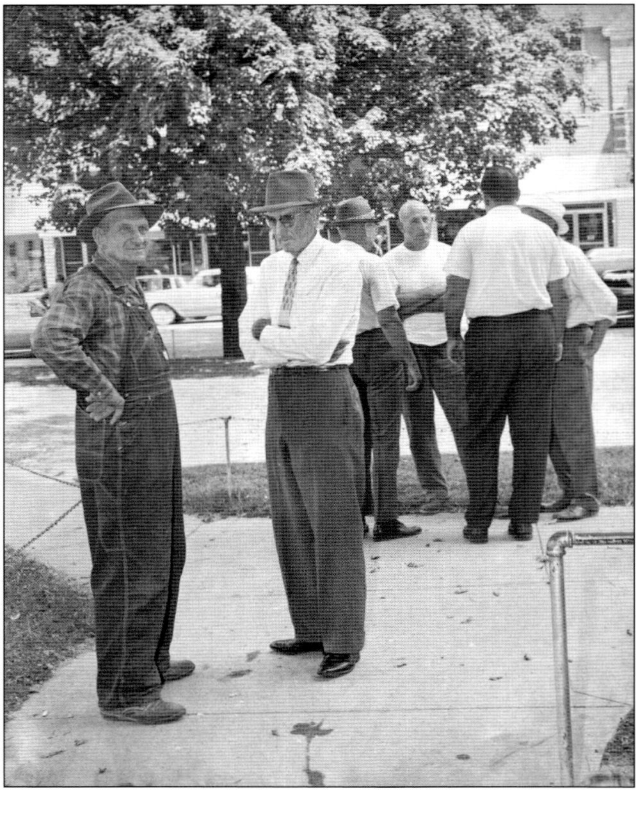

Generations of Sevier County citizens have gathered on the Sevier County Courthouse lawn in all kinds of weather to swap knives, discuss politics, and socialize with old friends or to simply observe goings-on. If one place could be called the heart of Sevierville, it would surely be the courthouse lawn. (Courtesy of the *Mountain Press*.)

Photographed in front of Newman's Restaurant, Alfred Newman (left) stands with US Congressman James H. Quillen. With a keen interest in politics, Newman served as campaign manager for Quillen in Sevier County. (Courtesy of Johnnie Faye McClure.)

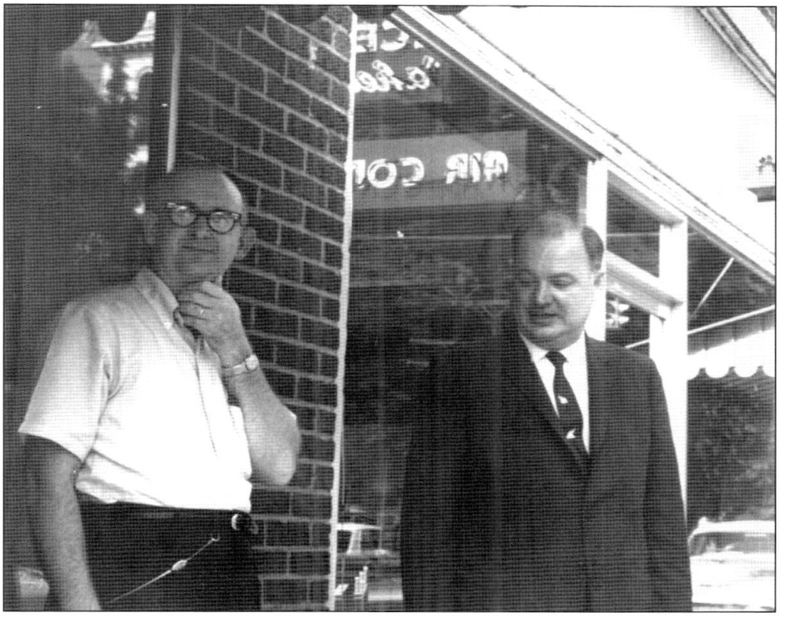

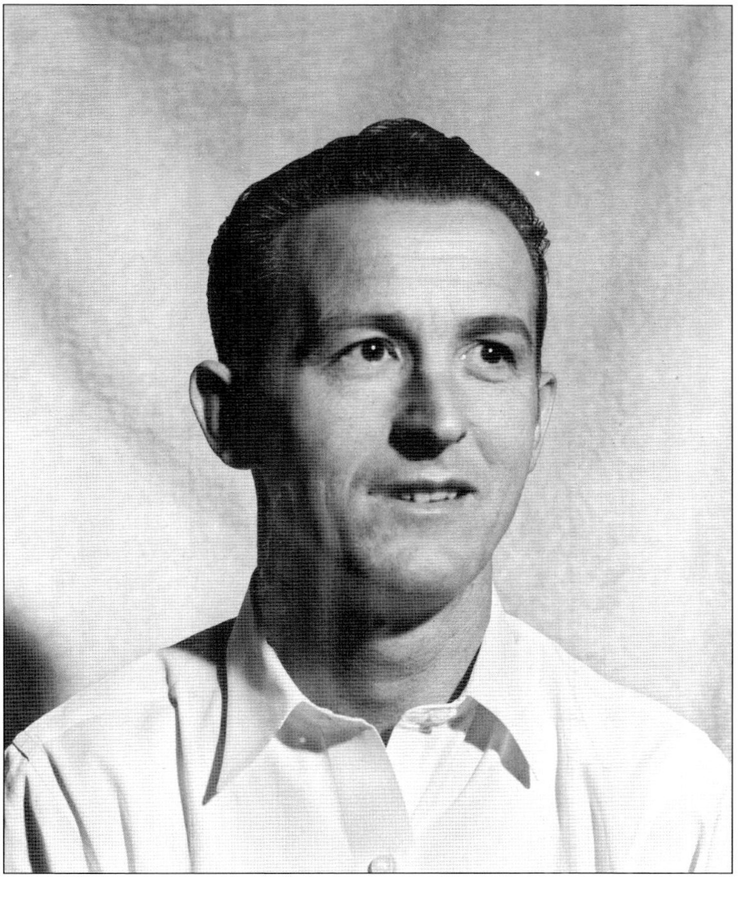

John Newman, photographed here, and his brother, Alfred, operated Newman's Restaurant on Bruce Street for three decades. While Alfred greeted the public, John was a legendary chef, a skill he began acquiring in the US Army. (Courtesy of Johnnie Faye McClure.)

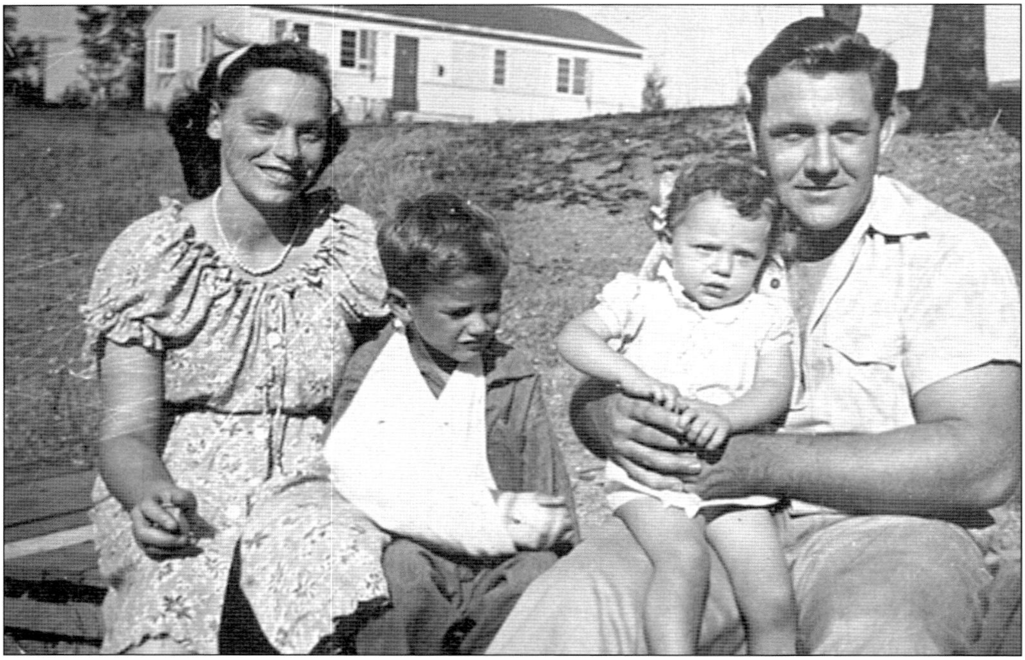

John and Ruby Fox were photographed with their children, David and Pat, before they moved to Sevierville. Although John Fox was a Sevierville native, he and Ruby were associated with Carson-Newman College in Jefferson City for many years. When they retired, they moved to Sevierville; John wrote columns for the *Mountain Press* and Ruby became director of the Sevierville Chamber of Commerce. (Courtesy of Sevierville Chamber of Commerce.)

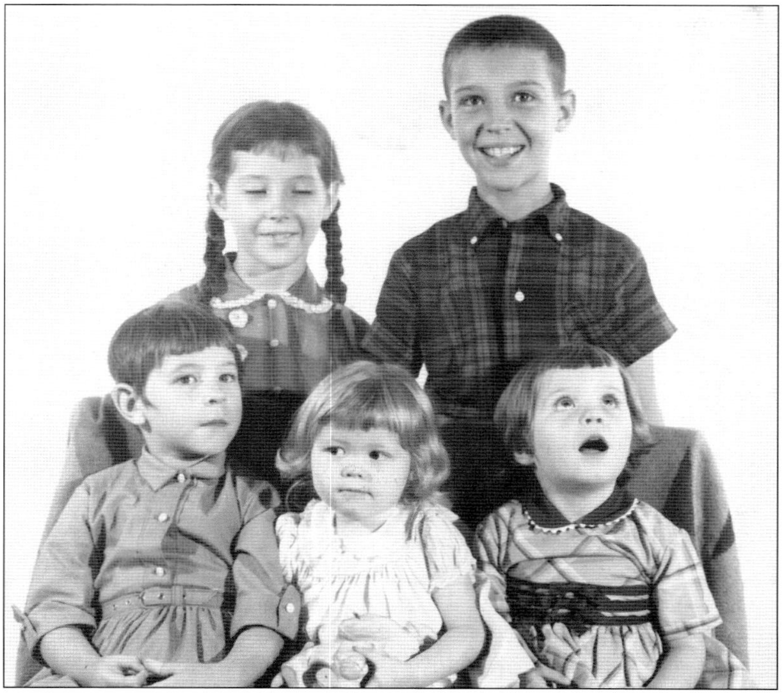

Captured here by well-known Sevierville photographer Marie Bashor in 1959 are five of the six children of Clyde and Louise McMahan. From left to right are (first row) Nina, Debbie, and Terry; (second row) Janice, and F. Carroll (author of this book). (Courtesy of the author's private collection.)

Six

Views from Above

If you don't scale the mountain, you can't view the plain.

—Chinese proverb

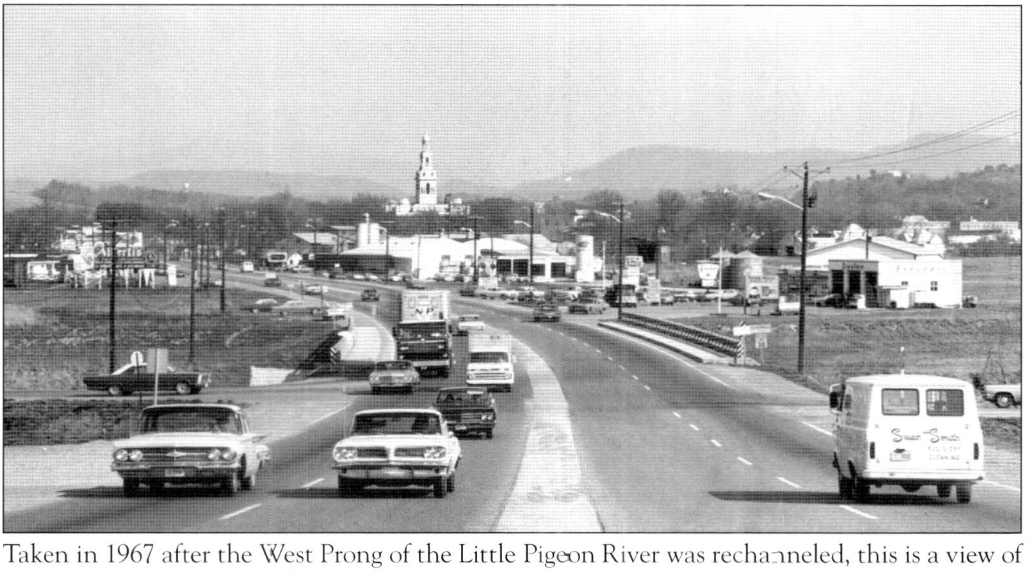

Taken in 1967 after the West Prong of the Little Pigeon River was rechanneled, this is a view of Sevierville from Jenkins Hill as you enter from Chapman Highway. Until Winfield Dunn Parkway (Highway 66) was completed, connecting Sevierville with Interstate 40, Chapman Highway was the busiest entrance to Sevierville. (Courtesy of the *Mountain Press*.)

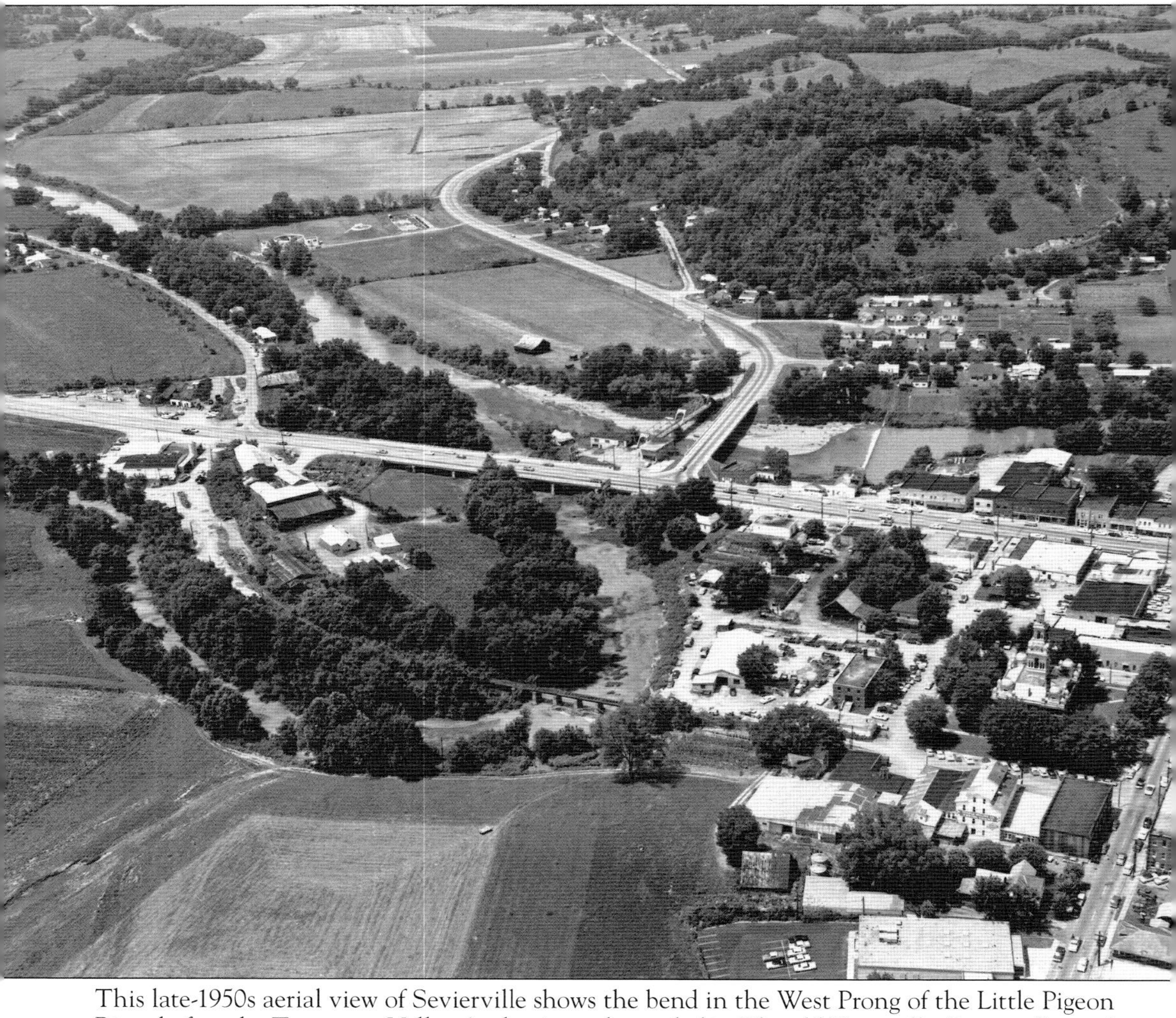

This late-1950s aerial view of Sevierville shows the bend in the West Prong of the Little Pigeon River before the Tennessee Valley Authority rechanneled it. The old Knoxville, Sevierville, and Eastern Railway trestle can be seen in the bend of the river. Rail service ended in the early 1960s. (Courtesy of City of Sevierville.)

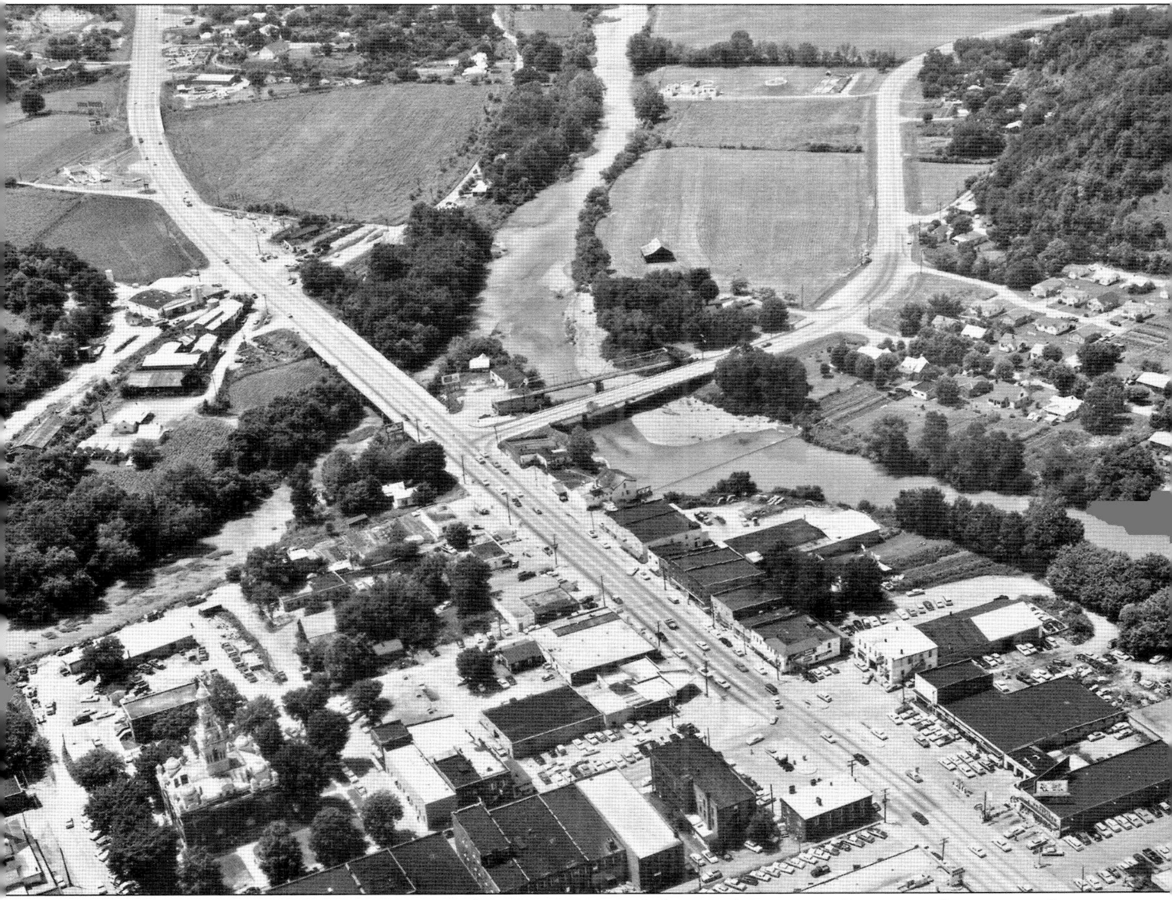

The confluence of the East Prong and West Prong of the Little Pigeon River is shown in this 1965 picture, along with the old five-span steel bridge and the adjacent Fred C. Atchley Bridge. (Courtesy of the *Mountain Press*.)

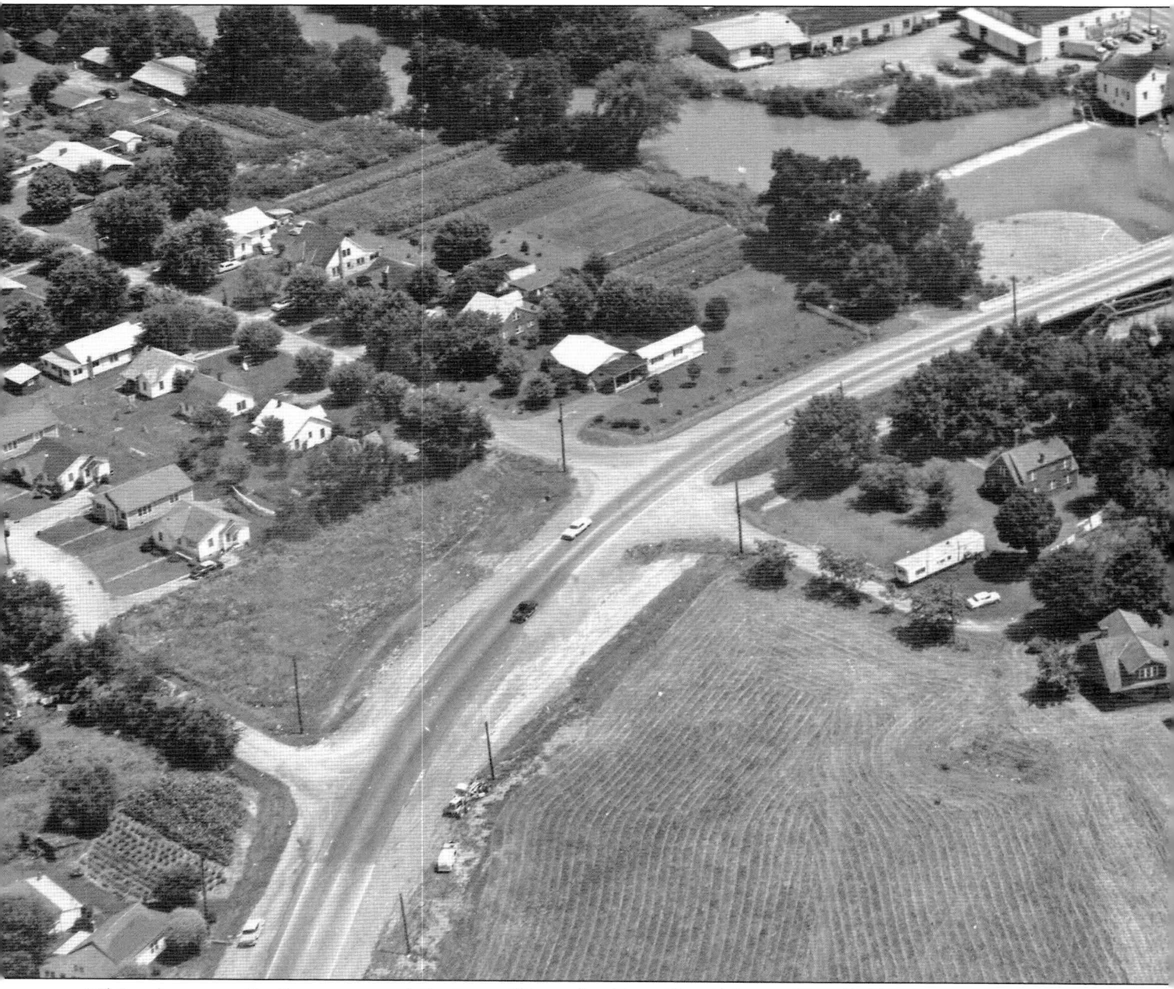

This photograph shows an aerial view of Douglas Dam Road (now Winfield Dunn Parkway), just north of the Fred C. Atchley Bridge. The old milldam behind the Frost Mills and Ice Company can be seen in the upper right. The dam was removed in 1966. (Courtesy of the *Mountain Press*.)

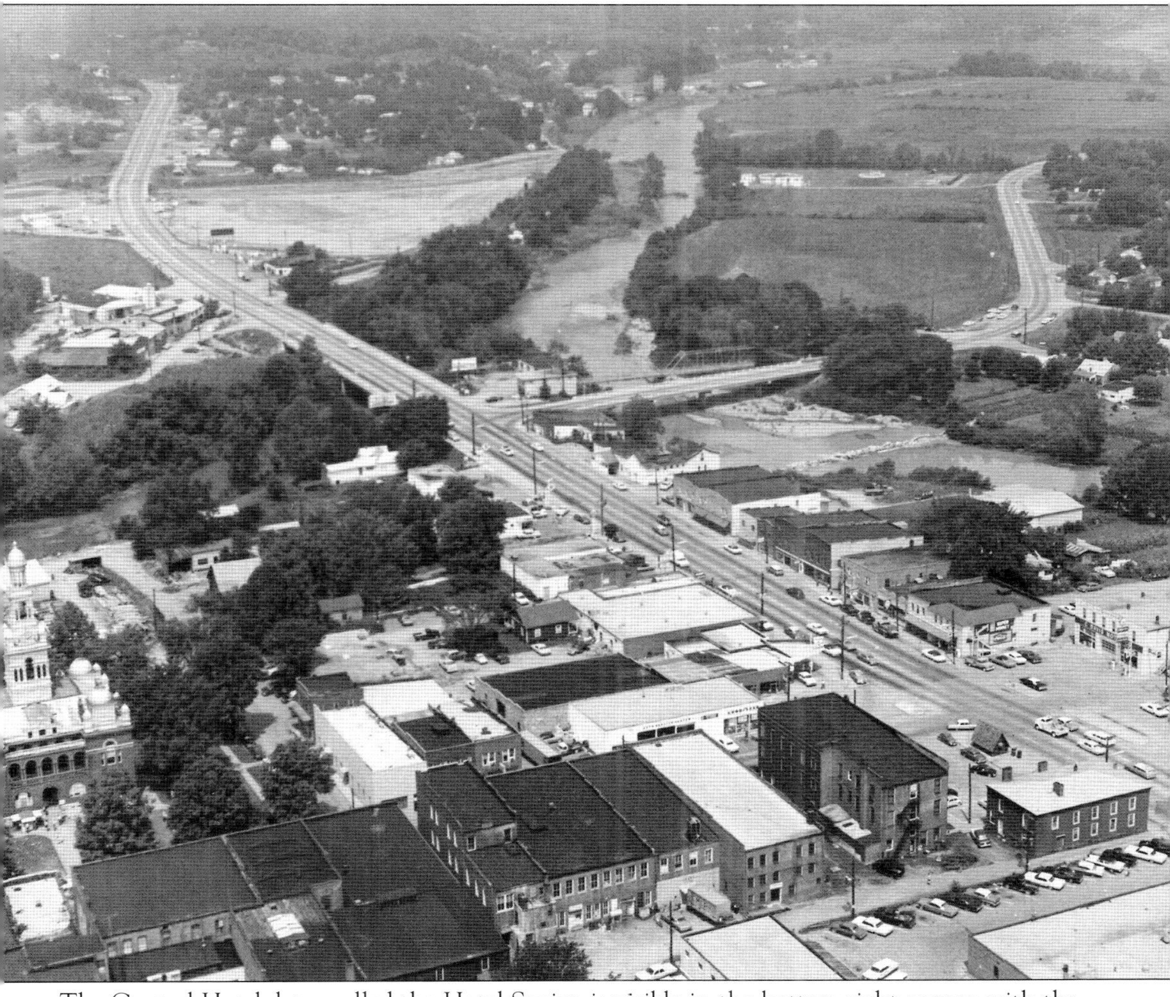

The Central Hotel, later called the Hotel Sevier, is visible in the bottom right corner, with the old Emert Brick Building to the right. The little chalet in front of the building was the first Sevierville Information Center. (Courtesy of the *Mountain Press*.)

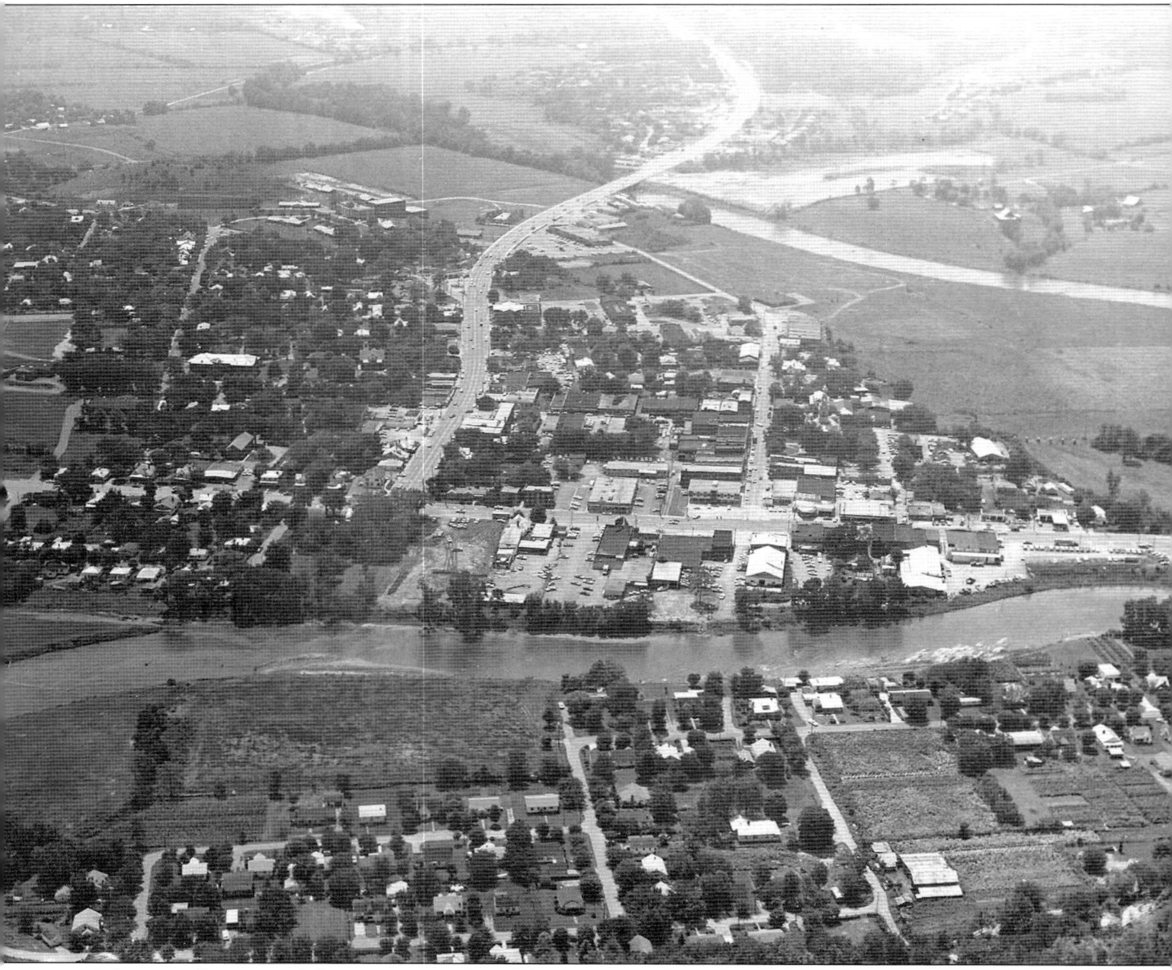

This south view of downtown Sevierville dates to the late 1960s, after the West Prong of the Little Pigeon River was rechanneled. The picture was taken before construction on the Forks-of-the-River Parkway began. (Courtesy of city of Sevierville.)

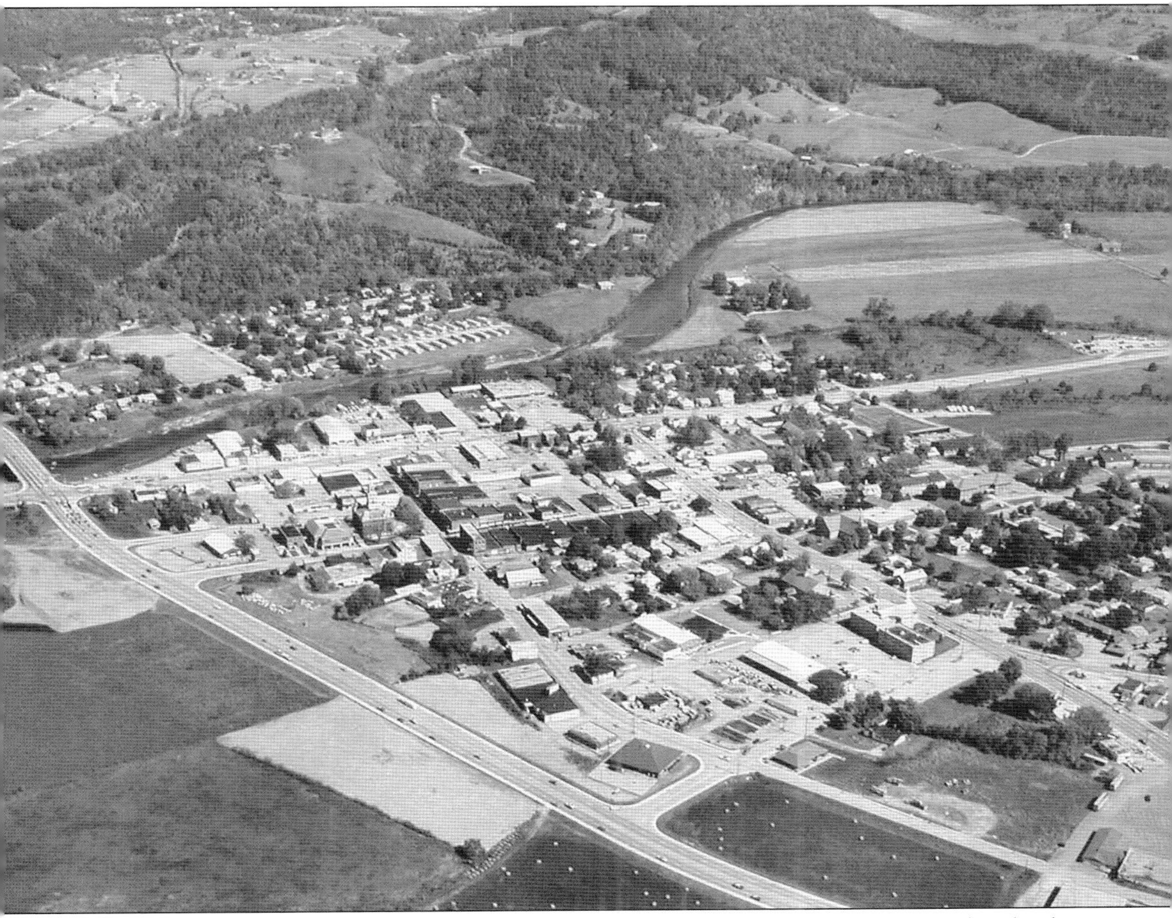

This aerial view shows the new Forks-of-the River Parkway shortly after it was completed. The New Sevier County Library is visible at the bottom left. The undeveloped area left of the new parkway is where the K-Mart Shopping Center is located. (Courtesy of the *Mountain Press.*)

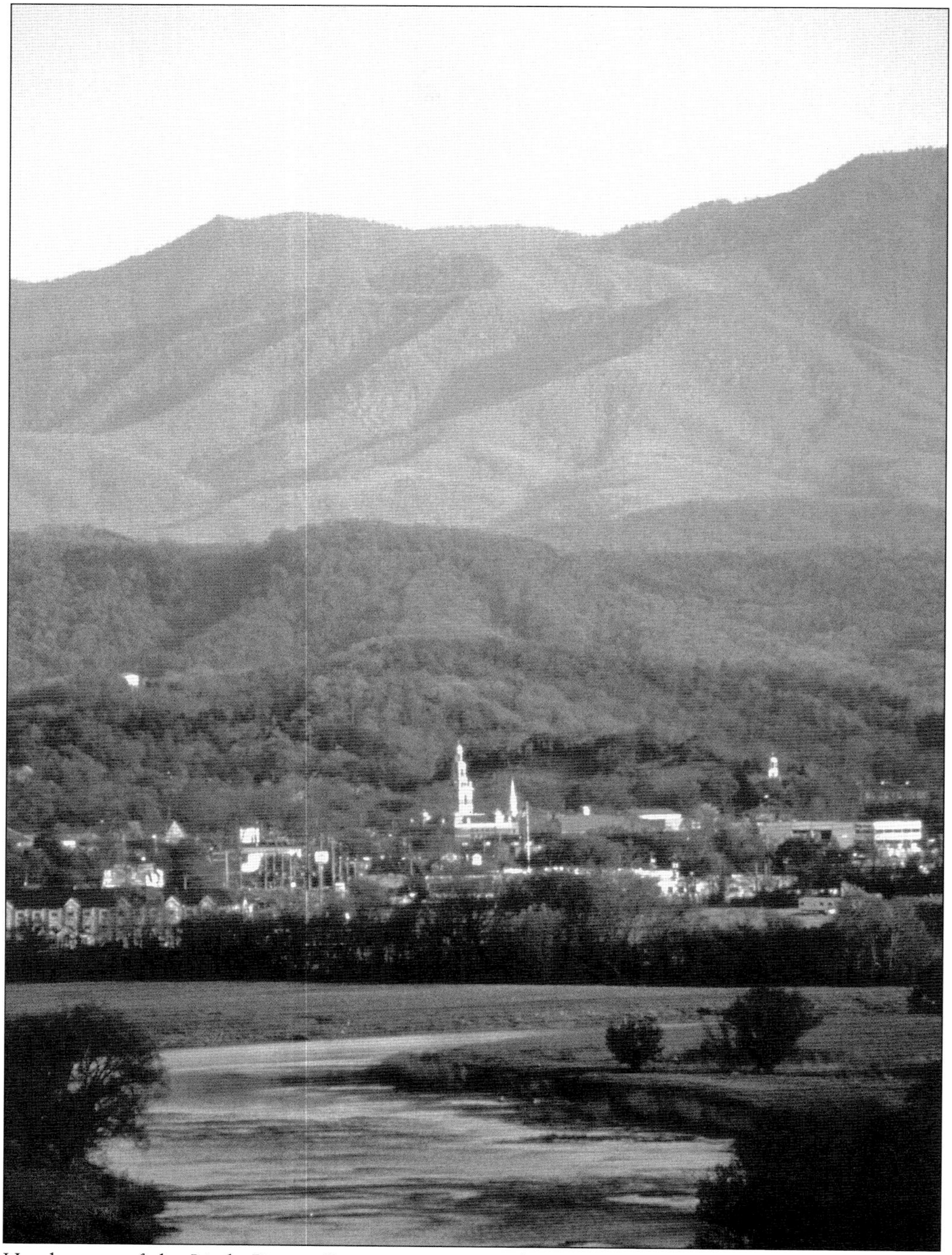

Headwaters of the Little Pigeon River originate in three areas of the Great Smoky Mountains before they merge in Sevierville. This spectacular view with the mountain peaks in the background shows the river flowing gently through town. Nothing man-made has ever surpassed the beauty of the mountains surrounding the city of Sevierville. (Courtesy of Sevierville Chamber of Commerce.)

About the Organization

While the Sevierville Chamber of Commerce promotes membership, tourism, commerce, and industry, the organization makes a special effort to preserve and celebrate the community's heritage as a way of both honoring the past and better understanding how to grow effectively for the future.

Formed June 18, 1963, at a special meeting of about 60 Sevierville business-minded men and women, the organization has grown to almost 600 members. With a primary mission to "advance the commercial, financial, industrial, and civic interests of the community, accomplishing collectively what no one can do individually," the Sevierville Chamber of Commerce has played a major role in developing much-needed year-round employment for the community's citizens. For the past half century, the primary source of employment opportunities has been tourism-related jobs.

Currently, the Sevierville Chamber of Commerce serves a dual role by providing business development opportunities for its active membership and serving as the tourism/marketing arm for the city of Sevierville.

About the Author

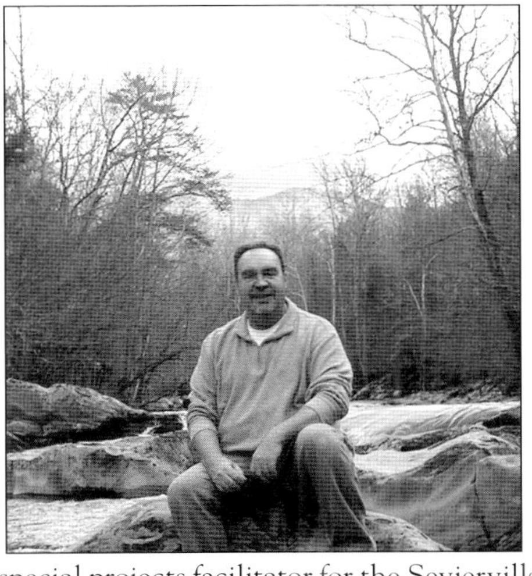

F. Carroll McMahan is the special projects facilitator for the Sevierville Chamber of Commerce. He has written this book for the purpose of preserving the history of his hometown. He is the recipient of the 2012 Community History Award presented by the East Tennessee Historical Society and the Historic Preservation Recognition Award presented on behalf of the National Society of the Daughters of the American Revolution, Spencer Clack Chapter.